A thriving family business needs a healthy
A healthy family encourages and supports a
and is more equipped to make decisions and support each other in
the process. I encourage all family members, not just family business
leaders, to pick this book up.

— Alicia Gerrits, Chairman, Grupo de Sola

This book offers hope, knowledge and practical resources for families
working to support members with mental health issues. Given that
this is a topic that is often avoided, the book can open new pathways
to healing and success in the family enterprise.

— Mary Nelson, ARC Leadership Associates, LLC

Whether you are a member of a family business or an advisor to one,
this book is a must read. It addresses an incredibly important and timely
topic, and it does it in a clear, compassionate, and realistic manner.
Using case examples, theory and practical advice, the authors show
the importance of mental health for a family business to truly thrive.

— Maria Jose Perry, Clinical Psychologist, 4th Generation
Family Business Member

This book delves into the crucial topic of mental health—a subject that
holds immense importance and relevance for everyone, not just those
involved in family businesses. Its insights are not only eye-opening but
also deeply resonant, making it a must-read for individuals from all walks
of life. I believe this book has the power to resonate widely and spark
important conversations.

— Nicolás Suárez-Inclán, Partner, Greenwood Family Advisors LLC

At last...a practical resource for family members, family business
staff and advisors who wish to be prepared for mental health
challenges in the family business ecosystem.

This book (i) identifies the wide variety of mental health challenges that
may impact the family business and its constituents and (ii) demonstrates
the importance of candid discussions and proactive planning for common,
yet often stigmatized, mental health conditions.

Mental health challenges are inevitable in any large, sustained group
setting—family businesses are not immune. Thanks to the authors for
providing guidance to those who accept that reality and want to be
prepared to identify and solve for those challenges as they arise.

— Sarah Kerr Severson, Partner, Arentfox Schiff LLP

From Stigma
to Strength

Cultivating Mental Health
for a Thriving Family Business

Edited by Andrew Keyt

Generation6 Innovation Series
A Generation6 Publication
Generation6.com

generation6
INNOVATION SERIES

Scan the QR code for more information
about the Generation6 Innovation Series.

Acknowledgments

In 2023 we established the Generation6 Innovation Series with the intent of addressing topics that we felt hadn't received adequate attention. The goal was to shine a light on these topics, introduce new thinking, and hopefully spur innovation that will help the families that we serve. This year, we chose to focus on the topic of mental health. It would not have been possible to explore this topic without the support, hard work and energy of many people.

First of all, I'd like to thank my co-founders of Generation6, Greg McCann and Joe Astrachan. They have been huge supporters of this project and tremendous colleagues that always inspire me to dream big dreams. Next, I'd like to thank all of my colleagues at Generation6 for providing ideas, referrals and the financial support to make this project successful. Specifically, I'd like to recognize Jocelyn Deamer our Project Coordinator, and Rodrigo Himiob our Managing Director for helping to manage all of the logistics behind the scenes to make this happen.

Our thanks also goes to Lisa Bennett, an author and award-winning journalist who was a consulting editor on this book. While we were the subject matter experts, Lisa was instrumental in creating a cohesive book, improving all of our writing, and making our ideas more accessible. Thank you to Kulvir Gill, our facilitator and Project Manager who led our retreat gathering and helped us share, collaborate, and connect during our authors retreat in Miami. Thank you to Anna Kline, our copy editor, and Rebecca DeYarman and the team at MatchPoint Partners who assisted us with book design.

This book would not have happened without the hard work and diligence of our authors who committed their time and talents to write a chapter and, in some cases, multiple chapters. The amount of time and emotional energy that they each contributed with the implicit goal of helping families cannot be underestimated. Each of them is as talented as they are generous.

My heartfelt thanks to Dr. Edward Monte, Dr. Ellen Astrachan-Fletcher, CEDS-S, FAED, Regional Clinical Director, Eating Recovery Center and Pathlight Mood & Anxiety Center, Dr. Joe Astrachan Co-founder Generation6, Dr. Gail Silverstein, Clinical Neuropsychologist, Anne Smart, Advisor Generation6 Dr. Fran Langdon, ABAM, Alyce Jurgensen LCSW, Trent Codd III, Ed.S, BCBA VP of Clinical Services for the Carolinas for Refresh Mental Health, Domingo Such, JD, Partner at Perkins Coie, and Diana Clark, JD, MA, President of Intent Clinical, Dr. Anneleen Michiels, Associate Professor of Finance, Hasselt University & Generation6 Advisor and Dr. Torsten Pieper, Associate Professor at UNC Charlotte and Generation6 Advisor.

I would also like to thank our gathering participants. These individuals are experienced family business and family office owners and leaders who devoted significant time to read and provide feedback on our chapters, and to gather together in person and virtually to discuss, debate, and develop the authors ideas, all with the goal of helping families. I would like to thank Ashley Duchossois Joyce, LCSW, Chair of the Duchossois Group, Veronica Maldonado, Chair of GEM Family Office, Sara Severson, Partner, ArentFox Schiff, Mary Nelson, ARC Leadership, Maria Jose Perry, Espinosa Organization, Jennifer Aguerrebere, Greenwood Family Advisors LLC, Nicolás Suárez-Inclán, CFA, Greenwood Family Advisors, Camilla Gallagher, Director Family Business Network Miami Hub, Alicia Gerrits de Sola, NACD. CD, Grupo de Sola, and Cristina Henriquez. We would also like to thank Gary Shunk, Family Wealth Advisor at Wells Fargo Bank for the input that he offered on several chapters.

Thanks to the Miami office of the Northern Trust Bank, for hosting our group in Miami in January of 2024. Your space allowed the authors and gathering participants a great setting to explore and discuss these important issues. We would like to thank Alexander Adams, President of South Florida, Maria Reese, Sr. Administrative Assistant, Robert Lugo, Vice President and Regional Director of Food Services, Joe Zayas, Vice President, Senior Associate, EUC North America Technical Services, Isaac Watkins, NA Field Services, IT.

Thank you to Erin Kuhn-Krueger, David Goetz, and Melissa Parks for their input and comments as we put together this book.

Finally, thank you to everyone who supported me through the process and the families that have trusted me to help them in their journeys. I will forever be grateful.

Andrew Keyt

Contents

Introduction

by Andrew Keyt

One of the true honors of working with family businesses is that you are invited into the life of a family in a very real and intimate way: their joys and sorrows, triumphs, and tragedies. Doing this work for over 25 years has taught me that abundant wealth and success do not guarantee happiness. I've learned that families we look at from the outside as the pillars of success and brilliance often have deep pain and sorrow hidden behind the veneer of that success. This pain and sorrow, strife, and struggle often find their origins in the challenges of mental health: depression, substance use disorder, narcissism, or family trauma. Yet, in the field of family business, we have spent little to no time exploring these issues. A recent literature review on the topic found that 73% of the studies of mental health in the field of family business have come since 2010.[1] (You can find more about the family business research literature on mental health in the Concluding Thoughts chapter at the end of the book.)

The reality is that mental health issues impact an estimated 58 million Americans[2] and almost 1 billion worldwide, and family businesses are not immune.[3] With the recent impact of COVID and the stressors of social media, economic strife, and political unrest, mental health has become a more significant and more visible problem for everyone. Research has shown that

---

1 Arijs, D., & Michiels, A. (2021b). Mental Health in Family Businesses and Business Families: A Systematic review. *International Journal of Environmental Research and Public Health/International Journal of Environmental Research and Public Health, 18*(5), 2589. https://doi.org/10.3390/ijerph18052589

2 *Mental illness*. (n.d.). National Institute of Mental Health (NIMH). https://nimh.nih.gov/health/statistics/mental-illness

3 World Health Organization. World Health Organization: WHO. (2022, June 17). WHO highlights urgent need to transform mental health and mental health care. *News Release*. https://www.who.int/news/item/17-06-2022-who-highlights-urgent-need-to-transform-mental-health-and-mental-health-care

there has been a 13% increase in mental health disorders over the last decade[4] and a steady increase in death by suicide over the same time.[5] This means that family businesses are experiencing these increases as well.

Despite the growth in mental health challenges in society and the world of family business, we, as advisors and the families we have worked with, haven't done enough to talk about these issues. This book aims to change that.

This book's central argument is that a family business's long-term success is inextricably linked to the family's health. While a family business may be able to survive without the health of the family, it won't thrive. We believe that most family businesses that fail don't fail because they can't solve the business problems. They fail because they can't manage themselves emotionally or navigate the complexity of the family relationships. Understanding and addressing mental health challenges is essential to the health of these family relationships.

Our hope with this book is to recognize that acknowledging the importance of mental health in the family business is the first step. Next, but just as important, we want to highlight the key mental health issues that most commonly impact family business leaders and owners and help those families find a path forward. We want to normalize talking about the challenges surrounding mental health. We want families to consider addressing these mental health challenges as a sign of strength.

Most families don't talk about these issues because of the societal stigmas that exist. The American Psychiatric Association has highlighted that there are three types of mental health stigmas.

Public stigma: The negative or discriminatory attitudes that society or those around us may have regarding mental illness.

---

4   Foy, C. (2023b, February 21). *Are mental disorders increasing over time? | FHE Health*. FHE Health. https://fherehab.com/mental-health-disorders-increasing

5   Garnett MF, Curtin SC. Suicide mortality in the United States, 2001–2021. NCHS Data Brief, no 464. Hyattsville, MD: National Center for Health Statistics. 2023. DOI: https://dx.doi.org/10.15620/cdc:125705.

Self-stigma: The negative attitudes or sense of shame that those with mental health may have about their condition.

Institutional stigma: The policies of government or businesses that may make it more difficult for those with mental illness.

These stigmas may make addressing the issues of mental health feel like an impossible mountain to climb.

To help us explore how proactively addressing issues of mental health can help your family business thrive, we gathered eleven authors with deep experience with these issues. These authors include family business advisors with decades of experience, medical and mental health professionals with deep clinical experience, and attorneys. The authors spent a year exploring these topics together and developing the structure for this book. We have tested these concepts by getting feedback from a group of family business and family office owners and family business advisors to ensure this book is relevant to you.

We have written this book to help you, the family business owner, the family business advisor, the family office professional, and the non-family manager in a family business, understand what you can do to address the mental health challenges that you face and strengthen your family enterprise. You can read this book cover to cover, but we anticipate that you may have specific issues that you are facing that draw your attention. We encourage you to focus on what is most meaningful to you. We recommend reading the first two chapters to understand some basic contextual issues around mental health and family business. Then, feel free to jump to the chapters that feel most relevant to you. Finally, we recommend reading Chapter 12 to help you understand how to develop meaningful conversations as a family around these issues.

This book will help you identify mental health issues when they arise and teach you how to talk about them. It will also help you understand these issues' impact on the individual, the family, and the business. But most of all, this book will give you hope, make you feel a little less alone, and help you develop a plan for the path forward.

In Part One of the book, you will learn about the unique challenges and stressors that family businesses face that may contribute to mental health challenges. You will learn how the stress of balancing the competing needs of the family and the business, sibling rivalry, and living in the shadow increases our vulnerability to mental health challenges.

You will learn that while many see the issues surrounding mental health as an "individual" problem, they are deeply connected to and impacted by family relationships. The mental health of one individual in the family system has a profound impact on the health and well-being of the entire family and the family business as well.

In Part Two, you will learn about specific mental health issues, how they affect the families involved, and what a healthy response to these challenges looks like. We will explore topics such as narcissism, anxiety and depression, substance use problems, dementia, and issues of attention (ADHD). Again, in reading Part Two, you likely will want to jump around and focus on the issues most important to your situation. We encourage that.

Part Three addresses treatment modalities that can be helpful when addressing mental health issues in family businesses (such as neuropsychological testing and dialectical behavior therapy) as well as significant practical issues that you will have to navigate as you bring the challenges of mental health into the light. These include practical legal issues and the very real challenges of how to start emotional conversations around mental health with your family.

We hope this book will become a guide and a resource for you now and in the future—that it will normalize what you are going through, make you feel less alone, and give you hope and practical next steps to build a healthier family and family business.

PART ONE

THE MENTAL HEALTH LANDSCAPE FOR FAMILY BUSINESSES

CHAPTER ONE

From Silence to Strength: Harnessing the Power of Family Relationships for Better Mental Health

by Andrew Keyt and Edward P. Monte, PhD

Jack lived the storybook life. Or so it seemed. He was young (36), the oldest child of three, and a member of one of Centerville's wealthiest and most successful families. He and his wife Sarah had two children, with another on the way.

It took only a decade for Jack to go from an entry-level salesperson to the top producer in the family business. Led by his father, Peter, now in his early sixties, Jones Packaging had grown to $125 million in revenue from $75 million in just a few years, largely thanks to Jack's relentless drive.

One late afternoon in early January, as Jack prepped for a presentation on the future of food packaging for the industry association, his father called, asking Jack to pop by the office. When Jack stepped into his father's office, the accusations flew.

"How could you lose our biggest and oldest account?"

"What?" said Jack. "Which client?"

"Centerville Foods. A $15 million account. I just got the call. They just signed on with one of our competitors."

"Are you sure?" Jack said. "I just talked with their VP last week."

"This is the problem," his father said. "How can I trust you with everything I've built when you don't even know what's happening with your biggest account?"

"I had no idea," Jack replied.

"That's the problem. You're not fully engaged in your work. You should have seen this coming."

"I –"

His father cut him off: "I can't talk about this right now. Just go."

Jack retreated to his office. He slumped on the sofa, his hands shaking. He took a deep breath and wanted to cry. He couldn't. He just felt buried. Losing the company's biggest client was crushing. His father was heartless but predictable. No matter what he did, the results weren't enough for his father.

Jack had felt hopeless before, having been berated by his father often, but for the first time, he thought: "My family would be better if I weren't around anymore." He thought about taking his life.

While Jack appeared to be living the American dream, no one could see the growing tension between him and his wife, Sarah. She often complained about his weekly trips to see clients and his travel's impact on the family. Jack also felt increasingly isolated from his siblings, who often referred to Jack as "the golden child," dad's favorite. Jack also felt deep exhaustion from the bickering between him and his father about sustainable packaging solutions. His father summarily dismissed Jack's concerns about the environment. In every facet of his life, Jack felt trapped. There was no place where he felt "good enough."

The story of Jack Jones is not an anomaly, but it is seldom told. The inability of the Jones family to surface and address issues related to their stress, anxiety, and depression has become a threat to their family relationships as well as their business. Their silence about their mental health challenges prevents them from leveraging the strengths of their family relationships and using their human and financial resources to seek support in addressing these issues.

Today, one in five adults in the U.S. is living with some form of mental illness.[6] This means that one out of every five family business CEOs, next-generation leaders, family business board members, or shareholders are experiencing challenges that will threaten their emotional well-being and the family unity and cohesion essential to their long-term success as a family business.[7]

Yet families, advisors, and the field of family business as a whole haven't done enough to understand the unique stressors and challenges that mental health challenges like Jack's create for family businesses.[8] They have chosen silence over proactively building strength by acknowledging that these issues exist and proactively seeking support to address the challenges they present. Families tend to choose privacy and protect the family image. Advisors may worry about whether it is their role or what it might do to their relationship with the client, and this leads many families to a point where they ignore and avoid issues of mental health until the pain becomes too great to bear. The field of family business is also complicit in that our research has not done enough to explore the impact of the issues and how to address them. In this book, we argue that the health of the family business is tied directly to the individual mental health of its family members and the dynamic between them. A family business is a family first and will be as healthy as the individual family members and the health of the family dynamics. Families need to prioritize their mental health to create a healthy and thriving business. There are

---

6   National Alliance on Mental Illness. (2024, May 16). *Mental health by the numbers | NAMI*. NAMI. https://www.nami.org/about-mental-illness/mental-health-by-the-numbers/#:~:text=22.8%25%20of%20U.S.%20adults%20experienced,2021%20(14.1%20million%20people).

7   Pieper, T. M., Astrachan, J. H., & Manners, G. E. (2013). Conflict in family Business: Common metaphors and suggestions for intervention. *Family Relations*, *62*(3), 490–500. https://doi.org/10.1111/fare.12011

8   Arijs, D., & Michiels, A. (2021). Mental Health in Family Businesses and Business Families: A Systematic review. *International Journal of Environmental Research and Public Health/International Journal of Environmental Research and Public Health*, *18*(5), 2589. https://doi.org/10.3390/ijerph18052589

rarely, if ever, simple solutions to mental health challenges. We can't give you a checklist or a magical treatment that will be the solution to the problems that mental health challenges create. In the following pages, we hope to provide a greater understanding of the unique issues that contribute to mental health challenges in family businesses and ideas about how to start a conversation within your family that will help you build a support system. We hope these strategies will help you leverage the strength of your family and break the silence around mental health.

A family needs to care about the mental health of the individuals and the family dynamic because the well-being of the family and the continuity of the family business depend on it. Despite how it looks or feels from the outside, addressing these issues is far easier than watching a family and business you love go down in flames.

In this first chapter, we want to provide an overview of the unique stressors on mental health that come from being a part of a family business, why we tend to ignore or overlook mental health issues, and what you can do to move from silence to strength to leverage the strength of your family relationships and resources to address these challenges before they become a threat to your family unity and the functioning of your family business.

What Do We Mean by a Mental Health Challenge?

Mental health challenges include everything from anxiety, depression, obsessive-compulsive disorder (OCD), bipolar disorder, addiction, PTSD, eating disorders, and more.[9] These can wreak havoc on one's self-esteem, self-worth, connection with others, and safety. A clinical definition that we can use for further guidance published by the American Psychiatric Association defines a mental health challenge as "a clinically significant disturbance in an individual's cognition, emotional regulation or behavior that reflects a dysfunction

---

9   *Mental illness.* (n.d.-d). National Institute of Mental Health (NIMH). https://www.nimh.nih.gov/health/statistics/mental-illness

in the psychological, biological, or developmental processes underlying their mental functioning."[10]

Discussing mental health means talking about the issues that impact a person's emotional, psychological, social, and spiritual well-being. The issues encompass how we think, feel, and act. Our mental health impacts how we deal with stress, relate to others, make decisions, respond to challenges, and perceive the world. Good mental health allows us to function effectively in daily life, cope with challenges, and be productive in our communities. To be clear, everyone faces issues of mental health, minor to major, at some point in their lives. It is on a continuum and can profoundly impact one's life.

If mental health is so important, why don't families and their advisors discuss it?

While there are a multitude of reasons that contribute to the fear of surfacing and discussing mental health challenges, the central reason is the meaning ascribed to mental health challenges. We, as families, advisors, and as a society, have developed the stigma that an individual who is experiencing a mental health challenge is deficient in some way. Often unwittingly, we view vulnerability as weakness and that the individual is wholly to blame for their challenge.[11] Advisors seek the solace of structure by encouraging families to put policies in place to manage behaviors that are being driven by the mental health challenges that the family is facing. Dealing with the complexities of mental health issues may overwhelm family members, leading them to ignore the issues, and the field of family business has spent more time studying the business and succession variables than seeking to understand how underlying mental health challenges may be impacting the family business.

---

10   American Psychiatric Association. (2022). *Diagnostic and statistical manual of mental disorders* (5th ed., text rev.). https://doi.org/10.1176/appi.books.9780890425787

11   *Confronting the challenge of Mental Health Stigma: A new report and a new national initiative.* Psychiatry. org - Confronting the Challenge of Mental Health Stigma: A New Report and a New National Initiative. (2022, October 14). https://www.psychiatry.org/news-room/apa-blogs/confronting-the-challenge-of-mental-health-stigma

When a sister who is struggling with ADHD misses deadlines, forgets meetings, or takes meetings off-topic, it is easier to label her as "the problem" than to be curious and try to understand what may be behind some of her issues. When a father is narcissistic and fails to recognize the contributions of the next generation and other non-family executives to the business, taking full credit for the success, the next generation, failing to recognize the narcissism and its origin, becomes insecure about their own abilities. They begin to orient all their work towards making Dad happy rather than developing their capacity to do what they think is right.

The reasons for the silence on these issues may vary depending on our roles concerning the affected individuals (see Table 1). But there are some over-arching reasons that we would like to explore.

Families	Advisors	The Field of Family Business
Societal Stigma	Fearing impact on the relationship by raising the issue	Most research emanates from business schools, not schools of psychology and psychiatry.
Protecting the image of the family with employees, customers, and the community	Lack of training or understanding of the issues	It is easier to measure business variables.
Cultural norms about the meaning of mental health challenges	Understanding that this will increase the difficulty in serving their client	Primary focus on succession and the business
Fear of dealing with vulnerability	The institutions they are a part of may discourage identifying or acknowledging these issues.	Complex and interdisciplinary nature of the issues involved

Table 1: Reasons for Silence Around Mental Health Issues

The Ambiguous Nature of Mental Health Challenges

One reason that families and their advisors don't talk about issues of mental health is that it can be difficult to identify and frame. Unlike physical ailments, mental health issues can seem mysterious, frightening, and simply *not to be believed*. They show up gradually rather than all at once. They are often dismissed as "all in the head," which is not meant literally, of course, but dismissively. There are often no clear physical manifestations that indicate that there is a problem. Yet, as *physiological, psychological, emotional,* and *spiritual struggles*, they exist, and their impact is most *definitely* real.

It is the ambiguous and mysterious nature of many mental health issues that can make them hard to identify and define. Exactly when does someone's depression become problematic? When is someone being narcissistic versus extremely self-confident? When does someone's drinking behavior become alcoholism? When does forgetfulness become dementia? The line and definition aren't as straightforward as diagnosing a broken arm.

For the Jones family from our opening story, Jack's depression didn't start the moment that his father yelled at him. The pressure of producing, maintaining the family image, and pleasing his father had been weighing on him for months and years before. His father's anxiety about sales and performance had been building as his father handed more and more responsibility to Jack over the years. Yet, neither Jack, his father, nor the rest of the family was able to identify and discuss the anxiety, emotional issues, or underlying vulnerabilities that had been building over time.

When someone breaks their arm, there is a distinct moment and event that lead to the break of the arm. Mental health challenges progress more quietly, building over time, making it harder for families to see that there is an issue that needs to be dealt with. The result is that the family may ignore the issue or even attempt to normalize it until there is a breakdown in either the family or business that forces them to confront those challenges. We hope this book will help you address these issues before you reach a breaking point.

Protecting the Family Brand

One of the more powerful reasons family business owners remain silent on mental health issues is fear of how the family image or brand may be damaged by employees, customers, or the public. What would happen if the perfect image of the family is tarnished? In that case, the fear that the business's success is threatened along with the respect and status of the family and, ultimately, the family's wealth. What would happen if the employees of Jones Packaging knew that the chosen successor was struggling with depression? Would they still have confidence in him as a successor? What would the community think if they saw the cracks in the Jones family's armor?

Maintaining the family brand is more than just an internal pressure within the family. Families in family businesses often find themselves in the spotlight in their communities or the nation. This spotlight comes with the idolization of the family and all that it has achieved, contributed, or perceived to be. The ethos built within the family is that to admit that you are struggling is to threaten the family's name, image, and legacy in the eyes of the community.

Aryan, a next-generation family member from a 5th-generation automotive parts company in India, struggled for years with undiagnosed ADHD. He was outgoing and gregarious. Everyone in the business loved him as a person, yet behind the scenes, they were angry and frustrated about his inconsistency. Some days, he was present and engaged; the next moment, his mind was elsewhere, and he failed to order parts on time or missed important supplier meetings. His mother and father didn't raise the issue for fear that the non-family employees might start to see the family as incapable or deficient in some way. Aryan, as is the case for many rising gens, was afraid to admit his struggles for fear of shaming the family. But the silence of not identifying and talking about the issue only worsened the problem. Aryan and his parents remained isolated from each other, unable to unlock the strength of their family relationships to address the mental health challenges that they faced.

Families in family businesses tend to be bigger than life in the eyes of those around them and, often, in their self-perceptions. Since everything is magnified, mental health issues are hidden away out of fear of the perceived damage they could do to the almost idyllic aura of the family. The family develops a family code that we "deal with our problems in-house," or if you are experiencing a mental health challenge, you just need to "buck up" and suppress the issues. This stands in stark contrast to how most family businesses approach business problems. When faced with business problems, they don't hide the problem in the attic. They proactively seek solutions. They find resources, consultants, and support to solve those business problems when they don't have in-house expertise.

Cultural Influences

A family's ethnicity and culture can also increase the stigma of talking about mental health challenges. These cultural barriers can form an invisible yet powerful barrier that prevents people from seeking and receiving help from professionals.

For Black and brown people in America, this can be attributed to being on the receiving end of inequities in healthcare and an overall lack of trust in the healthcare system. For others, like Asian communities, seeking help can be seen as a sign of weakness that could bring shame upon the family. In more Calvinistic cultures, these vulnerabilities are attributed to a failure to buck up, work harder, and overcome those weaknesses.

Gender is another powerful cultural factor that can impact how we are taught to approach issues of mental health. Men, for instance, may be less likely to seek mental health support due to the perception that expressing vulnerability goes against traditional gender norms. Women experience more challenges and discrimination about taking on leadership roles, leading to increased stress. These stressors range from women shouldering more of the burden for childcare and housework[12] to being perceived negatively for showing dominant or assertive leadership behaviors as men.[13] Finally, for family members in the LGBTQ community who don't identify with traditional gender roles, the stress, and discrimination that they feel may lead them to keep their feelings and experiences hidden.

The Cost of Our Silence

The silence of our families, the advisory community, and the field of family business comes at a cost. We could spend the rest of this chapter talking about the economic cost of mental health challenges to our society (an estimated $1 trillion a year).[14] We could extrapolate the financial impact that would have on family businesses based on the high percentage of family businesses in our economy[15] and what that means for our communities. But this would only be scratching the surface of the actual costs of this silence.

The real costs of our silence are the emotional costs, the fractured relationships, the feelings of being alone and unsupported, and the stress created. These are the costs that lead to family buyouts and breakups, family members being written out of the will, and sometimes the demise of the family business itself.[16]

To address both the economic and emotional costs, we must end the silence and start the conversations that will help us address these fundamental challenges. To see real change in mental health and the accompanying challenges,

---

12 Chavda, J., & Chavda, J. (2024, April 18). *In a growing share of U.S. marriages, husbands and wives earn about the same.* Pew Research Center. https://www.pewresearch.org/social-trends/2023/04/13/in-a-growing-share-of-u-s-marriages-husbands-and-wives-earn-about-the-same/

13 Kim, J., Hsu, N., Newman, D. A., Harms, P., & Wood, D. (2020). Leadership perceptions, gender, and dominant personality: The role of normality evaluations. *Journal of Research in Personality, 87*, 103984. https://doi.org/10.1016/j.jrp.2020.103984

14 World Economic Forum. (n.d.). *Strategic Intelligence | World Economic Forum.* Strategic Intelligence. https://intelligence.weforum.org/topics/a1Gb0000000pTDbEAM

15 Van Der Vliet, D. (2021, June 2). *Measuring the financial impact of family businesses on the US economy.* Family Business. https://familybusiness.org/content/measuring-the-financial-impact-of-family-businesses-on-the-US-ec

16 Kets de Vries, M. & Miller D. (1984) The Neurotic Organization. Jossey Bass. Kets de Vries, M. & Miller (1996). The Anatomy of an Entrepreneur: Clinical Observations *Human Relations, 49(7), 853–883.*

we need to acknowledge and openly discuss the existence and meaning of these mental health challenges for the individual and the family. We must leverage the strength of the family and its support system to help the individual, the family, and ultimately the business. Ignoring or avoiding these critical conversations and keeping mental health concerns behind closed doors only lays a foundation for catastrophe.

Unique Stresses on Mental Health from Being a Part of a Family Business

To move from silence to strength, we must understand that when we are a part of a family business, our family roles and relationships are more intertwined than those of a non-family-owned business. Professional, personal, and financial worlds overlap, which creates stressors on our mental health and well-being that are different from families in the rest of society. Some of the most prevalent sources of stress include challenges to the individual identities of family members, balancing the needs of the family and the needs of the business, sibling rivalry, the competition for power, influence, and approval, and the pressures to conform to the norms of family history.

Challenges of Identity

The pressure to live up to a family's mythology and maintain the family brand places pressure on conforming to one's identity in the family business context. Family business owners' lives are so intertwined that it's hard for the rising generation to establish who they are, separate from their families.

One successor we talked to shared how growing up in Germany, in a family that was well known, always wondered whether his accomplishments were his own or were because he was part of a prominent family. Early in his career, he worked for several years in the United States, where his family was unknown. He described those years as some of the happiest of his life because he knew that all his accomplishments were the results of his own work.

This story speaks to the human developmental challenge of differentiation. Differentiation is challenging for the rising generation to learn to stand separate from their parents with their thoughts and opinions (which may differ from their parents') while staying emotionally connected and having empathy. In family businesses, the enmeshment of family members' professional, personal, and financial lives make this stressful and difficult. For rising generation members, their financial lives and career trajectories are still deeply tied to their relationships with their parents. If they weren't working for their family business, they would have greater separation and agency over their lives and careers. We will explore this concept more deeply in Chapter 2.

Balancing the Needs of the Business and the Family

Over the years, many advisors have asked families, "Are you a family-first business or a business-first family?" This question speaks to the real stressor that families face in trying to balance the competing needs of the family and the individual family members with the business's very real and pressing needs. It is not a simple either-or, where we always choose to meet the family's needs first or vice versa. The real challenge and stressor for a family is to determine when we need to sacrifice for the family and when we need to sacrifice for the business.

This question overlooks the inextricable interconnectedness between the needs of individual family members, the family, and the business, implying that balancing the needs is a simple either/or equation. We know that it is far more complex and stressful than a simple either/or question. The challenge is to cultivate a family's ability to acknowledge the needs of all involved to the extent that we can and work to recognize the trade-offs that we may need to make for the good of the individuals, the family, and the business.

When a father spends all his time tending to the needs of a growing business and isn't available to provide support for his spouse or build relationships with his children, they become more vulnerable to mental health issues such as substance use disorder, anxiety, and depression.

In one family business we worked with, the oldest daughter has distinct memories of the family house being foreclosed upon when the family's first company went bankrupt. When she stepped into the CEO's role of their second business, which was thriving, she then experienced bouts of anxiety that paralyzed her from making important decisions, and she couldn't understand why.

These stories illustrate the need for families to foster open communication about how the business and the family impact each other. As we will learn in Chapter 2, families that foster good communication, collaborative problem-solving, and mutual support will be more resilient in facing mental health challenges.

Competition for Power and Control — Sibling Rivalry

One of the most common scenarios people think of when you talk about family business is sibling rivalry. The media loves to tell the stories of siblings scheming for power, control, and acknowledgment, witnessed most recently with the popularity of the HBO show *Succession*.

The reality is that sibling rivalry can foster unhealthy competition and isolation among siblings. The constant conflicts and power struggles can lead to stress and uncertainty, anxiety, attacks on self-esteem, feelings of hopelessness, and depression. Siblings pursue the prize of sibling rivalry (parental approval, power, love, respect, etc.) without questioning the costs. All these dynamics strain the family relationships vital to long-term family business success. It is the strength of family relationships that helps us marshal a healthy response to the challenges of mental health. We will dive deeper into the importance of the family dynamic and creating a healthy one in Chapter 2.

Pressure to Conform to and Sustain the Norms of Family History

Across generations, the stories we tell and don't tell about our families establish the family's narrative and sense of identity. Over time, this can develop into a mythology that shapes our growth as individuals and a family. These stories, however, tend to accentuate the positive while ignoring aspects of the family history that aren't as flattering for the family.

This mythology that builds up around a family business can be both a blessing and a curse. The power of these stories can create a system of values and beliefs that shape how the family, successors, and employees see themselves in relation to the company and its history. But they can also pressure family members to fit into the family mold and pursue the path others see for them rather than a path truer to their skills, talents, and desires.

The myths of a family business and its leaders set the tone for poor mental health. Seeing those who came before us—or those within our midst who deny their vulnerabilities—as heroes propels individuals and the entire family toward great pain and destruction. The myths primarily tell the stories of success, minimizing any notion of struggle, fear, or vulnerability, making it seem to the next generation that they must succeed without failure or vulnerability.

Mythology tells the stories of the legendary characteristics of the heroic leaders and founders of the family businesses. Stories such as placing endless hours at work and sacrificing beyond anything else, a natural and brilliant business acumen, the ability to see around corners, a killer instinct for winning, boundless energy and stamina, never giving up, a can-do attitude, never giving in to vulnerabilities, never saying you can't achieve whatever goal you set, never giving in to doubt or fear, never having doubt or fear—basically, doing it all without breaking a sweat. It looks impossible, and it is. So, we don't share our vulnerability. When we can't admit that we are in pain or hurting, then our pain and hurt go unnoticed, denied, and unsupported.

It is true of a family and family business that great success is achieved through talent, hard work, and a realistic knowledge of personal and familial limitations. It is the adage of learning to work "smart" versus just working oneself to death. This achievement is realized by acknowledging one's limitations and building a team where individual talents unite to accomplish balanced and long-lasting success.

To buy into the belief and history that says one should never share one's vulnerabilities buys into the myth that vulnerabilities are about weakness and not guideposts to success. Admitting that we have limitations allows us to work collaboratively with others to overcome these limitations. We don't have to have all the answers.

One successor we worked with had never wanted to lead the family business. He kept his desire to become a college professor hidden. While he experienced some success in the family business and felt increasingly trapped, over time, it led him into a deep depression where he was hospitalized for over a month. Keeping silent about his depression strained his relationships with family members, significantly hurt the financial performance of the business, and had a catastrophic effect on his health and well-being.

So, when mental health issues are seen as incompatible with the beliefs and history of a successful family business, families are forced to work hard to deny, hide, and or ignore these challenges. The result is secrecy and an absence of trusting communication. And, as any mental health professional (and common sense) would tell us, this reaction is precisely the recipe for disaster. Families feel that admitting that a family member is struggling is a betrayal of the mythic success of the family business. Combined with the high level of scrutiny paid to family businesses by the public, families may try to hide any issues that might tarnish the pristine image of the family or invite increased attention or scrutiny.

The reality is that mental health issues need not be viewed differently than any other health issue. They no longer need to be hidden away, judged, or ignored. With the current physiological, neurological, and psychosocial research, the diagnosis and treatment of mental health issues are improving. There is now a wide variety of approaches to understanding these issues and a wide variety of effective medication and treatment modalities to address and manage these issues.[17] All of this calls us as a family to work together to talk about mental health, support each other, and work to move from ignoring the pain and hurt of mental health challenges to leveraging the strength of our family resources for the health and well-being of both the family and the business.

How Do We Move Beyond the Stigma of Talking About Mental Health?

To move from silence around mental health issues to the strength of talking about and addressing them, we need to change the beliefs and mindsets of family members around mental health issues. We need to understand that the less connected we are as family members, the less we talk about mental health challenges, and the greater the likelihood that mental health issues will create problems for our family business. We need to:

1. **Identify the Problem.** The journey from silence to strength starts with identifying that there may be an issue. It begins with curiosity about the issues and how they are impacting our family members. We hope that the chapters to come will help you see the signs that the stressors of life and family business and how they may be impacting your family and family business.

2. **Understand and Assess.** Understand that mental health challenges are complex and that there are likely to be many contributing factors that will impact the severity of the problem and the effectiveness of your response. Again, there are no simple solutions; there is only a commitment

---

17   Vos, T., Lim, S. S., Abbafati, C., Abbas, K. M., Abbasi, M., Abbasifard, M., Abbasi-Kangevari, M., Abbas-tabar, H., Abd-Allah, F., Abdelalim, A., Abdollahi, M., Abdollahpour, I., Abolhassani, H., Aboyans, V., Abrams, E. M., Abreu, L. G., Abrigo, M. R. M., Abu-Raddad, L. J., Abushouk, A. I., . . . Murray, C. J. L. (2020b). Global burden of 369 diseases and injuries in 204 countries and territories, 1990–2019: a systematic analysis for the Global Burden of Disease Study 2019. *Lancet, 396*(10258), 1204–1222. https://doi.org/10.1016/s0140-6736(20)30925-9

to understanding what these issues mean to us as individuals and the conversations that will help us access the resources we need to manage the issues. It is imperative not to run away from the issue but to remain committed, curious, and creative in the face of it. As in our business, we identify the problem and seek the support needed to address the challenges.

It is also essential to understand that many influences contribute to the complexity and severity of the mental health issues we will explore in this book (See Table 2). As we will explore in Chapter Two, mental health issues are embedded in and a part of the family system. While we share common experiences and origins as a family, people from the same origin can have different outcomes.[18]

The role that the affected family member plays in the business system will also contribute to the severity of the impact of the mental health challenge on the business. A CEO with a substance abuse problem will have a more drastic impact on the family business than a shareholder not working for the business. A next-gen member with anxiety will have a different effect than a family council chair with anxiety. While all these challenges will impact the fabric of the family and, thus, the family business, their proximity to essential decision-making processes will be a key determining factor in the severity of their impact.

The size and scope of the family and the business will also contribute to the size of the impact of the challenge. A mental health challenge facing a family business of four, where all family members are working for the business, will present a more significant challenge for the business than one facing a family with a hundred shareholders working both inside and outside the business.

---

18   Von Bertalanffy, L. (1950). AN OUTLINE OF GENERAL SYSTEM THEORY. *British Journal for the Philosophy of Science*, *1*(2), 134–165. https://doi.org/10.1093/bjps/i.2.134

Regardless of the severity of the challenge, we need to understand that family interconnectedness and cohesion are a central factor in determining the quality of our response to the issues. It is our family orientation to mental health challenges and the meaning that we make of mental health challenges that will increase the effectiveness of our response. Do we see mental health challenges as a deficiency and as shameful, or do we see them as health issues that can be dealt with through courage, empathy, and treatment?

If we deny and hide mental health problems, they won't improve, and family members will suffer. We deny our family members access to the strength of the family. Suppose we instead acknowledge the issues and deal with the stressors? In that case, we offer hope and opportunity to manage the issues better, limit their negative impact on the family business, and empower the family member to lead a more engaged and fulfilling life.

3. **Address the Issues.** Understanding the issues is not enough. To ensure that mental health challenges don't become a threat to the family or the business, we need to work together and build a support system to address the mental health challenges that we face. It's not if we have mental health issues in our family—it is how we respond to them. Families that rally both the tangible and intangible resources of the family can support the individual with mental health issues more effectively.

Returning to the story of the Jones family that we started with. The presence of suicidal thoughts was the pivotal moment for Jack. It was at that moment when he was thinking about taking his life that he knew he needed help. Jack called his wife,

"Honey, I need help."

"What's wrong?" said his wife, Sarah.

"It's all just too much. I lost our biggest account; my father hates me, and I can't do this anymore."

Sarah suddenly realized that this was serious. She began by checking to see if Jack was safe and worked with him to agree on a plan to meet at the hospital to seek help. Sarah then reached out to Jack's mom, who helped Sarah with childcare to get Jack the support he needed. Now that the issue was out in the open, the family was using all its resources to support Jack and work through the problems together. For Jack and his family, the process of healing began that day.

Conclusion

We hope that by moving from silence to strength, understanding the issues and how they impact our families, and looking at ways that we can find treatment and support, we can build and sustain healthy families and healthy businesses across generations to come.

Beware that a family business can exist without the health of a family, but it will not thrive. Family businesses usually fail not because family members don't know how to run a business but because they cannot manage themselves emotionally or their relationships.

We invite you to discover effective ways to frame mental health issues and understand specific mental health challenges that family businesses face. By exploring and understanding these issues, we will be better able to build support systems for the mental health of the individuals and the families and the business's health.

Influencers on Mental Health	Description
Genetic Factors	Certain genetic factors may contribute to a vulnerability to mental health challenges.
Brain Chemistry and Structure	Imbalances in brain chemistry or abnormalities in structure can contribute to mental health challenges.
Environmental Stressors	Stressful life events can be contributing factors, such as work stresses, traumas, and loss of a loved one.
Biologic Factors	Physical health conditions, hormonal imbalances, and changes, or chronic illnesses impact many mental health challenges.
Childhood experiences	Unmet needs and traumas, such as abuse or neglect
Psychological Factors	Personality traits, coping styles, and individual differences in how people perceive and handle stress
Traumatic Experiences	Exposure to traumatic events, such as violence and accidents
Family Patterns	Families often have maladaptive patterns that result from unresolved issues from previous generations. These patterns become learned behavior within the family and can contribute to mental health challenges across generations.

Table 2: Factors that contribute to the state of mental health for individuals

For Family Working in the Business	For Family Owners	For Advisors	For Non-Family Executives
If you don't talk about these issues, they typically don't get better.	You may have a more objective viewpoint at times on these issues than those inside the business.	It can be hard to identify what is a mental health issue and what is a family dynamic.	It can be hard to identify what is a mental health issue and what is a family dynamic.
Strong communication will limit the negative impacts of mental health challenges.	Your health and well-being are just as important as those working for the business.	You may need to enlist the help of family members and professionals to raise the issue.	You may have a more objective viewpoint on the situation than family members.
Look at the cost of working around the issues that the mental health challenge is creating.	Look at the cost of working around the issues that the mental health challenge is creating.	Understand your role in the system.	To address serious issues, work to create a team that includes family members and non-family.
Is the mental health challenge an issue that can be solved, or is it an issue that needs to be managed?	Is the mental health challenge an issue that can be solved, or is it an issue that needs to be managed?	Is the mental health challenge an issue that can be solved, or is it an issue that needs to be managed?	Is the mental health challenge an issue that can be solved, or is it an issue that needs to be managed?

Table 3: Implications

CHAPTER TWO

Thriving Together:
The Interdependence of the Individual, Family, Business, and Mental Health

by Edward P. Monte, PhD and Andrew Keyt

"Poor Peter." From early childhood, that was the family name for the brilliant son of a renowned family. Raised in the 1950s and joining the family business in his twenties, Peter was rarely referenced without this unfortunate pre-fix. He had struggled throughout his early life, seemingly either being so out of control that no restraints or boundaries on his behavior worked or so withdrawn and sad nothing anyone did could rally him. Despite his obvious intellect, he barely made it through school. His very frustrated father reluctantly brought him into the business without any plan as to what to do with him.

His father put him in the back office where "he couldn't do any damage"— effectively quarantining him. No matter the task assigned to him, his erratic moods and lack of consistency—in both work ethic and follow-through—resulted in his failure. His talents and passions were never known or explored, and the family business essentially was used as a holding tank for him.

There were periods when Peter performed well, but his drinking and absenteeism increased over the years to the point of non-functioning. And, with each step downwards, his father's disgust grew. His home life completely fell apart; his wife divorced him, and, at age 57, while drunk, Peter killed himself with his father's favorite hunting rifle.

Peter, similar to many people with mental health issues, became a stereotype and an anecdote in the family. His pain became his identity—"just the way he is." Any curiosity about how to help fell by the wayside. The family was burned out, and so was Poor Peter.

In actuality, Peter had bipolar disorder, a mental health condition little understood in the 1950s. His illness terrified his father, who had a grandmother with similar symptoms. His father once cruelly joked that if they had an attic, he would rehab it and hide Poor Peter there. To be fair, they did not know what to do with him. They tried to give him a role in the business and an income they maintained no matter how seldom he showed up for work. They simply handled him.

The irony is that the very system designed to support the young man also perpetuated his illness. Not intentionally, but from a lack of awareness. The fault did not lie with one person but with a family system that failed to be curious and pay attention to the needs of one individual who desperately needed empathy and help. There was no room for Peter.

Thinking of a family member as hopeless or crazy without identifying or understanding their mental health challenge is a classic example of a family system that is not functioning as it should. In this case, a mental health problem existed not only in the individual but in the context of a family system that ignored, dismissed, and tolerated it until it became intolerable for the individual who was suffering. It wasn't simply his problem; it was a family problem with a devastating impact on the individual, the family, and ultimately the business.

To effectively deal with mental health challenges in a family business, we must understand that mental health issues aren't just a function of an individual's problems. They are also completely interdependent with the family system in which they are embedded. We simply cannot live apart from a context. No one truly lives entirely alone. "Even a hermit needs a crowd to avoid." The stressors on an individual will affect the entire system, which, in turn, impacts the individual.

The reality is that mental health challenges are often hidden in plain sight, so much a part of the system that it is no longer recognized as a problem. They are redefined as eccentricities that are normalized—whether as family oddities or individual quirks. Often, with genetic origins, unaddressed mental health challenges such as anxiety can become generational patterns that can shape the culture of the company. The most obvious and important realities are often the ones that are the hardest to see and talk about. It's hard to see the big picture if you're in it and can't step out to gain some distance and perspective.

In the case that started this chapter, no one saw the smaller piece—a relative with mental health issues—in the context of the bigger picture—the family system. The family was afraid of what publicly acknowledging that there was a problem would mean. The progression from bipolar to addiction to death was accelerated by the inertia of a family system not equipped to deal with it. We need to understand the family system to understand how this can happen. What is it about the family system that creates this situation?

In this chapter, we will explore what a family system is, the complexity of the interdependent relationship between the individual and the family, and what this all means to address the mental health challenges we will explore later in this book.

The Individual Within the Family Context

To be human is to be in a relationship with each other. We are born into a family system that existed long before our arrival and will exist long after we are gone. Yet, our presence changes the system. In a family system, each person's thoughts, emotions, feelings, and behaviors influence and are influenced by the other family members. Families are interdependent, dynamic, and constantly adapting and changing in response to events.

This means that changes in one family member impact the entire family. When a father (CEO) experiences the stress of losing a significant customer and expresses his frustration by yelling at his spouse and kids when he gets home, the family is changed. When a sister with a problem with alcohol gets drunk at an industry event, it doesn't just affect her; it affects the whole family.

It follows that addressing the mental health challenges of an individual requires us to understand both the experience of the individual, the experience of the family system, and the dynamic between its members. To understand an individual, we must understand the family system that they grew up in. To understand a family, we must understand the individuals who are a part of it. To understand the family system, we must understand the family dynamics and patterns and how they influence the relationships within the family. A family business is a family first and will be as healthy as the individual family members and the health of the family relationships.

To understand these family dynamics, we must understand some fundamental psychological principles that guide human interactions[19] and how families create meaning.

1. **All human experiences are unique.** Each of us experiences the world from a unique perspective that can't be experienced exactly in the same way by anyone else.

2. **All human experience is sharable.** Despite being unique, we can share parts of our experiences with others. How we share our experiences changes our dynamic as a family and how we make meaning of our experiences.

3. **All human experience is temporal**—it happens and changes over time. It is generational.

---

19   Lauer, Quentin. *Phenomenology: Its Genesis & Prospect.* New York, NY, Harper & Row, 1965.

The extent to which a family can understand these principles can help guide us as we look at family dynamics.

Creating Healthy Family Dynamics

There are many frameworks to understand what contributes to healthy family dynamics. It's important to note that healthy doesn't mean perfect. Being healthy is the state of creating, supporting, and promoting well-being. It demands constant attention. Though challenging, becoming a healthy individual and family is attainable. Healthy families create shared meaning and build strong belief systems; they have a clear structure and organization that is stable and flexible, and they have open and transparent communication.

These concepts, rooted in the work of Froma Walsh, are the characteristics that allow a family to face challenges and emerge from them stronger and more resourceful. Like the family they exist within, these characteristics are interdependent with each other. Strong communication can help create shared meaning, and shared meaning can help develop structures that support the family's adaptability and resilience. [20]

Shared Meaning and Beliefs

We are what we believe. Or, more precisely, we do what we believe. Our actions most accurately reflect our deepest beliefs. Put another way, our beliefs determine our behavior. If I believe the world is out to get me, my behavior will follow accordingly. I might become isolated, defensive, and maybe even paranoid. Conversely, if I believe the world is my oyster, an opportunity and not a threat, I will proceed with confidence into the world. Just as an individual has beliefs, so does a system, and the two are interdependent. The beliefs of one create the meaning in the other. The family system's beliefs sustain and support an individual's beliefs. They work in tandem and reinforce each other to encourage or discourage certain behaviors. When families create a sense of

---

20   Walsh, Froma. *Strengthening Family Resilience.* The Guilford Press, 2016.

shared meaning and purpose, this can help them make meaning of adversity.[21] An absence of this shared meaning will make responding to mental health challenges more difficult.

For example, one shared belief that is powerful in healthy families is a belief in benign intent.[22] This is the belief that no one is out to intentionally hurt me. It is the belief that relationships are valuable and not burdensome and that we must fundamentally understand each other's experiences. A brother might say hurtful things about his sister's performance at work, but he doesn't wake up in the morning to make her life miserable. Doing a stupid/foolish thing fundamentally differs from intent to cause harm. Suppose we interpret the brother's comments about his sister's performance as evil, a malicious attempt to undermine his sister's performance. In that case, we can expect a response that is more reactionary and defensive.

A belief in benign intent is powerful because it acknowledges our propensity to do or say foolish things while presuming the best of the other person in the relationship. Thus, it creates opportunities for conversation, growth, and change. It also opens one up to forgiveness and trust.

Clear Structure and Organization

Healthy family systems have a clear structure and organization that creates a sense of stability that helps a family face adversity. They are not so rigid that they can't adapt and change to meet those challenges. There is a clear power structure, the ability to be heard, and clear boundaries. This starts with building a sense of mutual support and connectedness.

Mutual support and connectedness require finding the right balance of closeness and distance in our relationships. The tendency in most family businesses is to become enmeshed. Because so many aspects of our lives are

---

21 Walsh, Froma. *Strengthening Family Resilience.* The Guilford Press, 2016.

22 Beavers, W. Robert. *Successful Families: Assessment and Intervention.* New York, NY. WW Norton & Co. 1989.

interconnected, we end up in groupthink, with insufficient individual sense of identity. The opposite end of the spectrum is disengagement. If we are completely disengaged from each other—we won't care enough to work together to respond to problems. Working collaboratively to build shared meaning is one avenue to creating a sense of support and connectedness.

If meaning underpins motivation for our actions, structure is how we organize our actions as a family. Having a clear structure (clear roles and responsibilities, clear lines of authority) helps us manage the flow of information to members of the system. A clear flow of information allows us to respond more effectively to challenges. To resolve differences, the most basic demand of a system is to be brave enough to have hard conversations and finish them! When we don't resolve issues, problems convert to impasses, and without resolution, it can lead to depression, anxiety, pessimism, and hopelessness.

With clear structure, adaptability, and shared meaning we can work to accommodate the mental health issues of family members. We know one family that runs an extremely successful company where several family members have ADD. Their CEO is a brilliant visionary, but she simply can't stay focused. Becoming aware of this, the family finally hired an exceptionally bright assistant for her whose primary assets are organization skills and meticulousness. Among the assistant's many responsibilities, one critical one is to take notes so the CEO could listen and interact with whatever was being said rather than having to try to remember everything by taking notes.

In most cases, the belief is that brilliance equals being able to do anything and handling ten things at once. That belief had to be challenged by testing and research which showed the CEO that multitasking was only going from one focus to the next with much being missed and little getting the full understanding it deserved. Once that false belief was addressed, the meaning of "brilliant with certain limitations" could be inserted and the structure to meet the family member's needs in the family business could happen. Again, to start with the underlying beliefs often will reveal what is both the problem and a possible solution.

Communication

A family cannot respond effectively to a mental health crisis without healthy communication. In the case example that started our chapter, rather than identifying and getting curious about the mental health challenges Peter faced, the family chose to deny and pretend that the problem didn't exist.

Responding effectively requires clear and consistent messaging. It demands vulnerability and the open sharing of emotions and opinions. Shared meaning, stable and flexible structure, and clear communication enable the family to move to collaborative problem-solving. None of this is easy and is often counterintuitive if one is purely in a defensive or attack mode.

Take the example of a next generation member who comes to their parents and says they want to become a professional actor. In one family that we worked with the father's response was, "that's a stupid idea, you'll never make any money at that, you are going to come into the family business." We started working with this next gen family member who had fallen into a deep depression. In another family that faced the same issue, the parents' response was, "That's an interesting idea, and we know you are passionate about this, so let's work together to create a plan." Engaging and communicating around the issue lead to a 5-year plan for this next generation member to pursue an acting career. The parents then offered to fund half of the first two years of that plan. The end result was a next generation member who pursued an acting career and later made a choice to come back to the family business. That young man came back feeling loved and supported and was excited about the opportunity to build a career at the family business.

Barriers to Responding to Mental Health Challenges in a Healthy Way

While there are many varied and complex things that can prevent a family system from responding in a healthy way to mental health challenges, there are three we will explore: how we frame or label the mental health challenge, the family's desire to maintain homeostasis, and developmental breakdowns in establishing a healthy sense of individual identity.

Framing the Challenges of Mental Health

How we frame the mental health challenges that we face has a dramatic impact on how we respond to them. For example, if a mental illness is perceived to be a weakness, the system will treat it as such: ignore it, contain/quarantine it, push it aside, or even pretend not to see it. As with "Poor Peter" mentioned at the beginning of this chapter, the system will do everything to NOT deal with a mental illness.

The system organizes itself—consciously or unconsciously—around the issue to avoid dealing with it directly. It accommodates and works around it. (When this happens, it's extremely difficult for an individual within the system to change the meaning and shift the system.) And, conversely, once the system takes the wrongheaded stance to not deal with the issues at hand, those individual issues will never go away—they will fester.

In Peter's case, he could not make meaning of his bipolar illness. Conceding to the belief of the system (the family) that he was "just crazy," he dealt with it by drinking. Alcohol was his escape / his medication.

In a family business, the system is organized to support the business, analyze, assess, troubleshoot, and problem-solve. We search for certainty, which leads to labeling or diagnosing our family members. We reduce a mental health issue to a diagnosis or a label, thus losing the ability to be curious and creative in their problem-solving. The problem becomes insurmountable and, therefore, easier to avoid, deny, or dismiss.

An example can be seen in a family in which the father was labeled as narcissistic by the rest of the family. He became pegged as cruel, egotistical, and even evil. It allowed any minor misstep made by this father to be interpreted through the lens of self-centeredness and eliminated all curiosity about the insecurities that lay beneath his narcissistic behaviors. In cases like this, we lose all empathy for the person involved when we aren't curious about deeper, underlying issues. We lose the opportunity to understand his vulnerabilities and possibly make healthy inroads into building connections.

When your children are young, if your child hits you and says they hate you, you don't think of them as sociopathic or narcissistic. You wonder what's wrong with them. You empathize with them and seek to understand what is happening to cause them to act like that. You differentiate between their behavior and its causes and between them and their behavior. We do that for children. We tend not to do that with adults, and we rarely do that with men. Bad behavior is used to define adults as bad, eradicating any need to be curious about their vulnerabilities.

No one is arguing that bad behavior should be overlooked. There are consequences for being abusive. But the minute you turn to a narcissist and say, "Are you ok?" Developing a curiosity about their experience, you open the door to change in the way you view and understand them. And you invite them to walk through that doorway of change into a different way of relating to the family. It invites participation from all the members of the family system so they can truly listen to one another, seek to understand, and find points of agreement even as they highlight areas of disagreement.

Homeostasis

Family businesses are portrayed and celebrated in our society as pillars of stability. Families that have existed across generations laud the importance of tradition and protecting the legacy. Although magnificent concepts, "legacy" and "tradition" can be words used to keep a family stuck in the present when it needs to adapt to meet future challenges.

Theorists from the field of family systems psychology have highlighted the natural tendency of families to establish comfortable and consistent patterns that work to ensure a stable environment. They identify this tendency to return to what is familiar, regardless of its impact on the system, as Homeostasis.[23] For some family businesses, homeostasis helps define the core of who they are and the values they share that will guide them for others. This becomes an absolute belief that for the system to survive, it must *always* remain the same. When the meaning of change equals loss, rather than opportunity and growth, the family will seek the comfort of homeostasis.

While the stability of familiar family patterns can feel comfortable, families are not static. Families are always changing, children are growing, parents are aging, and the business is evolving. Healthy family systems change and adapt to meet these challenges. As we explored earlier, a healthy family system has stability and the flexibility to adapt. The challenge is determining what we need to hold onto that is essential to who we are and what we need to change to survive and grow.

It becomes a stuck system when a family faces change and seeks the comfort of familiar patterns over changing and adapting to meet new and evolving family needs. For a generational family business, this often shows up in the stalemate when the next generation pushes to find new ways of doing things while their parents seek stability in doing things the way they've always done them. If a family business is stuck, it may survive but not thrive. Nor will the individuals who maintain it.

A family that is stuck will find it hard to address mental health challenges. They may seek to normalize the behaviors and symptoms rather than confront the problem in the system. An example is a fourth-generation family business going into its fifth generation of leadership. This family can trace much of its dysfunction over the years to undiagnosed depression. The depression has been normalized. Rather than seeking treatment, family members are told to "Soldier on!" They want to do better, but it's been 110 years of distorted

---

23   Ludwig Van Bertalanffy, Karl. Zu einer Allgemeinen Systemlehre. Blätter für deutsche. Phiosophie, ¾. (1945). Extract in: Biologia Generalis, 19 (1949), 139-164). 1950. An outline of General System theory. British Journal for the Philosophy of Science.

thinking about depression. Changing will take a seismic shift in thinking and doing. This family is fighting homeostasis. This is a system that is striving to maintain the comfort of seeing depression as normal, failing to understand that affect disorders like anxiety and depression have a strong genetic component, but can also be treated.

Homeostasis underscores the interdependence between the system and an individual within the system. When an individual within the system changes, the family resists, trying to keep them in the role they've always played. The system feels safe but strangles the family's growth and adaptability.

We worked with a family where the father, who was the chairman of the board, had signs of early-stage dementia, which his wife was great at masking. She would jump in and answer when he was asked a difficult question. She kept him out of stressful situations that might reveal his symptoms. She hid the truth of his condition, protecting the image of her husband as a fearless leader, denying the reality of the effects of aging from siblings and cousins until it was too late. The company drifted because no one was running it, forcing them to sell.

The family system organized to maintain homeostasis, ultimately creating chaos for the entire organization. The irony is that the one person who knew about the dementia and had the most reason to address it—the CEO's wife—refused. This is the power of homeostasis. Others who didn't know came up with other explanations. "He's tired. He's overworked. He's being his usual cranky self." The family system, organized to protect the person having the problems, creates chaos and, in this case, demise.

In a healthier system, perhaps members of the family and the board would have shared their concerns about cognitive decline and a plan that would address the CEO with compassion and care while protecting the company.

The Challenge of Human Development: Developing a Healthy Sense of Identity

A healthy family system needs family members to have a strong sense of self. It needs to have healthy individuals striving to be more fully realized who can both support the system and receive support from it. Next-generation members need to have enough self-confidence to speak their minds, and parents need to know who they are and where their identity starts and ends to foster healthy, individuated children. This is the developmental challenge of differentiation.

Differentiation is the normal lifelong process of an individual developing their sense of self in relation to others. It is about knowing who you are within and apart from your primary relationships—particularly your parenting figures. As children grow up, this means developing the ability to stand separate from their parents, with their ideas and opinions, while staying emotionally connected with empathy.

Those two last words, with empathy, make this the most difficult life cycle task. As anyone knows, any two-year-old or fifteen-year-old can stand apart from their parent(s) by simply saying "No!" That is not differentiation; it's rebellion. It is an attempt to exert power and explore one's own individuality. Differentiation is being able to stand with someone of authority, someone you may look up to or even feel some contempt for, and say, "I hear what you are saying, this is how I see it, this is where I agree with you, and this is where I don't….and I hope this doesn't hurt your feelings."

When families resist their members' attempts to differentiate, family systems can manifest in two unhealthy extremes: infantilization and parentification. Infantilization is the result of a psychological need in the family to continue to view the successor as a child and not a fully grown adult. The British royal family—a family system enmeshed in an archaic system of governance—provides an example. Until he became king at 73, Prince Charles was the perpetual little prince while his mom sat on the throne.

Parentification—the other extreme—is when a young successor is thrust into a position of authority without any background or experience to be successful. Both extremes lead to unhealthy behavior. The adult family member treated like a child can't do anything of consequence; the young family member vaulted into leadership too soon is expected to work wonders.

While these two basic patterns reflect unhealthy behavior in general, they can directly impact mental health. For example, giving a title to a child who has had a lifelong anxiety disorder can be rocket fuel for the ego but is terrifying for the child. They will compensate by concealing their anxiety and going the way of power and narcissism; often, other family members will grow to despise them. We have seen this happen with tragic results.

Infantilization and parentification oversimplify the transference of leadership within the family: from one extreme—daddy knows best—to the other—you're the wunderkind who's going to save us. They also oversimplify the people involved. We see traces of these patterns in mental health issues, where individuals are not seen and understood as complex and multifaceted.

It is essential to know that the concept of differentiation is aspirational, and an individual's identity and the system are constantly evolving and hopefully growing. It is a goal one works toward one's entire life without ever fully realizing it. It's similar to self-actualization or reaching a state of Zen. Knowing and trusting oneself, feeling valued, knowing one's influence, and having a conscience as a guide are all part of being differentiated.

Differentiation can also get distorted or truncated when the system can't meet the needs of the individual in key developmental moments. When the family system is unable to meet the needs of a family member, these experiences become little traumas that compound over time and impact how that person interacts with the larger system, which in turn affects the system's health. When a family cannot identify or address these traumas, they can linger in the background, tearing at the fabric of family unity.

A Healthy Response to Mental Health Challenges

Marshaling a healthy response to mental health challenges requires us to understand that these issues are complex. They can't just be reduced to a diagnosis or a label. Mental health issues are full of ambiguity and can't be treated with a pill, one session with an all-knowing therapist, an amazing family business consultant, or just "powering through" the problem.

A diagnosis may provide some level of clarity and certainty, but dealing with mental health issues doesn't have a quick fix. To be effective, the individual and the family must work together to understand the emerging complex causes and effects. Families need to engage professionals to understand how to address these issues effectively. As illustrated in Chapter 1 (Table 2), causes for mental health challenges can range from biological and genetic factors to traumatic experiences and patterns. Most often, it is a combination of several. When we don't address the mental health issues, they often become a problem that repeats itself in the next generation.

Another layer of complexity that we face in dealing with mental health challenges is that they often appear in a symbiotic cluster. Bipolar illness can trigger substance abuse. ADHD works in tandem with narcissism, as we have seen. With human beings, it's rarely simple and clean. Once you accept that, the messiness can pull for curiosity, leading to a fuller understanding and more creative solutions. We will cover these more in-depth in future chapters, but for now, it's important to understand that experiencing the stresses of one mental health challenge may lead to other mental health challenges emerging.

The Courage to Act

To be aware of mental health issues, to bring them to the surface, and to deal with them is not an admittance of weakness but a show of strength, bravery, and intelligence.

Change requires doing something differently when we are used to doing the same thing. It is especially hard when we believe that change equals loss rather than opportunity and growth. It takes courage to push against patterns that may have existed across generations. It takes courage to change a mindset, admit vulnerability, and seek help.

Turn towards each other rather than away.

Turning towards a family member who has a mental disorder is a small and powerful action, a fulcrum on which the entire system can begin to reorganize around mental health. It is a turn towards hope and health and away from helplessness and "stuckness" of homeostasis.

When we turn towards each other and work together, we leverage the strength of the family so that no family member must face an issue alone. When a family shifts its mindset from fear to curiosity and seeks to explore and understand what is behind the problem, mental illness is no longer something left to fester.

And where does a family find courage? In themselves and their love for each other. We rarely talk about love and its generative power to create change. Love is fundamental to healthy relationships, but it's never discussed and is always awkward to address in a family business—all the more reason to discuss it.

Love is probably the most important driving force in a family business and the reason you work with your difficult sibling when the business could hire someone more "qualified." Or a robot. Love is also the fire in the heart of the family business. The secret sauce that shouldn't be kept a secret. Love will make a way when there seems to be no path forward because it prioritizes relationships over everything else. The story of our lives is less about what we build and more about who we build up, starting with the family.

Work Together to Understand the Dynamics

With curiosity and connection, we can face mental health challenges together. If we work collaboratively, with love, to research and explore the diagnosis, the challenge, and the family dynamics surrounding it, we build connection and cohesion that will sustain our family business for generations. When we look not just at the mental health challenges that an individual is facing but also the role that family dynamics have played, we create the opportunity to break the homeostasis of our family patterns and find hope in a new way forward together.

Develop Your Support Team

Family businesses are often reluctant to seek help. The thinking goes, "Our family built it, and we can sustain it. We've done well so far by ourselves, and we will continue." This is, of course, a myopic view. If help is available, why not seek it for the good of the family? If we can change our belief that asking for help is a weakness, we can open new paths to healing and connection.

The adaptability of a family and family business demands the awareness that some things are beyond one's expertise. As with a founder building a small hardware store into a national chain, there is a point where she understands the business has outgrown her, and she needs help. When faced with a new problem, such as an impactful mental health issue, getting on top of it can only be achieved by bringing in the best help possible.

Ideally, a support team will include professionals to address the specific mental health challenges of the family dynamic and the complex legal and business issues that may emanate from the challenge of mental health. The advisors, the family as a whole, and the individual family members with the diagnosis must work together to cope with what they are facing.

Hope Has the Last Word

If a family has learned to be helpless in the face of mental illness, it can also learn to be hopeful. Moving the business from silent inertia to hopeful action can galvanize support around the person or people suffering from a mental disorder and build the family's resilience to emerge stronger and more resourceful. For a family business, it is just good to face these issues head-on and increase the possibility that the business will survive for more generations.

The Rest of the Story

We started this chapter with the story "Poor Peter," who struggled with bipolar syndrome, was exiled within the family system, and eventually committed suicide. We find hope in how the family learned from Peter's tragedy through the story of his son Jordan.

Jordan was diagnosed with bipolar disorder a year after he left college. Jordan's symptoms surfaced in high school, where his persistent, mild form of mania pushed him to need little sleep and created a high energy level that Jordan focused on academics and sports. It was his superpower. Then, graduating with honors from college and having little sense of what he wanted to do, Jordan plunged into a deep depression that lasted a full year. His mother, frantically watching a rerun of her time with his father, got him to an excellent psychiatrist, which resulted in a short in-patient hospitalization to establish his medications. When he came home, he announced that he would like to join the family business since he had a marketing degree.

His father's brother, Uncle Ray, was the Chairperson and CEO of the company. He was a solid, even-tempered, and empathic man who loved his nephew and recognized much of his older brother's "demons" in him. Unlike his total lack of influence over the handling of Peter's situation, he was now in the position to do something different with Jordan than what his father had done with Peter.

Before bringing Jordan into the family business, he invited him for a weekend where Ray asked him to tell him about his life, his struggles, and ambitions. Ray spoke openly about his love for his brother and his frustrations over the tragedy of how his brother suffered without help and ultimately succumbed to his lack of self-care. Ray's anger was not at his brother but at his parents' denial. What was the most outrageous for Ray was how the family dismissed his brother's struggles and subsequent behavior as "normal," repeatedly saying, "Well, that's just Poor Peter." Peter's missteps and failures were the focus, and the horror was how the family looked at the outside world.

Jordan was amazed that his uncle spoke so openly about his father without judgment and with understanding and love. Ray told Jordan how much he loved him and, surprising to Jordan, how much he wanted him in the business. But Uncle Ray noted his offer was not without strings. Jordan would remain in the business for as long as Uncle Ray felt Jordan consistently shared how he was feeling, and if he sensed he was headed for trouble, he immediately sought help. Jordan had to commit to a life of self-responsibility, self-valuing, and self-care despite how difficult that would sometimes be. He had to commit to assessment therapy and faithfully take whatever medications he and his psychiatrist agreed upon. Most importantly, Uncle Ray insisted that Jordan lean on him and the family when times get rough. If he needed a break, the family would be there, and the business would alter his work schedule and expectations to accommodate his level of functioning. He could be assigned special projects without deadlines that would affect day-to-day operations. Ray particularly shocked Jordan when he said, "If you had diabetes or MS, we would all be there for you without shame. This is no different."

That was fifteen years ago. Jordan has flourished, the business has flourished, and the family has remained an example of mental health for its members, its employees, and the community. Over the years, the Peter Lancaster Foundation for Bi-Polar Disorder has also raised over $10 million for research.

PART TWO

WHAT TO KNOW ABOUT COMMON MENTAL HEALTH ISSUES

CHAPTER THREE

The Connection Dilemma: Narcissism in the Family Enterprise

by Joseph H. Astrachan, PhD, and
Ellen Astrachan-Fletcher, PhD, FAED, CEDS-S

*Note to our readers: We strongly recommend you read Chapter 10
on Biotemperament before reading this chapter. Many of the terms
and ideas presented in that chapter are used here to help us understand
narcissism and the things we can do to improve systems and
relationships where narcissistic traits are present.*

The litany of complaints is endless: "My dad never listens to a thing I say." "We don't want to get my mom angry. Her silent treatment can last months." "Succession won't happen as long as Dad's alive, so we'll wait until then to deal with the big issues." "I tried working with my father once, and that was more than enough," "My mom just surrounds herself with yes-people. There's no challenging her—or you're out." "If my father ever said he was proud of me, I think I'd lose it!" These paraphrased quotations are from some of the many families we've encountered who have had a common problem: a powerful figure who acts from what seems like a strong sense of what is right, someone with a "be reasonable and do it my way" attitude, a person who acts as though they don't care about the feelings of anyone else, in short, what the general public refers to as a narcissist.

That term grossly simplifies the complex leaders in family business who act in ways that put family and others at a painful emotional and relational distance. A simple definition of a narcissist is someone who acts like they think very highly of themselves and seems to seldom listen to others or take their feelings and interests seriously.

Diagnosable narcissistic personality disorder (Narcissistic Personality Disorder) occurs in some 6.2%[24,25] of the population. Some speculate that almost all great leaders have narcissistic traits.[26] Their success in business might be because they persist when others give up and give in, and they have an almost uncanny ability to face failure and stay committed to a course of action.[27] While we may all think we know a narcissist when we see one, the medical definition is fairly precise. Peruse the list below. It may seem eerily familiar; someone with five or more of the following traits might be diagnosable as a narcissist.[28]

- A grandiose sense of self-importance

- Preoccupation with fantasies of unlimited success, power, brilliance, beauty, or ideal love

- Believing that they are "special" and unique and can only be understood by, or should associate with, other special or high-status people (or institutions)

- Requiring excessive admiration

- A sense of entitlement (unreasonable expectations of especially favorable treatment or automatic compliance with their expectations)

24 Lowenstein, J., Purvis, C., & Rose, K. (2016). A systematic review on the relationship between antisocial, borderline and narcissistic personality disorder diagnostic traits and risk of violence to others in a clinical and forensic sample. *Borderline Personality Disorder and Emotion Dysregulation, 3*(1). https://doi.org/10.1186/s40479-016-0046-0

25 Fromm, E. (2010). *The Heart of Man: Its Genius for Good and Evil.* American Mental Health Foundation.

26 Post, J. M. (1993). Current concepts of the narcissistic personality: Implications for political psychology. Political Psychology, 14, 99-121.

27 Wallace, H. M., Ready, C. B., & Weitenhagen, E. (2009). Narcissism and task persistence. *Self and Identity, 8*(1), 78–93. https://doi.org/10.1080/15298860802194346

28 American Psychiatric Association. (2022). *Diagnostic and statistical manual of mental disorders* (5th ed., text rev.). https://doi.org/10.1176/appi.books.9780890425787

- Being interpersonally exploitative (taking advantage of others to achieve their own ends)

- Lacking empathy (unwilling to recognize or identify with the feelings and needs of others)

- Often being envious of others or believing that others are envious of them

- Showing arrogant, haughty behaviors or attitudes

This chapter explores Narcissistic Personality Disorder's causes and consequences. Our primary goal is to provide you with ideas so you, individually and as a family, can cope with others who display these characteristics or seek ways to change yourself, as having these traits can lead to significant loneliness. We also try to provide a deeper understanding of what causes Narcissistic Personality Disorder behaviors in hopes that you can use that understanding to generate ideas for coping, managing, and changing yourself and others appropriately. The most positive outcome might be overcoming your biases, insecurities, triggers, and fears while you develop deeper connections. In that way, you might be able to see what is driving emotions and behaviors to overcome old scripts and creatively adapt and change.

A Case-in-Point

Seventy-three-year-old Buck Bingham was 34 when he was named CEO of the family company his father ran for nearly 50 years. His father, a hobby pilot, died in a horrendous plane wreck just two weeks prior. Growing up, Buck felt he had two dads: the one who was fun-loving, thrill-seeking, and a best buddy, and the one who was stressed out, drank too much too often, and lashed out at those who did not immediately agree with his insights, his need to be right or at least appear so, and his seemingly unending need to find fault. Buck never quite came to terms with how his father handed out praise like a miser hands out money.

Buck remembers feeling like he always had to care for his younger sister and brother and shield them from their father's behavior. "Come to think of it," he once said in confidence to his hunting buddy, one of the few people he trusted in the world, "I remember thinking that if I just went with him on his jaunts and did all I could to make him happy, he'd leave the others alone." Of course, that was not enough. Buck also exerted enormous pressure on his siblings to act perfectly whenever their father was around to keep him from exploding. Buck felt like his mom was sweet and kind but incapable of ensuring things were shipshape enough to keep the father volcano from erupting. As he got older, Buck kept looking for things, especially in detail, that would cause his tiger of a father to pounce and maul him.

Without realizing it and without anyone seeing the connection, Buck had become a narcissist himself. He had an endless appetite for compliments from those who worked for him. It wasn't so much to make him feel powerful as it calmed him down. He liked mobilizing large groups to do what he thought was essential (and sometimes acting like they were life-or-death issues). Whenever he thought of leaving the top position, he shuddered and changed his internal dialog, generally focusing his attention on where mistakes were easy to spot rather than more meaningful, finding problems in details that didn't matter.

On the family front, Buck had not done much better. He alienated his brother and sister. As he explained it, "They just couldn't do things right. It felt like Armageddon was around the corner every time one of them had real responsibility!" While his marriage started with deep love and what he felt was ultimate understanding, he saw his spouse as incompetent with even the simplest tasks after the children arrived. Of course, it didn't help that his own father was overly critical of Buck's babies. Buck and Anne divorced when their youngest, now 41, was 12.

All three of Buck's children were in the business at one time or another. Only his oldest, Graham, remained in day-to-day management, and Buck thought that while Graham tried hard, he never admitted or accepted responsibility for his mistakes, and he just couldn't keep others from making them either. He was afraid he'd have to stay in the business until he died, always hoping for a miracle to make someone who knew how not to make mistakes appear.

Buck's children felt about their dad like Buck felt about his own father. They took to having endless arguments about what was right when Buck was not around and pretending to be aligned when he was. All the topics family business experts say should be discussed were kept from Buck because none of his children wanted to be on the receiving end of a Buck-bashing. Taboos included succession, ownership transfer, having a board of directors, and even the idea of family get-togethers where business would be discussed. His grandchildren, as well as his nieces and nephews, were kept at a far distance from Buck, and most had no idea why. As the cousins grew older, they would joke about whose parents had the most outlandish expectations, asked the most bizarre questions, needed the most praise and reassurance, or, in short, as they put it, "was crazier."

What Is Narcissistic Personality Disorder?

As in Buck's story above, one can easily see how a successful and lucrative family business can be a nursery for narcissistic traits. He seems to display many traits of Narcissistic Personality Disorder—inflated feelings of self-importance, excessive cravings for admiration, and a lack of empathy for others' feelings. In Buck's case, as in many family businesses, the endless supply of agreeable employees, praise from employees and community leaders, and the ability to command and mobilize tremendous resources make scratching the narcissistic itch easy indeed. What's more, people with Narcissistic Personality Disorder often have depression, bipolar disorder, and substance abuse, as they can have trouble coping with their emotional loneliness.[29] It might be due to

---

29 Ronningstam E. Pathological narcissism and narcissistic personality disorder in Axis I disorders. Harv Rev Psychiatry. 1996 Mar-Apr;3(6):326-40. doi: 10.3109/10673229609017201. PMID: 9384963.

the pressure they put on themselves, their need for success and praise, their need to avoid criticism, or countless other reasons. Or it could be due to the need to have deep connections with others, which rarely happens because narcissistic behavior pushes people away, especially when they begin to get close!

According to the DSM 5[30] (Diagnostic Statistical Manual of Mental Disorders, Fifth Edition, which is the bible for all psychological disorders used by medical and psychological professionals), there are three subtypes of Narcissistic Personality Disorder that have some empirical support and can help us understand why some people with Narcissistic Personality Disorder can present and function very differently than others. For example, some are completely controlling and have to be involved in every detail to the point where people stop communicating and acting in ways that might draw anger and disappointment, while others might present as so fragile that you often feel compelled to change what you do to not upset them, and others might show themselves to be free-spirited to the point of chaos who take offense at the slightest challenge to their creativity or freedom. They all share in common that their emotional outbursts or quiet intensity shapes the behavior of those around them. We will discuss a few of the different types of narcissism later in this chapter.

Narcissism is a misunderstood term and a common catchall to describe people who seem to care far more about themselves and little to not at all about others, except perhaps as some actions of caring might support their larger-than-life self-image. But is it really narcissism or just plain old self-ish-appearing behavior driven by fear? Is Buck Bingham, in the example, a narcissist? Are his kids destined to be as well? What emotions might underlie this behavior? We explore this and what family members, as well as people who think they might have narcissistic tendencies, can do to cope, manage,

---

30   American Psychiatric Association. (2022). *Diagnostic and statistical manual of mental disorders* (5th ed., text rev.). https://doi.org/10.1176/appi.books.9780890425787

and even work toward changing the conditions that trigger and stoke narcissistic-appearing behavior.

Traits of Narcissistic Personality Disorder are diametrically opposed to what needs to happen for long-term continuity in families and businesses: achieving and maintaining relational strength and strong emotional bonds. How does this happen? To help answer this question, we need to explore the connection paradox: people who deeply want connection yet are unaware of their incompetence in developing authentic and open relationships. They often have huge emotional hurdles to being vulnerable, being emotionally available, and allowing themselves and others to have real responsibility for how they feel and act; the obstacles may be so large that they don't allow themselves even to understand what this is. Left unaided, systems with such personalities often spiral into deep conflict (sometimes over years, decades, or generations) that causes some kind of generational catharsis (once or more a generation), where a conflict erupts and causes an irreconcilable shattering of the family fabric. But don't panic. There are things we can do to change our family's course and one place that is helpful to start, as discussed in Chapter 10, on biotemperament.

Human beings are social by nature; we need each other to survive. Physically, we can survive alone, but emotionally, without real connection, we are quickly ungrounded, easily unbalanced by others, increasingly misinterpret the actions and communications of others, and are destroyed emotionally. When people exhibit narcissistic traits, they often socially signal in ways that communicate "you're an idiot," "I know best," "I am better than you," "What I think matters the most," "What you want does not matter" "I don't care if my desires or needs cause you an inconvenience or pain." To be clear, the person does not necessarily intend to signal those messages, but it is still what gets signaled, and it pushes people away. For Buck Bingham, trying to make things perfect so he does not feel out of control is such a strong motivator that he pushes away all who might want to get close to him.

Another example is Susan, an adult child of alcoholic parents, who was driven to be responsible and achieve as a child. She was constantly reinforced for managing the family, taking control, and not showing vulnerability or emotions. In adulthood, she started a successful business that she often referred to as her "baby." She sold it ten years in, intending to stay on to help the company continue. However, she did not like the direction the new owners wanted to go, and instead of trying to work it out, she left to start a new company that she could run "in the right way." Susan also had two children, her eldest daughter, and her youngest son. While her daughter was incredibly competent and able to be independent, her son struggled with big decisions and was often impulsive when feeling pressure. While Susan received feedback from many consultants about this, she decided to put her son in an executive position because she believed "he just needed to be pushed into seeing how competent he is." She let her daughter take a back seat, stating that "she would be fine no matter what she does." Susan's daughter moved away, and her son bankrupted the company.

Two Frameworks: Biotemperament and Multi-generational Psychodynamic Perspective

We now turn to one of two frameworks for helping understand and deal with narcissists and coping and managing inside family and business. This is the psychodynamic framework that explores how life experiences shape perceptions and how these shape behavior. The other framework, biotemperament, is covered in much more depth in Chapter 10 and only briefly reviewed here. The second is psychodynamics; we will focus on that framework later in this chapter.

Biotemperament and Narcissistic Subtypes

Understanding a person's temperament can help us understand and have more compassion for how to grow in one's areas of need. For example, if you know you have high threat sensitivity, you might work on engaging your social safety system before interacting with authority. Importantly for families in business, it can help us understand others so that we can communicate with and act in ways that communicate clearly, as the intended messages, verbal and non-verbal, are likely to be more accurately received. Remember, someone might be extremely threat-sensitive and react defensively to even the slightest cues of a threat (like a lack of eye contact), and knowing their sensitivities can help when framing messages, choosing words, and being sensitive to other nonverbal cues. As discussed in Chapter 10, when talking about temperament, we are looking at threat sensitivity, reward sensitivity, novelty seeking (meaning how much a person likes new experiences), detail focus versus globally focused processing, and inhibitory control (indicating how much a person can choose to not respond to their urges). Susan was driven by her fixed mind state, her resistance to change, and her belief that she knows best for everyone, and with all of this, she pushed everyone and her business away.

Let's look more closely at three subtypes of narcissism[31]:

- Grandiose "Overt" Type

- The Fragile/Vulnerable "Covert" type

- The high functioning "Exhibitionist type."

First is the Grandiose "Overt" Type. They can show more of an emotional undercontrolled temperament ("look at all the amazing things I am doing" without bringing their projects to completion) or an explosive overcontrol biotemperament (a classical "that's wrong, I can't believe you are so stupid" kind of reaction). Second is the Fragile/Vulnerable "Covert" Type ("I'm fine with that " even though I am furious inside, and I will find a way to take revenge that you might never find out about). Finally, the third type is the High-Functioning "Exhibitionist" Type (where appearing competent is most

---

31   Kim, J., M. D. (2019, June 12). *The Three Subtypes of Narcissistic Personality Disorder*. Psychology Today. Retrieved June 22, 2024, from https://www.psychologytoday.com/us/blog/culture-shrink/201906/the-three-subtypes-of-narcissistic-personality-disorder

important, and they will argue that they are right, even if they know they are wrong).

The Grandiose Overt Subtype

Behaviors that are most significant and potentially destructive occur with the grandiose overt subtype, which, at its worst, becomes the "malignant type." This person is prone to angry outbursts and views children as extensions of themselves. They can be emotionally uncontrolled with high threat and high reward sensitivity, leading to a more chaotic presentation focused on the attainment of reward at all costs ("You don't trust me to get this done, but I already have achieved so much, and we will succeed so stop worrying about the level of debt."). Conversely the grandiose overt subtype can be emotionally overcontrolled overly disagreeable, with high threat and low reward sensitivity, leading to the need to appear competent even if they are not ("I am not angry," or "I am not being defensive," followed by "but if you changed one or two details you might have a chance of making what you are doing work," implying to the other that the Narcissistic Personality Disorder is competent while the other is not).

Both grandiose types put personal success (will plan revenge and easily betray others) and a sense of happiness (multiple affairs, substances, etc.) above all else. They can be extremely destructive in family businesses. They often signal their contempt for vulnerability and total disregard for others' needs. This type is also the most unwilling to seek consultation or any other help, stating, "I know my business best, and I know how to take care of it." This pushes others away (especially people with competence), causes people not to bring problems forward, and stops all creativity save for that which can be claimed by the Narcissistic Personality Disorder leader. When challenged, they react strongly, shut down conversation at best, or at worst fire people. Pro tip: First reassure and compliment to calm threat sensitivity, and compliment to calm reward needs, then use words like, "Is it possible that …..," to attempt to have them listen to and engage ideas that might otherwise be perceived as rejecting their position and transitively, them.

Let's consider Tommy, one of four brothers running the company their father had started. While there were also three sisters in the family, they were not allowed to join the business because the longstanding family belief communicated by their father and uncles was that "only men can lead." While Tommy loved women and had multiple affairs to prove it, he was raised to believe women were not as smart as men. When Tommy's third brother passed away, he allowed his nephews to remain part of the company, but none of his nieces. Tommy clearly communicated that he was the person in charge. One of his nephews was called Tom, as Thomas was a family name. Tommy decided that he should be called Tom because it was a more respectable name, so he told everyone in the company to call Tom "Zarta" (which means "fart" in Turkish). Only people in the family truly knew what an insulting Turkish name he gave to his nephew. Tommy's reaction to the name was not the only way people in the business knew not to take Zarta seriously; the fact that his uncle required him not to be referred to by his proper name also reinforced his nephew's lack of authority and status. Not only did this contribute to his nephew's ever-worsening poor self-esteem, but it also signaled to others in the family that Tommy could be cruel so no one would defy him, and, as a result, Tommy's loneliness grew.

When interacting with the grandiose overt type, it can be helpful to remember that their high threat sensitivity can make them perceive a threat from the slightest of signals and feel a threat even when it is not there. People with high threat sensitivity feel it first and justify it later, sometimes with outlandish and highly threatening beliefs. For example, they may believe others want their jobs, romantic partners, money, or lives. They are likely to have confirmation bias, meaning they will pay attention to the things that reinforce their beliefs and discount everything contrary. They push people away even as they want to feel closer to people. Try to be clear that you care about them and want to help them. Ask them if they are open to feedback, and do not give it if they say no. Remember that, in general, unwanted advice rarely helps, and it is always best to ask permission before giving advice, especially with people with narcissistic tendencies!

The Fragile/Vulnerable "Covert" Type

This type tends to be quieter, contained, and shy. They tend to be viewed as "super feelers" and often communicate indirectly. Social signaling fragility tends to get others to back off, not give feedback, nor make explicit expectations. ("You never treat me fairly" would be one message they signal, as well as other messages that imply victimization: "I should be treated specially because of my struggles in life"). Their sense of self-importance is hidden, and they can appear incredibly nice and caring on the outside but be resentful, bitter, and even vindictive on the inside. Their bitterness and vindictiveness are likely seen in passive-aggressive behavior. When they feel badly about their internal thoughts and feelings, it can turn into self-hatred and depression. This might be seen in them "disappearing" for days at a time. They have many judgments about others but will not voice them unless pushed to an extreme, in which case their judgments are communicated in ways that seem intended to hurt others. Abandonment is their solution; they will leave situations or even families when pushed too far. It is not too hard to see how such behaviors would make for very confused employees.

Natalie was not allowed to be part of the company (her father experimented with only one daughter, the first in several generations to be allowed to work in the company). While she was generally very quiet and withdrawn, if she got fed up, she would have angry outbursts for which she often felt shame. She believed her emotional outbursts only proved her family's belief that women are too emotional for business. So often, instead of expressing her anger, she would work to sabotage others. She believed her sister Judy was not advocating enough for women to get a role in the company because, historically, women were excluded from company business. Natalie wanted to prove that Judy was ineffective, but that was a Judy thing, not a female thing, so she hid Judy's hearing aids in the basement of the house. Judy found her hearing aids only years later, and it did not help Natalie, or their other sister get consideration in the family enterprise.

When interacting with a loved one who is the Fragile/Vulnerable "Covert" type, it can be helpful to realize that when they are uncomfortable, they are going to escape or, in other ways, try to disappear. This is bad for family and business alike, and for the sake of family and business, it is advisable to try not to let them run away. Try to communicate that they do not have to be perfect to be loved and valued. When they are honest about their feelings, thank them for being honest, especially if it was a difficult truth to admit or if they risked making you upset by being honest.

The High-Functioning "Exhibitionist Type"

In a non-family business, the high functioning "Exhibitionist type" tends to be the most successful subtype of narcissistic personality disorder. This type functions at a high level and they have more flexibility in their behaviors. They are the ones who are beloved at work because the more they are upheld and revered, the better they feel. But at home, they are likely to be very different, showing their Narcissistic Personality Disorder traits of lack of compassion and contempt for "weakness." They can be outwardly demanding at home, lacking compassion, and dismissive. Substances "to unwind in the evening" can make that difference even greater. The nuclear family might feel both the need to protect the reputation of the loved one to support the family's ongoing financial success and fear the likelihood that others might not believe such an unfavorable representation of a person who they see very differently anyway. In these cases, the person with Narcissistic Personality Disorder might use the fact that "others love me, at work" as evidence that they are a good person, and the feedback the family is trying to give them "must not be true."

In the family business, where the high functioning "Exhibitionist type" cannot separate work and family, we often see the family and leader trying to have a soundproof wall between family and business communications. There may be many family-only meetings and lots of talk on the importance of keeping things from employees. However, they try, the truth seeps out, and employees are left anxious, not knowing the truth from rumors, not feeling trusted, and not knowing if big changes are around the corner.

When interacting with the high functioning "Exhibitionist type," it can be helpful to remember that it likely takes a ton of energy for this person to put on a show every day at work and that they let loose at home where they feel safer. It can be helpful to validate for them how well they are doing at work while asking them if it is possible their dedication and commitment to that could be taking a toll on their family. One can try to be curious about their values, whose admiration matters most, and why. But don't push too hard on this if there is discomfort. Small doses repeatedly at a slow pace are more likely to produce change, whereas large, overwhelming ones often produce stronger and stronger resistance to change.

Narcissistic traits are present with all subtypes, although some are more visible or expressed. The sense of self-importance, the belief that no one really understands them because they are so special, and the sense of entitlement all interfere with their ability to be open to truly and to connect with others. In a family business, these traits can destroy what took generations to build.

Now What?

So, we understand Narcissistic Personality Disorder and its subtypes. Now what?

First, let's look at those who might have Narcissistic Personality Disorder traits. We do this to help those who want to help themselves, assuage fears if you think you might have tendencies and are now filled with fear, and help those who want help dealing with those with narcissistic personality traits to be able to see through the real eyes of those who vex them and not just a simplistic or overly self-defined version of why they act the way they do. We then offer actionable advice for those dealing with people with narcissistic personality traits. Lastly, we will turn our attention to those who want to have better interactions with people with Narcissistic Personality Disorder traits using a different frame that is a little more oriented to stopping the pattern of multi-generational narcissism.

If you might be starting to recognize yourself in some of the above examples, fear not. Your threat sensitivity and need to take care of yourself and your needs first and foremost do not have to rule your actions so that you can have deeper connections. You might think, "If I do not care for myself, no one will." Unfortunately, that is only true when you stop caring for others. What are your values? Do you have relationships as a value, whether it is a value of family, a value of friends, or a value of connection in general? Is this a value, even if you are a person who knowingly or unknowingly pushes people away? Is knowledge or education a value? Do you sometimes signal competency because you believe that will get you the most respect, even if you do not feel competent? Is it possible people actually respect you less when they feel you are not genuine? Are you a person who feels stressed when interacting with others? Do you see any of this as a potential problem? Would you be open to learning and growing?

If you are willing to consider the possibility of growth, you must be open to feedback. To be truly open to feedback, and not open in a way that you will listen and then defend yourself as though you are being attacked requires that you make yourself open to consider the possibility that there might be something for you to learn from the feedback or the distress you feel when receiving the feedback. Remember, we tend to get more distressed about feedback that hits home, especially if it is something that we would not want to acknowledge about ourselves. To do this, there must be openness to healthy self-doubt to learn and grow versus unhealthy self-doubt that keeps us stuck. Unhealthy self-doubt is just beating ourselves up. Healthy self-doubt enables us to feel the pain of realizing we do something that does not align with our values and then to learn and grow, deciding to do something different.

If you are a family member of or working with someone with Narcissistic Personality Disorder traits, there are things you can do even if the person does not want to change. When interacting with someone with Narcissistic Personality Disorder, it can be helpful to understand that they are threat-sensitive. This means that they are more likely to perceive threats in the world than rewards. To keep themselves feeling safe, they can throw up huge defenses that end up pushing others away and imprisoning themselves in loneliness. People with Narcissistic Personality Disorder do not like being told about themselves as they are the experts, especially on themselves. It can be helpful to enter into a true stance of curiosity. (This means not thinking, "I know the right answer, but I will ask a question expecting them to say the right answer"). Do not assume they are wrong, just like you would not want them to assume you are wrong. Remember that the mind states, discussed in Chapter 10, are prompted by feedback or things changing to protect a person's perfectionism while preventing them from having to change. When giving feedback, it can be helpful to ask the person with behaviors consistent with Narcissistic Personality Disorder if they are open to feedback before giving it. If they say "no," ask if they might be open to feedback later. When giving the feedback, give it as the gift it is, with kindness and the intention to help this other person learn and grow.

Hopefully, this section on biotemperament and Narcissistic Personality Disorder has been helpful, adds valuable perspective, and provides avenues for immediate action to improve situations. We next turn our attention to a more psychodynamic perspective to help gain a deeper understanding of the causes, consequences, and range of responses available to improve the current situation and help keep it from repeating in future generations.

Multi-generational Narcissistic Personality Disorder and the Psychodynamic Perspective

As we saw at the beginning of the chapter, in the case of Buck Bingham, the behavior of Buck's father caused a range of behaviors and the interpretations of others that led Buck himself to display Narcissistic Personality Disorder behaviors. His desire to not hear his father's scolding voice, and his mind's eye, led Buck to be harsh, demanding, and unforgiving with his own children. The likely consequence of Buck's actions towards his children will be that they will repeat the pattern. It may be that they want Buck's love, or simply they want to avoid harsh criticism, or perhaps both and more. They will likely behave similarly to their children, causing the cycle to repeat.

So, let's spend a few moments looking at what has caused Buck's behavior and his way of interpreting the actions and words of others. This will help us develop ideas for how to behave around the Bucks of the world and how to hopefully keep our children from suffering the same fate. While we will provide ideas, the real power of this section is for you to engage your creative minds to come up with different ways of behaving that are ultimately avenues for real multi-generational change. While we will build off the example of Buck, not all with Narcissistic Personality Disorder have the same root causes. Your job as a member of a system with Narcissistic Personality Disorder will be to figure out root causes and use that understanding to develop your own repertoire of behavioral and communicative changes to improve your situation and, hopefully, the situation for all in your family.

One last note: It may be very hard for you to give up on your version of the person with Narcissistic Personality Disorder in your life, as a demon. It may be hard to give up on the dream that the person with Narcissistic Personality Disorder in your life can be the person you always wanted them to be. It may be hard to stop being tormented by the idea that you have some control over how you are viewed. (For example, if you achieved more, you would have received some fantasized version of love, for example). As the old saying goes, to make a real change with your parents, it is necessary to grieve for that parent you will never have and accept the one you do have.

Buck was raised in an environment with little control and even less ability to predict what would happen. The threats he faced were real, and as a child, like most children, he could not interpret his father's behavior and saw them as coming from the context they were in, meaning that Buck believed all his father's behavior was due to things happening in the household as he hadn't a clue about his father's life outside of the home. As a child, he would happen upon avenues for protecting himself and his siblings, meaning there were likely no deep thoughts or considerations for how he should behave to elicit reactions from his father that would improve the situation. Such circumstances lead people to believe in magical thinking or the idea that if "My siblings and I only do everything right, we can avoid the dangers presented by their father." However, given that their father probably had a similar character as his father, it was unlikely that any behavior from him or his siblings could substantially reduce the risks. (That's the thing with such characters; they are responding to their parents when alive and still long after they are gone). Furthermore, it was also likely that their mother did little to step in to protect them, making that sense of threat all the more powerful. The feeling of threat consequently increases the passion one feels toward the importance of proper behavior, not making mistakes, appearance, or whatever bugaboos are instilled in childhood. With such a pervasive, deep, and profound feeling of being under existential threat, is it any surprise that Buck is a man who pushes people away with his perfectionism, criticism, and harsh attitude? Essentially Buck was pushing people away with the overpowering need to protect himself.

Is it surprising that Buck can't seem to form meaningful, deep, authentic friendships or relationships? Just look at some things he might be contending with about himself. If he makes himself vulnerable, all the childhood feelings of threat and fear will be inescapable. How caring might someone have to be before he'd even be willing to give them a peek at his real vulnerabilities? This is likely a man who felt that if he showed fear of any kind, if he were ever wrong, or if he was weak in any way, his life and the lives of his brother and sister would be in danger. So powerful are such childhood conclusions that they generally persist well beyond their usefulness!

Before we get into ideas about how to interact effectively with someone like Buck, let's look at what he might really want in a relationship. Above all else, he probably would want someone who could truly protect him from danger. His need for protection and to feel safe might be so great that if he were to latch on to someone who promises such protection, he would feel easily betrayed when they cannot provide it (even when it is out of their control to do so). He might want someone who calms his fears, not by trying to argue that they are unrealistic (which he might interpret as a possible threat), but who would understand them, normalize or agree with them, and want to maintain a relationship, nonetheless. As a person always looking for reasons to distrust others (trust is a source of threat for some), he might wait to be communicated with rather than reaching out to bond or talk. The fear of rejection if the person reaches out is so great that they would rather not connect than potentially be rejected, without realizing that when others don't reach out, they feel rejected. We all know people who don't reach out and maintain that those who don't call them don't really care about them, and in Buck's case, there would likely be no way of arguing him out of that point of view—so why try?

We have established that while people with Narcissistic Personality Disorder likely want a comforting, authentic, and meaningful relationship, too many things about their past keep them from being able to establish such relationships. Before looking at what we can do to have a chance at a relationship, it might be helpful to look at a few general rules for establishing good relationships, which come from a synthesis of years of psychological research.

There are four rules to follow:

1. First, all else being equal, the more often you communicate with someone, the better your relationship. Face-to-face communication is the best since it has been shown that over 70 percent of communication comes from non-verbal cues (such as body posture, eye contact, tone, tempo, and volume of voice). If you want a relationship, you need to figure out what might keep a person willing to talk, and such topics are generally non-threatening and interesting. The more you know about another person, the more likely it is that you can choose topics that might be of interest and communicate in ways that do not signal a threat.

2. The longer you talk, the better your relationship. The idea here is only to cover topics people have a genuine interest in and do not press your personal agenda.

3. The more you make yourself vulnerable, the better the relationship. Here, we start with vulnerabilities in which the other person has no role. So, for a parent, for example, we must avoid any topic that the parent could even begin to think they have any responsibility for. Neutral topics of vulnerability include relationships that are distant from the one you are trying to build. Fears that clearly attribute to others (teachers, supervisors outside the family business, coaches, etc. might all be usable examples).

4. Finally, the fewer taboo topics you have, the better your relationship. Eliminating taboos takes time, and one tactic is to bring up a topic and change the subject, wait a few weeks, and try again if not met with receptiveness. It may take months or years to remove taboos since it can take a long time to desensitize someone to the fears associated with a variety of taboo topics.

In general, if you talk all the time, for long periods of time, are comfortable with being vulnerable, and have no taboo topics, then the chances that you will identify, discuss, and resolve all problems and challenges grow astronomically.

Now, let's return to Narcissistic Personality Disorder. Here's one recipe for making things better. The first task is to note how often you communicate and then increase the number of times you communicate to at least three times per week. To start, try to discuss only light topics, avoiding topics that are likely to be perceived as threatening. Now that we know more about the person we are trying to communicate with, we can develop neutral, non-threatening, yet interesting topics. Avoid family and business as topics. Do not talk about anything that might imply you are judging or disapproving of the other person. Steer clear of topics that they might feel compelled to try to fix. Do not touch on topics that might imply that the other person owes you something or is obligated to you. Do not trigger their insecurities, even if you have a history of believing they have no insecurities, have faith that they do have them and try to be aware of them. In general, people are better communicators when they are calm. Be sensitive to the other's emotional state. If they are not calm when you reach out, don't try to calm them by being reassuring; this may backfire. If they are willing to talk to calm themselves, welcome that. If they are calm when given compliments, give them compliments. If you know something else that will calm them, use that. Give yourself a few months to increase the frequency of communication, and don't be put off by weeks and weeks of a lack of response. Remember, a person with deep fears and high threat sensitivity needs time to get used to a new pattern of behavior. The time it takes will depend greatly on the height of the other's emotional walls built by their experiences and their biotemperament. Here are a few more ideas as well as suggestions from above for an action plan.

- Increase Communication to 45 minutes a week—this can take a few months.

- Avoid threatening topics.

- Avoid discussing business.

- Anticipate some skepticism and remain consistent.

- Increase vulnerability once you are talking regularly for 45 minutes a week.

- Ask questions and listen to the answers.

It is important to recognize that in these conversations, the person with narcissism might say things that activate your threat sensitivity, as they are prone to do. Remember that people often do not intend to signal what they are signaling, and if they do, it is likely a defensive reaction to somehow protect themselves. If you respond from that activated place, you will likely find the suggestions above much more difficult. You can also always respond with "I am not sure how to respond to that." or "Is there a particular response you are looking for?"

Once you are up to having three or more conversations a week, the second step is to increase the amount of time you talk during each conversation. Find topics that they have the energy to talk about. It may not be pleasant for you in the beginning since those topics may not be urgent for you and may not be of interest, but in forming and building relationships, especially with Narcissistic Personality Disorders, we need to set our own wants and desires aside in the short run to build a more meaningful and open relationship in the long term. It may take six or more months, but if you can get to 45 minutes weekly, you are ready to move to step three.

The first two steps are all about establishing comfortable communication. Now that you are at 45 minutes a week, the other person can start listening more freely. You can now slowly introduce personal vulnerabilities into your conversations. If you detect hesitance to listen, return to topics that put the other person at ease. The more non-threatening vulnerabilities you can work into your conversations over time, the more likely the other person will start to feel comfortable enough to open up and be more authentic. This may be extremely challenging at first as they have likely had very few situations in which they have been open and authentic, and at first, it will likely be extremely frightening to them to do so. If and when they express any fears or vulnerabilities, just listen. (Do not offer solutions, comfort, or opinions; try to relate them to yourself by talking about your own experiences or normalizing their feelings or fears in any way.) Try asking a non-threatening question or two, and if they start to shut down, go back to a more comfortable topic and try again some other day. Don't ask about fears and vulnerabilities; they must emerge naturally in conversation. And as to the time it takes to get to this stage, please remember they took decades to build their emotional shielding. It may take what seems like an inordinate amount of time for such armor to soften.

Now, perhaps a year or more has passed. You likely have a more trusting relationship. It might be possible to bring up important topics. By this point, you will likely have a good feel for this and know, almost intuitively, how and when to move the conversation to topics that only a few months ago might have been too threatening to broach. If your relationship has gained sufficient depth, you might become aware of the other person's logic; those things that made no sense to you now are understandable, even if you do not have the same way of looking at the world. Once you understand their logic, you may be able to work inside of it to get movement on formerly troubling issues. For example, some people with Narcissistic Personality Disorder traits are compulsive collectors, even to the point of threatening their businesses and families. In such cases, when trust has been built, it might be helpful first to ask if it might be possible that some of their collections can be shed to keep collecting newer and more important things and, by doing so, not challenge their need to collect but affirm it.

You may always have to stay hypervigilant in monitoring the other person's emotional state when communicating. That is an unfortunate reality of having a relationship with a person with Narcissistic Personality Disorder traits. Even though it might be arduous work, the benefit of a comfortable relationship far outweighs the drama and chaos when a person desperately wants meaningful relationships but has none.

We hope this chapter has provided insight and hope. We hope you find strength in the ideas of this chapter and never lose the desire to improve the situations for yourself and your loved ones, now and for future generations. We are reminded of the words of Medal of Honor awardee and Vietnam prisoner of war survivor Admiral James Stockdale: "You must never confuse faith that you will prevail in the end—which you can never afford to lose—with the discipline to confront the most brutal facts of your current reality, whatever they might be."

Summary of Key Points

In this chapter, we learned:

- Narcissistic personality disorder can have a significant negative impact on the family enterprise.

- The term narcissism can be used as a weapon and as justification for writing someone off.

- There are three general types of patterns of behaviors with NPD: Grandiose "Overt" Type, The Fragile/Vulnerable "Covert" type, The high functioning "Exhibitionist type."

- Undercontrol and overcontrol biotemperaments show up in different patterns of narcissistic behavior. Identifying and understanding the nature of these patterns further increases our effectiveness in relating to, connecting to, and managing people.

- Understanding psychodynamic intergenerational trauma can enable us to work on changing patterns of behavior.

- There are steps to take to begin relational transformation.

CHAPTER FOUR

The Role of Anxiety in Family Business

by Gail Silverstein, PhD

Sanjay's father summons him to a meeting. His eldest son has been implementing a new initiative for the family business and knows, by his father's prior silence, that he and his leadership team are unhappy with how things were going. Sanjay has felt over his skis as a senior vice president for the past few years. When his team asks questions, he deflects and tells them he will get back to them. He tries to avoid his father even though he reports to him. As a result, his team, like him, often feels uncertain about what to do.

He's thought of leaving the company, but his father would never accept that. As his oldest son, his father expects him to become the family leader and president of the company in ten years. This expectation has been drilled into him since he was a child. Now, at 35, he is more anxious than ever. He takes antacids on an hourly basis for an acid stomach. Every night, he comes home, unloads his worries, and frets to his wife. The real trouble isn't the work. It is uncertain how exactly his father wants him to carry it out. Uncertainty drives his anxiety, which leads to a suite of performance problems.

Anxiety

Anxiety is a funny thing. A little anxiety is motivating, but too much anxiety can be counter-productive at best and crippling at worst. Anxiety can be what gets us out of bed in the morning and drives us to do our best. If your goal is to complete a project, a little anxiety can get you to work harder, stretch your abilities, and try one more thing to improve your final product. Too much anxiety can lead you to overthink, procrastinate for fear of failure, and maybe never try to do the project at all. If you are anxious, you may have trouble focusing and concentrating, and it's unlikely that you'll do your best problem-solving. If you aim to impress someone, some anxiety can get you to be on your best behavior. Too much anxiety can lead to you being tongue-tied or blurting out the wrong thing. When anxiety consistently and significantly interferes with your life, it is better thought of as being an anxiety disorder.

How Do You Know if You or a Family Member Have Anxiety?

Some people are all too aware that they are anxious, which may be evident to people around them. They may constantly ruminate and have trouble relaxing. They may be hypervigilant, always looking for something that could go wrong. They may obsess about what they should have said but didn't. They may have trouble sleeping because they can't shut their brains off and stop thinking about the day, including all the things that have not gone well and all the things that they felt OK about at the time but are now thinking were a disaster. Then, the lack of sleep itself may lead to further anxiety.

Other people are not entirely aware of the anxiety that may underlie some of their habits and tendencies. Many people, most often men, experience anxiety as anger and may lash out. Some people who work long hours every day may be doing so because it is necessary to get the job done or because they enjoy it. An underlying fear of failure may drive other people. Unrealistic expectations due to perfectionism may lead to procrastination or "paralysis by analysis." Overthinking and second-guessing make everything take longer than necessary, so long hours become "necessary." People who have learned unrealistic expectations for themselves may take on too much work. They may be afraid to say "no" or to establish appropriate boundaries for fear of disappointing others or revealing their hidden incompetence.

The father in a family I worked with had been the victim of a horrendous crime in which he experienced a complete lack of control. He was never able to talk about what had happened, and he suppressed the consequent anxiety. However, it emerged anyway, as these things tend to do. In this case, he tried to control every aspect of his children's lives, including doing all their college assignments. As a result, although the children graduated from college, they knew very little about the subjects they had majored in and were essentially helpless when it came to "adulting"—paying bills, finding needed resources, etc.

Sometimes anxiety is expressed through the body in a variety of symptoms such as gastrointestinal problems, headaches, backaches, difficulty breathing, heart racing, dizziness, lightheadedness, etc. Fidgeting, nail-biting, and hair-twirling can all be manifestations of anxiety. Expressing anxiety through the body is more likely when people are reluctant or unable to admit to themselves that they are anxious.

Anxious people can be challenging to be around, both in personal relationships and in the work environment. As noted above, they may be irritable. This tendency may be particularly hard for people around them, who often spend time trying to understand why the person is angry at them and what to do about it. As with Sanjay, second-guessing leads to inconsistent responses to others; thus, guidance may need to be clarified to employees. It is hard to provide leadership to others when someone is uncertain about themselves. They may repeatedly ask for reassurance, directly or indirectly, but then reject any that you try to offer. People with unrealistic expectations for themselves often also have unrealistic expectations for others. Therefore, they can be too critical or demanding of employees. Anxious people may be preoccupied with their own concerns and so neglect the needs of co-workers and employees. These difficulties are multiplied and magnified when co-workers are also family members.

Anxious Thoughts

We all have thoughts and patterns of thinking that we learned sometime during our lives and continue circulating through our consciousness, whether or not they still make sense. In addition to the feelings and behaviors described above, anxious people generally have thoughts that revolve in some way around the premise that the world is a dangerous place and they do not have the resources to cope. The danger can range from major to minor, and a big part of the problem is that the person with anxiety is often unable to tell which is which.

Several less adaptive patterns of thinking can plague people with anxiety. Here are some of them, slightly exaggerated for effect:

- **Catastrophizing,** or making things more important than they are. For example, someone may think, "I made a mistake. Now, the whole project will be ruined. Everyone will find out. I will be fired. I'll never find another job. Then my spouse will leave me, and I'll never see my children again."

- **Discounting the positive.** For example, someone may think, "Well, yes, I did succeed at that one thing, but it wasn't that big a deal. That doesn't mean I will succeed at the next thing. Other people have had more success. I'm a loser."

- **Mental filter** or picking out one flaw and letting it dominate the whole picture. For example, someone may think, "Everyone said my presentation was great, but I forgot to mention that one thing. How could I have forgotten that? It ruined the whole thing. I am deeply ashamed of myself for totally blowing the presentation."

- **Personalization.** For example, someone may think, "The company lost money this year. It's probably because I didn't work hard enough."[32]

---

32   Burns, D. (1980). *Feeling Good: The New Mood Therapy.* Avon Books.

What Causes Anxiety?

There are many potential causes of anxiety. Some are biological. Anxiety can be hereditary. Some medications and or recreational drugs can lead to feelings of anxiety. Sometimes, the reason is situational, such as being a victim of a crime, having health problems, being involved in a motor vehicle accident, and being impacted by fires, floods, etc. All of these can lead to long-lasting and significant anxiety. In the business context, you may feel anxiety after losing a client, making errors in your work, or being criticized by a parent, sibling, or cousin.

Many times, the source of the anxiety lies in family dynamics and relationships, especially for those who work in a family business. For example, your parents may have placed unrealistic expectations on you as a child. Or you may have been told that "You can do anything," and, as a result, feel obligated to try to do everything. Since no one can do everything, you will likely fail under these impossible expectations and feel anxiety about your failure.

If you were praised too much, whether you have earned the praise or not, you may grow up feeling anxious because you can't tell what your abilities are. On the other hand, when some kids get a 98 on a test in school, their parents want to know what happened to the other two points. You can never please them no matter what you do, so you grow up anxious about never being good enough. The problem can be compounded if you think your parents see a sibling as better than you.

Anxious parents often produce anxious children. The parents may feel that they are not good enough and see their children as a reflection of themselves who must make up for their parents' deficiencies. Or they may compete with their children. If the child can accomplish something, the parent may feel anxious about not having been able to achieve the same thing. Anxious parents model anxiety for their children as a way of coping with the world.

How Anxiety Affects Family Businesses

People in family businesses may have additional sources of anxiety, especially if the family or the business is well-known. You may need to present a façade to the world where you have it all together and can effortlessly handle everything. This may be especially challenging if other family members currently working in the business or ancestors who founded or worked in the business presented the same type of façade to the world. How can you live up to Great Uncle Joe, who invented the product or started the business? This type of anxiety makes it very hard to seek help.

Impostor syndrome can also be a significant cause of anxiety in a person in a family business. If you believe that the only reason you hold the job that you do is because of your last name rather than any of your attributes or the education/experience you have had, how can you not feel anxiety? What qualifies *you* to be an executive in a major company? And what if "they" discover that you are secretly unqualified, incompetent, stupid, etc.? You may overlook the possibility that you can be a talented person who also has the "right" last name.[33] Depending on the family, another source of anxiety can be the fact that you have known at least some of your co-workers since birth. Family relationships are complex, with a mixture of love, sibling rivalry, anger, etc. You have a history together and may carry warm feelings or lingering resentments about something that happened when you were eight. Whatever the relationship, your family is important to you.

If you work in a non-family business, your family may only partially understand what you do for a living. They may judge your success or failure solely by factors like whether you can earn a living, hold a job, etc. If you work in a family business, everyone may know whether you said something stupid in the last meeting, failed to complete a project on time, etc. You can't leave work

---

33 Maenpaa, J., Presentation: *Working with High Functioning Anxiety: Supporting Our Overachievers.* May 2022.

at work and relax in the bosom of your family. There is less privacy, and you may get questioned about something that happened at work, at a family event, or the dinner table. You may get flak if your performance directly affects other family members' jobs and financial well-being.

Treatment for Anxiety

If you have anxiety, for all of the above reasons, it is easy to think that you have to suffer in silence, keep a stiff upper lip, etc. However, this will only increase your isolation and make the anxiety worse. If the anxiety is mild, it can be lessened by talking to a good friend, exercising, eating well, spending time in nature, practicing mindfulness, meditation, etc. But if the anxiety is chronic and does not respond to those types of interventions, and if it is interfering with your well-being, the best thing to do is to see a mental health provider. They can determine whether anxiety is indeed the problem and help you decide which treatment or combination of treatments are right for you. Anxiety is one of the most common mental health issues, and many effective treatments are available.

Family or couples therapy can be enormously helpful in dealing with the interpersonal aspects of anxiety. A good therapist can help people discuss past and present interactions, not to engage in blame, but to illuminate patterns and better understand how things got to be the way they are. Sometimes, this insight alone results in changes. More often, the therapist will need to help the family learn new patterns of behavior, which will result in the kinds of change that everyone wants to see. Changing the family dynamics and interactions can majorly affect your well-being and personal relationships, how people interact in a family business, the work environment, and the bottom line.

Sometimes, the family or some family members cannot or will not change. Some people are unwilling or unable to take the steps to go to family therapy or to involve family members in the therapy. Luckily, there are many routes to a goal. You don't *need* to get other people to change to change yourself, even though it often *feels* that you do. For example, you may think that if your parent stopped criticizing you, you would feel less anxious. While that may be true, your parent may *never* stop criticizing you because of their own issues, personality, or background. Why let your well-being rest entirely in someone else's hands?

Individual therapy is also an excellent treatment modality for anxiety. With individual therapy, you can learn to handle things differently so that they no longer affect you as they used to, even if the behavior that precipitates your anxiety continues. Taking excessive criticism from a parent as an example, you may initially assume, consciously or unconsciously, that if your parent criticizes you, they must be right. This is a belief many of us have, left over from childhood, a time when we think our parents are *always* right. This belief is particularly common when a parent is an impressive, high-achieving person, like the head or founder of a business. But, in reality, they are not always right because no one is. Therapy can help you to understand and internalize that reality. Then, even if they continue to criticize you, you can learn to look at what they have said more objectively and decide for yourself if what they are saying has merit. Perhaps your parent is a person who is impossible to please no matter what you do. Realizing that and stopping trying to do the impossible can be enormously freeing. Or perhaps your parent is criticizing you because they are anxious themselves about the project you are working on; their criticism of you may be an indirect way of expressing that anxiety rather than a sign that they think you're doing a lousy job, that you're stupid or incompetent, or that they hate you.

Cognitive behavioral therapy (CBT) is usually done with an individual and is a highly effective treatment for anxiety. It is based on the idea that rather than feelings causing thoughts, as many people think, thoughts cause feelings. If I hear a noise in the night and attribute it to a branch of a tree rubbing against the house, I will roll over and go back to sleep. If I attribute the noise to a burglar breaking into my house, I will become anxious. CBT focuses on helping the individual learn to challenge and change the types of unadaptive and unrealistic thoughts discussed above. The goal is not to make the person into a Pollyanna, seeing only the bright side, but rather to make the anxious thoughts more realistic. For example, the person will not learn to deny having made mistakes, but they will learn to create a more accurate appraisal of the effects of their mistakes on the situation and other people. Thus, anxiety will be reduced or eliminated.

Some people benefit from medication for anxiety. If you think you may want to try medication, it would be better to consult a psychiatrist than to go to your family doctor, even if you have a good relationship with them. Family doctors need expertise in many ailments—sore throats, broken bones, etc. Depending on the doctor, they may or may not have in-depth knowledge of psychiatric medications. Especially if you are older, have unsuccessfully tried taking medication before, and or have other medical problems, prescribing this type of medication can be complex. So, why not go to the best person for the job?

How Can the Family Support the Member with Anxiety?

Probably the most important thing a family member can do is not to minimize or disparage the anxiety or the person who is feeling the anxiety. Many people think that if you just explain the reality of the situation, the anxious person will stop worrying. But, even if you think that they are worrying about something insignificant, illogical, or even ridiculous, telling them that is only going to make them feel worse. Now they have new things to worry about—your apparently low opinion of them and how they can hide their anxiety from you in the future. Even if the situation or issue they are worrying about is not "real," the feelings they are experiencing are quite real and probably also painful. It would be much better to sympathize with how badly they must be feeling and to ask how you can help.

Different people will have different needs. Maybe they just need to know that you care about them; asking how you can help will help to convey this message. They may need some time alone to sort things out. They may need a sounding board to help them think things through or provide support. The sounding board could be a family member, friend, or therapist. If they feel overloaded and overwhelmed, you could assume or delegate someone else to take some of their responsibilities for a while. Or perhaps the anxiety is a sign that they *are* trying to handle too much and *should be* relieved of some of their responsibilities permanently. Alternatively, it could be helpful for you to help them break down overwhelming tasks into smaller, more manageable steps and to plan how and when to tackle each one.

It will be important not just to take over and do things for them, as avoidance will only perpetuate the anxiety. Supporting them in doing scary things for themselves would be much better. If the person is in treatment, you can help them to implement the coping strategies they are learning. The only way to know which, if any, of these things is best is to talk it over with the anxious person.

It will probably be helpful both for the anxious person and for you, the family member, for you to educate yourself about anxiety. If you understand better what they are going through, it will be easier for you to support them. It will also be easier for you to refrain from taking things they may say or do personally. Similarly, depending on your relationship, it may be helpful for you to learn the signs or behaviors that show that the person is anxious. Then you can help them to see that for themselves. This should be done gently and carefully so as not to make the person feel criticized or invalidated.

Conclusion

All in all, anxiety can be highly detrimental, not only to the well-being of the person experiencing it but also to their performance at work and to the people around them. The effects are magnified in a family business and can affect leadership, the business's ability to engage in new initiatives or necessary course adjustments, and succession planning. Luckily, once the problem is identified, many treatments are available. Intervention with the family can go a long way to reversing and alleviating the problems.

CHAPTER FIVE

Depression and the Impact on Family Business

by Alyce Jurgensen, LCSW-C

Niles was at the helm as CEO of the third-generation family business and was frustrated with his siblings. He believed they were taking too many vacations, leaving work too early, and should have been working on weekends when he asked them to. Depression can cast a shadow for generations. Like his grandfather, Niles believed running the family business meant all work and no play. What Niles did not know was that his grandfather suffered from depression, a depression that caused him to have a mindset where work was everything in life. Unfortunately, the business's success legitimized and encouraged this imbalanced approach. While business success was seen as a great family legacy, it masked the debris field left by untreated depression — the other family legacy. While Niles may not have been depressed, he embraced the mindset of his depressed grandfather. Unknowingly caught in this inherited approach, Niles' singular focus on business caused conflict with his siblings, who saw value in the business and their sibling relationship.

Family business can be all-encompassing. It is our identity and, at times, our financial means, and most notably, a point of pride. The pressures that accompany these highly charged dynamics magnify stress exponentially. This creates a ripe environment for depression to take hold, although that is only one way depression can enter our families. The focus of this chapter is to support those in the family business arena dealing with depression and to provide guidance and resources to help navigate the next steps. We will be discussing the most common types of depression and what can be done to assess and address mental health in the family.

Depression is a natural and very normal part of life; there is nothing bad or wrong with someone who is experiencing symptoms. It can vary in strength and length depending on the circumstances surrounding the individual and their genetic heritage. However, depression can be challenging to recognize in ourselves and others because it can hide out just under the surface of our lives, papered over by our busy schedules. And the line between manageable depression and debilitating depression is whisker thin. In its most crippling forms, it is an illness that can feel like life is unmanageable. Or for some, it shows up as everything is "fine" when they are just numbly going through the motions with minimal to no feeling attached to anything. Depression becomes unmanageable and requires treatment when day-to-day life becomes troublesome; routines dissolve, eating habits drastically change, and it is difficult to experience feelings of happiness.

The question arises, why is it important to look at depression as it relates to family business? Depression generates a gravitational pull on the family and the business, making it essential to recognize and address. As children, we learned that gravity is invisible yet impacts everything we do. We have evidence of its force, even though we cannot see it. Depression operates similarly; however, most people do not perceive it as a force that will impact the family and its business until it is too late. Take the example of Watson, a fourth-generation owner and president of sales at the family business. He was constantly working and overperforming; it was what the family expected from him. However, he tended to be erratic, late to meetings, scattered, and impulsive in his decision-making.[34] Occasionally, he was verbally aggressive with a few employees and even lost a long-standing customer after firing off

---

34 "Depressive Disorder (Depression)." World Health Organization, World Health Organization (WHO), 31 Mar. 2023, www.who.int/news-room/fact-sheets/detail/depression.

an angry email. A few colleagues were concerned for his well-being but felt uncomfortable bringing it up; after all, he was a family member.

His undiagnosed depression also impacted his relationships. Watson was 52, twice divorced, and had three children. He had friends, but no one knew how he was doing. His peers envied his bachelor lifestyle, but little did they realize depression was at play, keeping him alone and isolated from trusted connections. To feel something, he engaged in high-risk adventures but was often left feeling empty.

Because Watson worked at the business, he was more pressured to keep up appearances and fulfill unrealistic expectations. Untreated depression hindered Watson's ability to assess realistic expectations and kept him entrenched in survival mode. Many of the behaviors he exhibited resembled his mother's behaviors. She was also isolated when feeling down and didn't express her emotional pain. Watson unconsciously learned how to ignore the signals of depression.

Depression can diminish our ability to tolerate frustration, manage our emotional relationships with others, and generally feel good about ourselves. Depression can also cause a family to adjust to a family member in unhealthy ways. Family members often react to anger, tears, and withdrawal in ways that further harm rather than help relationships. Anger, frustration, and resentment begin to pile up on all sides. If families had the tools necessary to understand how depression might be affecting their work together, they would gain greater resilience and increased capacity to grow together rather than apart. When the family incorporates mental wellness into their work, their relationships deepen, and goodwill takes root. As the family builds emotional coherence, the business only stands to benefit. The family's mental well-being should be considered a key driver to the business's success, not separate from it.

Impacts on the Family Business

A family business is an expression of a family and its enduring legacy. So is depression, albeit a more secretive one. Families can become less productive as a working group when they are absorbed in the dynamics of a family member facing depression. Depression can cause someone to self-medicate with alcohol or drugs. Depression can cause someone to try to avoid their feelings with obsessional behavior, be it work, exercise, eating, or a whole host of addictions, unhealthy and healthy alike. Depression can cause someone to withdraw or to inflict harm on themselves or others. Lastly, depression can cause someone to start thinking about suicide. Clearly, this can cause families to unite to try to support their loved one, or more likely, engage in a host of dysfunctional behaviors in an unconscious effort to normalize the situation. One of the many harmful impacts of normalizing emotional and psychological pain is the next generation learning to do the same. Given these possible negative scenarios and given the longevity of a family business, depression can negatively impact family leadership for many generations.

It's important to know that depression does not discriminate; it can affect people of all ages, races, ethnicities, and genders. The National Institute of Mental Health states, "Globally, it is estimated that 5% of adults suffer from depression, with a 50% higher propensity among women than men, and a slightly higher percentage among adults older than 60 years (5.7%). Approximately 280 million people in the world have diagnosed depression, and many others suffering from diagnosable depression that goes entirely unreported. [...] Because men may be less likely to recognize, talk about, and seek help for their feelings or emotional problems, they are at greater risk of depression symptoms being undiagnosed or undertreated."[35]

---

35 "Persistent Depressive Disorder (Dysthymic Disorder)." National Institute of Mental Health, U.S. Department of Health and Human Services, www.nimh.nih.gov/health/statistics/persistent-depressive-disorder-dysthymic-disorder. Accessed 25 Feb. 2024.

As implied earlier, family businesses can be a breeding ground for depression. One common theme we see in family business is individuals suffering under the weight of expectations. They typically feel pressured to sacrifice parts of themselves and their identity to fit the norms and expectations of the family. Either the guilt of not meeting those expectations or the sacrifice of one's identity to do so can be heartbreaking and understandably lead to a depressive state.

Families do not have to suffer in the hope that the emotional turmoil will subside; it will likely only worsen. Actions can be taken to find relief for the individual, family, and business. Treatment helps rebalance and support one in being more energized, creative, and engaged. Family members can influence their loved ones to engage in treatment. Not only can they take action and find help, but they can also be an ally by offering consistent understanding, empathy, and encouragement, all of which impact healing for the better. Acknowledging and treating mental health challenges is crucial to living a fulfilling and engaged life. Dedicating our time and resources to healing can support one in not only surviving the extraordinary demands of the family business but thriving within it.

Understanding Depression

So, what is the difference between being sad and being depressed? Sadness and grief are natural responses to life, and they tend to recede with time, while depression is an illness.[36] A clear indication that sadness has shifted into depression is when one can no longer engage in life in the way they would like to. It's like tasting your favorite meal and noticing it's lost all the flavor, but you continue to eat, hoping the flavor returns. At some point, you realize the

---

36 Substance Abuse and Mental Health Services Administration (SAMHSA). "Table 3.19, DSM-IV to DSM-5 Adjustment Disorders Comparison - Impact of the DSM-IV to DSM-5 Changes on the National Survey on Drug Use and Health - NCBI Bookshelf." Impact of the DSM-IV to DSM-5 Changes on the National Survey on Drug Use and Health [Internet]., U.S. National Library of Medicine, June 2016, www.ncbi.nlm.nih.gov/books/NBK519704/table/ch3.t19/.

flavor of life is not returning. It becomes increasingly complex to get through the days because there are fewer and fewer internal resources to function. That is a clear signal that intentional action needs to be taken to seek treatment.

Depression, because of its very nature, can be challenging to talk about, even more so in the blending of family and business. It is worth first taking a moment to talk about why the topic is often avoided in families, making it challenging to address. Below are a few of the reasons why depression is frequently not discussed:

- Shame about perceived inadequacies is often present with depression.

- Families may avoid talking about depression out of fear that it will tarnish the family legacy and reputation and, subsequently, hurt the business.

- Boundaries within family business are more complicated and intersecting. Family members may hesitate to voice concern for their loved ones, believing they may violate their privacy. "I will let them approach me if they need to talk."

- Many people lack an understanding of depression and the emotional language to express it.

- Fear is a significant factor blocking communication about depression. On the one hand, there can be fear that the depression will become more critical if discussed when, in fact, that would arrest both its growth and impact on the system. On the other hand, there might be fear that acknowledging the depression will expose a person or the family as "weak" and thus incapable of managing or functioning within the family enterprise.

- Some families value the productivity of an individual over their well-being. Therefore, as long as the family member with depression continues to be productive, the subject is not broached.

Depression, to the profound detriment of many, is cast as an illness of the "weak." This notion is fed by the pull-yourself-up-by-your-bootstraps and snap-out-of-it culture embedded in American and other societies. Essentially, depression is a series of signals being ignited to generate awareness of an emotional and psychological imbalance. Ignoring them is not the path forward; these signals must be recognized, and action taken. Treatment, among many things, will lead to a greater capacity to experience emotions without being toppled by them. It is said that depression is not a sign of weakness; rather, it means *you have been strong for far too long*.

What can cause depression? Many things can increase our risk factors: traumatic events, childhood trauma, drug and alcohol abuse, physical illness, grief, loss of identity, and chronic stressors. We can also be genetically predisposed to depression. In fact, "studies suggest that approximately 40–50% of the hazard of developing depression is genetic."[37] If your grandfather suffered from depression, you have a higher risk of also developing depression. In a study of three generations, it was found that biological children with two prior generations suffering from major depressive disorder (MDD) had a three-fold increased risk of MDD.[38]

Types of Depression

People fear being labeled with a mental health diagnosis, but it is a necessary step to receive treatment and begin the healing process. The three most common types are situational depression, dysthymia, and clinical depression.

Situational Depression. Situational depression occurs some three months after the onset of an intense life stressor. It is common and can be

---

37 Alshaya, Dalal S. "Genetic and Epigenetic Factors Associated with Depression: An Updated Overview." Saudi Journal of Biological Sciences, U.S. National Library of Medicine, 29 Aug. 2022, www.ncbi.nlm.nih. gov/pmc/articles/PMC9232544/.

38 Weissman, Myrna M et al. "A 30-Year Study of 3 Generations at High Risk and Low Risk for Depression." JAMA psychiatry vol. 73,9 (2016): 970-7. doi:10.1001/jamapsychiatry.2016.1586

considered a natural part of life. In situational depression, the capacity to hold perspective and hope for the future remains intact.

Sitting over coffee, Prune confided in her friend Beth, "I feel so lost and sad since retiring as chair of the board. I don't know what to do with myself; honestly, I feel like I've lost a piece of my identity. I enjoyed my leadership role, but I didn't realize how much it was a part of me until I retired. How else can I stay connected to the family business now?"

Beth listened and offered support and understanding as Prune expressed her grief, sadness, and hope that these feelings would pass.

Dysthymia. This type of depression may initially feel like "I'm just stressed out," but the feelings are pervasive regardless of the situation, and they continue for at least two years.[39] It is similar to having a chronic low-grade fever where you can still function, and few, if any, would notice. It is not as severe as major depression, yet it can still have a profound impact on health, relationships, and work.

It can be challenging to assess and address this type of depression because it is mainly invisible to others and sometimes to yourself. It seeps into your life gradually, making it difficult to notice. However, family members, especially within the walls of the family business, may recognize a shift in mood or energy levels in a loved one suffering from this type of depression. Additionally, a person struggling with this type of depression can do their job and go about their day-to-day life but with little joy or optimism for the future. David worried about his younger sister, Nina. She used to meet friends for dinner and travel frequently and always came up with creative ideas about how the family could engage with employees throughout the business. However, these traits seemed to fade away gradually. She was now sad at times for no apparent

---

39 "Depression." National Institute of Mental Health, U.S. Department of Health and Human Services, Sept. 2023, www.nimh.nih.gov/health/topics/depression.

reason, frequently tired, and constantly expressed worry about how she didn't think she was doing a good enough job. Initially, David thought it might have been stress brought on by her new role in the business, but he'd begun to suspect it was more than that.

Paradoxically, work can fuel this type of depression because it provides a break from the non-stop battering of emotional pain, low self-esteem, and feelings of unworthiness. The more one works, like any obsession, the easier it is to ignore pain. You look successful because over-performing is valued and applauded, particularly in the family business. Consequently, these unhealthy behaviors are being rewarded, but they also contribute to the depression you are unconsciously trying to avoid.

Clinical Depression. Clinical depression, also known as Major Depression, is the feeling of looking down a dark hallway and never being able to see the end of it. It is isolating, lonely, and frightening and barricades you from the kindness, warmth, and affection of others. It can make you believe that joy is only reserved for others. David Letterman once described his experience with depression as "a sinkhole."

One of the distinguishing factors of Clinical Depression is the severity of the symptoms and the degree to which it impacts day-to-day activities. With Major Depression, it is challenging to work and focus on anything other than how you are feeling. The extremes become more extreme: greater irritability, potential drug and alcohol use, and feeling detached. Additionally, this type of depression also increases the risk of suicide. Treatment should be immediate.[40]

Enduring depression can sometimes shift the shorelines of our minds, and we begin to imagine what it would be like not to feel the emptiness and agitation anymore. That is when suicide starts to look like the answer, even though it is a form of self-harm that goes against every fiber of the body.

---

40   American Psychiatric Association. (2022). *Diagnostic and statistical manual of mental disorders* (5th ed., text rev.). https://doi.org/10.1176/appi.books.9780890425787

Thoughts of harming oneself under the weight of hopelessness and despair is an attempt to find relief; understandably, one would seek to ease the onslaught of pain. However, the goal here is to find life-affirming relief, not relief that causes more harm. That goal cannot be achieved by pulling yourself up by your bootstraps. A healthy way would be to engage in medical interventions such as psychiatric medicines, psychotherapy, ECT, and, if needed, an inpatient hospital stay.

Symptoms of Depression and What It Feels Like

The author Andrew Solomon aptly describes depression as "the aloneness within us made manifest, and it destroys not only connection to others but also the ability to be peacefully alone within oneself." [41] Depression robs us of the connection to ourselves and others while also demanding we function within paradoxical extremes; everything feels like too much or too little. There is too much sleeping, crying, eating, or not enough. Saturated with overwhelming feelings, or the opposite, numb to all feelings. Depression operates in the realm of extremes because the emotional, psychological, and physical ecosystem is out of balance.

It can be helpful to view depressive symptoms as a series of alarms. Depression has a domino effect on the body, meaning if you feel depressed, your thoughts are depressed, your physical functions are depressed, and your actions are depressed.

When a clinician is assessing depression, they will take into account many factors, including the severity and prevalence of symptoms, the individual's overall health, genetics, and social influences. The following is a list of symptoms a clinician will be looking for to determine mild to severe depression:

---

41   Solomon, A. (2015). *The Noonday Demon: An Atlas of Depression.* Scribner.

Emotional Changes	Thinking Changes	Physical Changes	Behavioral Changes
Persistent feeling of sadness	Confusion	Enduring fatigue	Loss of interest of pleasure in activities
Excessive guilt	Difficulty making decisions	Lack of physical motivation	Tearfulness/ crying
Irritability	Overwhelm with simple tasks	Sleep disturbance (difficulty sleeping/ sleeping too much)	Decline of physical hygiene
Sudden outburst of anger	Decreased concentration	Weight-loss or gain	Social withdrawal
Hopelessness- feeling like life will never change	Thoughts of suicide	Never fully able to relax	Substance abuse
Mood swings	Self-criticism	Unexplained aches and pains	
Low self-esteem	Lack of creative energy	Agitation	

Depression can manifest differently in people who identify as male and female. While men often exhibit symptoms of rage, anger, and isolation, women tend towards sorrow, confusion, and desperation. Women also have the added influence of hormonal fluctuations, which can have a cascading effect throughout their lives, particularly post-partum and during perimenopause.

Other mental health disorders, such as anxiety and substance abuse, can also accompany depression. Estimates show that 60% of those with anxiety will also have depressive symptoms.[42] Similarly, those with addictions to

---

42   Salcedo, Beth. "The Comorbidity of Anxiety and Depression." NAMI, 19 Jan. 2018, www.nami.org/Blogs/ NAMI-Blog/January-2018/The-Comorbidity-of-Anxiety-and-Depression.

substances might also be dealing with the impact of depression. It can feel easier and safer to self-medicate one's pain than acknowledge or talk about the pain that is driving the depression.

Coping with Depression in the Family Business

Due to the societal stigma around mental illness and a great fear of hurting the business, families follow the impulse to tuck depression away, favoring an ecosystem of isolation, shame, and secrecy. Shame, so often the culprit sitting below the mantle of depression, creates feelings of loneliness and causes individuals or families to suffer in silence and continue the legacy of secrecy. Secrets negatively impact the family business by generating invisible forces that disturb proper functioning. And where there are secrets, there is also loneliness.

Families that are dealing with depression cope in healthy and unhealthy ways; some utilize the resources of the family and seek treatment, while others ignore it, deny it, vilify it, or treat it as normal. When doing that, they injure the trust and connection within the family. In the earlier example with Watson, he didn't realize that he was swimming against the tide of the genetic component of depression that was passed on from generation to generation. Watson's family continued to ignore and deny the red flags of depression. As a result, the gravitational pull of depression harmed the family and the business. Those experiencing depression in the family continued to suffer, both personally and professionally, along with the people surrounding them.

At times, depression can go unnoticed by the family at large because it is being experienced by a family member who doesn't feel safe to express their feelings.

"If I were you," Lee told Brian, "I would stop attending those meetings about your family's business. You always seem down and exhausted when you return. Can't you just say you don't want to go anymore and leave it at that? What's the worst that can happen?" Brian has asked himself the same questions. He is aware of the toll these meetings place on his mental health, but he also feels a responsibility to the success of the business that few understand. Adding fuel to the fire, he fears the criticism and potential punishment from his family. The distress increases when questions arise about how his relationship with the family might change if he didn't meet the expectation of attending meetings. In other words, Brian feels threatened by the loss of connection to his family. All of this keeps him feeling trapped and alone with feelings of depression.

Guidelines for Addressing Depression

"Anything that is human is mentionable, and anything mentionable can be more manageable," Fred Rogers famously said. "Talking about our feelings makes them less overwhelming, upsetting, and scary. The people we trust with that important talk can help us know we are not alone."[43]

Now that we've defined depression and its impact on the individual, family, and business, we'll now discuss diagnosis, treatment, and the importance of self-care.

Depression can be diagnosed by several healthcare professionals: general practitioners, psychiatrists, psychologists, licensed clinical social workers, licensed mental health counselors, and psychiatric nurses.

The two main medical treatments for depression are psychiatric medicines and psychotherapy.[44] However, due to the complexity of depression, it also requires a holistic plan of treatment (body, mind, and spirit) that includes a combination of lifestyle changes, social support, education, and physical activity. It should be a plan suitable to the needs and resources of the individual. What works for one person may not work for another. Also of note, if you or a family member meet with a psychiatrist, try a new medicine, or work with a

---

43 "What Is Mentionable Is Manageable: Mister Rogers." PBS Learning Media, WUCF, 6 Feb. 2022, whyy. pbslearningmedia.org/resource/mentionable-manageable-mister-rogers-video/meet-the-helpers/.

44 *Depression Treatment for Adults*. (2019, August). apa.org. Retrieved June 23, 2024, from https://www.apa.org/depression-guideline/adults

therapist and do not find relief, keep going until you find the right fit. It can take multiple attempts to benefit from the help that is needed.

Depression is not an illness that is necessarily life-long. However, it may take years to treat, depending on the type of depression, as well as other potential diagnoses. Treatment helps one create a greater capacity to handle stressors while expanding into feelings such as relaxation and joy. Managing depressive symptoms is not about forcing one's way through to the other side. Still, it is a deliberate effort to feel better, with self-compassion as a key relief driver.

Psychiatry and psychiatric medicines. The positive impact of medicines cannot be overstated. Medicines can be a great first step, as they work for many people. Antidepressants and other psychiatric medications have the potential to deliver immense relief. "Studies show that the benefit generally depends on the severity of the depression: The more severe the depression, the greater the benefits will be. In other words, antidepressants are effective against chronic, moderate, and severe depression." [45] Those with mild depression may not need antidepressants, and some might need a different type of medication. It's best to find a qualified professional to support you in finding the medicine that is appropriate for you.

They provide greater emotional and psychological bandwidth to address the underlying emotional and relational issues.

While primary care physicians are capable of prescribing some psychiatric medicines, it is highly recommended to seek care from a psychiatrist. Your primary care doctor will be able to give you a referral. Psychiatrists are specialists and are equipped to assess what medications will best reduce and manage symptoms. If you are experiencing a heart issue, you see a cardiologist; if you have a toothache, you go to a dentist; and if you have a mental health issue, you go to a psychiatrist.

---

45   Institute for Quality and Efficiency in Health Care (IQWiG). (2020b, June 18). *Depression: Learn More – How effective are antidepressants?* InformedHealth.org - NCBI Bookshelf. https://www.ncbi.nlm.nih.gov/books/NBK361016/

Unfortunately, a barrier to treatment is the stigma associated with getting medical care from a psychiatrist. There is a belief that only "crazy people" see psychiatrists when, in fact, going to a psychiatrist is simply about getting the most experienced help possible. There is also a stigma connected to taking psychiatric medicines, as it is believed to be a sign of weakness. Again, there is no shame in seeking relief and support. It takes great courage.

Psychotherapy. Otherwise known as talk therapy, psychotherapy is designed to treat one's condition by talking with a mental health professional. Several professionals are trained to treat the underlying causes of depression and administer psychotherapy, some of which include psychologists, licensed clinical social workers, and licensed clinical professional counselors, each with their approach. Be sure to work with a therapist who specializes in depression. And while going to a therapist for individual therapy is highly recommended, it can be helpful to engage a therapist for family sessions, as well.

Therapists can help you work through many areas of your life, including:

- Symptom management
- Learning coping skills
- Identifying negative belief structures
- Learning self-compassion
- Setting boundaries
- Coping with relationship challenges
- Increasing self-confidence
- Modifying behavior
- Setting realistic expectations
- Supporting you in feeling seen and heard
- Processing complicated emotions
- Alleviating guilt and shame
- Providing perspective
- Processing grief and loss

Many effective treatment modalities can work, but most importantly, there must be a good connection with the therapist—one where you feel understood and valued. Studies confirm that the relationship between the therapist and client strongly correlates to a positive outcome.[46] Moreover, the therapist must understand the pressures and complexities of family business. In the example given earlier with Brian, it would be vital for him to work with a therapist who is nuanced in their approach. The therapist must understand the challenges involved when an individual sets a boundary within the complicated family business landscape. It can threaten Brian's connection to the family, the business, and, potentially, his financial well-being.

It sometimes feels daunting to find a therapist and begin psychotherapy, but there are resources available that can help with this process. First, it is worthwhile to ask trusted friends and colleagues. The best referrals often come from people you know. The website "Psychology Today" is also a great place to begin researching for a mental health provider in your local area. You can click on the globe icon to find resources in many countries outside the United States. Their website is *https://www.psychologytoday.com/us/therapists*. Your primary care provider may also be able to assist with referrals, and it's essential to keep them in the loop regarding your mental health. Moreover, if you are engaged with any community, industry, or professional organizations, for example, the Young Presidents' Organization (YPO), they may also be able to provide referral sources.

In recent years, psychotherapy has become available online. Some individuals benefit from meeting with a provider in person, while others benefit greatly from working with a provider remotely.

While we all hope the person experiencing depression will choose to receive care, not everyone does. If this is the case, the loved ones often ask for help for themselves. It can be painful to witness someone struggling, and it's

---

46 Flückiger, C., Del Re, A. C., Wampold, B. E., & Horvath, A. O. (2018). The alliance in adult psychotherapy: A meta-analytic synthesis. *Psychotherapy*, *55*(4), 316–340. https://doi.org/10.1037/pst0000172

wise to receive support to prevent you from struggling, too. You'll also be in a better position to support your loved one if they choose to get help later.

Hospital and Residential Treatment. Clinical depression may come to the point of requiring inpatient treatment for the adjustment of medicines and psychotherapy. Inpatient stays offer an opportunity to reset, reestablish boundaries, restore, and quickly receive relief by administering medicines. You can reach out to many organizations for information about treatment centers. The "Psychology Today" website listed above has a treatment center search option. You can also ask your local hospital, medical center, or mental health providers for recommendations. Government agencies related to mental health and substance abuse also offer resources to help find treatment.

Team Approach. A team approach is the best approach. Depression can feel like the floor you are standing on is constantly undulating. In other words, your emotional and psychological foundation is unpredictable when depression is on board. Your primary care doctor, psychotherapist, and psychiatrist should all work in a coordinated fashion to support you in achieving your goals and finding relief. In addition to your medical care team, the family can be a phenomenal support with anything from making medical appointments, filling out paperwork, and coordinating workloads or time off. Administrative items and creative thinking can be most challenging to the person suffering from depression. Again, it is important that the family does not take over the process but coordinates care alongside the struggling family member.

Self-Care. Unfortunately, self-care can be viewed as a luxury reserved for those who have the leisure to take care of themselves. But self-care is made up of daily routines and rituals carried out in service of one's physical, mental, emotional and spiritual wellness. Self-care efforts promote positive health on all levels of wellbeing. It is the connective tissue that binds your life together. If you neglect it, you begin to experience psychological, emotional, and physical pain. Caring for yourself is a preventative measure, as well as a way to manage symptoms of depression. However, self-care routines are not enough to manage symptoms of moderate to severe depression. Adapt a self-care routine specific to your work with the family and the business. For example, if you know the upcoming meeting with the family will be stressful, consider your pre- and post-self-care activities to ensure resiliency.

Prioritizing rest, time in nature, and physical movement are some suggestions to help prevent, manage and heal from depression. Below is a list of helpful self-care tips.

- Focus on simplifying your life.

- Build in short units of restoration during the workday.

- Find a creative outlet.

- Move your body.

- Talk to deeply trusted people.

- Spend time outdoors.

- Have FUN.

- Limit your obligations.

- Avoid or limit your time with toxic people.

Advice for People Witnessing a Family Member Struggling with Depression

When observing a loved one whom you believe is being impacted by depression, your instinct may be to throw the book of wellness at them.

"Here," Sarah said to her husband Torsten, "Read this book about depression. This is what you need to do to get better!" Torsten had already been struggling with keeping up with his work and family responsibilities and now felt even more discouraged and overwhelmed by all the pressure to "get it together" and stop feeling down following the loss of his mother two years ago.

The goal is not to rush the person to wellness but to listen more intently to what is being expressed. They might be speaking their truth and feeling profound guilt. The ally's job is to listen with a compassionate mind, not a fix-it mindset. Although it may feel like depression has taken the wheel of your loved one's life, it is not up to you to grab the wheel. Instead, you should focus on the support they need and work to implement the support infrastructure. During this time, the family can create an ecosystem of kindness that focuses on support, generosity, care, understanding, and empathy for their family member. It is also the ally's job to get the support they may need to support their loved ones. It can be difficult to be a compassionate ally, as coping with a depressed person often causes hurt feelings, anger, and resentment. The ally must have their support system where they process their intense feelings, so they are prepared to show up as a compassionate and caring ally when needed.

As stated earlier, mental illness impacts everyone in the system to varying degrees and can echo through generations. Recognizing depression within the family business system allows for informed choices that support individuals in getting treatment for the betterment of both the family and the business.

In the case of a prominent third-generation mid-western family business, there was an awareness that depression bloomed on the family tree. So, when Albert became more irritable, he stopped attending in-person meetings and began ruminating about minor mistakes at work. The family, recognizing their mental health legacy, acted early to make sure Albert received the treatment he needed. They gathered around him, each utilizing their strengths to support his treatment needs. His sister worked with his psychotherapist to locate the best treatment center for depression. His cousin found a retreat center that would support aftercare and restoration, while Albert's aunt, as CEO, coordinated workflow and informed select team members, ensuring work responsibilities were maintained. This gave Albert the time he needed to begin to recover from a depressive episode. This is an example of an integrated family system coming together, without judgment, to support their loved ones while utilizing the business's and the family's resources.

Unique Challenges and How to Deal with Them

Not everyone needs to know you or a family member is experiencing depression. Health can remain openly discussed and private at the same time. It is vital in the family business to determine what needs to be said and to whom it needs to be said. For example, it might be necessary to share with the chairman of the board, the CEO, or the family advisor. The question is always, who are the key players that need to know what's happening? They are the ones who are in a position to protect the individual and make the necessary adjustments to the workload.

What do you say to others who do not need to know details but might know there is an issue? The following suggestions below may be helpful:

- I need greater flexibility with my current schedule.

- I need to recharge my batteries.

- For health reasons, I need time to reorganize my priorities.

Conclusion

Mental fitness is also the family's legacy, and one could argue, perhaps a more enduring one. So much time, attention, and finances are poured into strategic plans, the next move for the business, the next big opportunity, and succession planning. What if families poured that kind of attention and determination into the mental health of their family? Why should mental health be viewed as secondary, or worse, not seen at all, when it is the epicenter of the family business? The hope is that your family feels inspired to invest in mental wellness and bring the discussion to the forefront. Mental health in families deserves as much attention as the bottom line, for if our mental health is rattled and unsupported, what is all of this for? The fruits of your labor within the family business cannot be harvested if there is suffering.

Implications

1. **For the individual with depression.** Your health impacts the family and the business, including your roles or responsibilities. Seeking treatment can be a game-changer, both personally and professionally. Stigma often keeps us from this, but seeking support takes strength and courage.

2. **For family members supporting an individual with depression.** As much as we'd like to "fix" our loved ones, we need to be realistic and meet them where they are. You must first assess the level of their awareness. Do they realize there is something wrong? How open are they to getting help? One of the most painful and frustrating things to experience is to have a loved one suffering but not ready to get help. In these situations, your self-care becomes a priority. If they are open to help, you become the ally supporting their healing efforts.

3. **Advisors supporting the family business.** Advisors are in a position of strength; they can see what the family cannot and advocate for change. They are also a non-threatening ally to employees and management and can help provide resources where needed. Should management have concerns, they have someone to go to who is not a family member and who is in a better position in their role as the conduit between all groups.

4. **Non-family executives.** Non-family executives can sometimes be in a delicate position, having a leadership role within another family's business. Find an ally, an advisor, or a family member to express your concerns. Be familiar with mental health resources you could provide if asked for and support the struggling person and assist how you can.

CHAPTER SIX

The Impact of Substance Disorder on Family Business

by Fran Langdon, MD, ABAM, and Anne Smart

One early spring day, Gary Williams Jr, a 4th generation owner and employee at Williams Holdings (WH), took a company truck, got drunk at lunch, and nearly killed a co-worker as he returned to work. This wasn't the first time he'd violated company policy and the law by using or drinking on the job. Previous incidents had earned Gary formal warnings and even a suspension. This time, there were too many violations to ignore: the accident brought an ambulance, law enforcement, and media stories naming the company and Gary. The ensuing liability, which included lawsuits and increased insurance premiums, would cost the company real money.

The next day, the Williams leadership team, comprised of Gary's Uncle Joe Williams, CEO, and his father, Jack Williams, COO, Heather Smith, Safety Director, and Joe Johnson, CHRO, held a safety debriefing meeting. Shockingly, what started as an understandably tense review of the incident by the leadership team quickly escalated into a physical altercation between Joe and Jack, and two employees had to pull the brothers apart. Everyone was shaken by the violence and anger between the two men.

The Williams family is a typical but hypothetical 3rd/4th generation family business currently experiencing a crisis in their business and family. The family's story is one of predictable and repeating behavioral patterns present in families experiencing the chronic and recurring condition of addiction.

Addiction has far-reaching consequences for a family and family business. It strains relationships, confounds communication, creates financial burdens, and brings reputational risk. It's also often ignored, untreated, and prevalent in generations and contributes to the destabilization of the family business.

In this chapter, we will highlight the vulnerabilities and amplified risks of enterprising families experiencing substance use disorder (SUD). We will use the Williams family story to illustrate both healthy and maladaptive coping mechanisms used in addressing addiction in a family and a business.

Substance use disorders and behavioral addictions profoundly affect the family and the family business systems and are not unique to any one culture. They are treatable, chronic medical diseases involving complex interactions between genetics, brain circuitry, the environment, and an individual's life experiences. People with addiction use substances or engage in behaviors that become compulsive despite harmful consequences.[47]

Developing an awareness and acceptance that addiction is a chronic, recurring, and treatable disease can bring hope to families as they learn to manage effective intervention, treatment, and recovery. In this chapter, we will share some of the bio-psycho-social contributors of SUD[48] and the best and current research for effective treatment. We'll offer a hopeful treatment model, including the public health model of longitudinal recovery and stringent medical treatment. Appropriate treatment can leverage the best characteristics, often endemic to a family business, offering hope and resources for the whole family as they address addiction in the family and its impact on their business.

Addiction Impacts the Whole Family Business System

Let's explore how the Williams family begins to address and understand the genetically influenced and generational disease impacting their business and

---

47 Smith, D The evolution of addiction medicine as a medical specialty. AMA J Ethics 2011; 13: 900

48 Skewes M, Gonzalez V, Chapter 6 - The Biopsychosocial Model of Addiction. Principles of Addiction. Elsevier Inc, 2013. 61-70. http://dx.doi.org/10.1016/B978-0-12-398336-7.00006-1

family. Aided by psychological, social, and business resources, they secure effective treatment for Gary and the whole family. They will also integrate what they learned into guidelines and training for the benefit of their employee and family systems.

Williams Industry was founded 60 years ago by Gary Williams, a 3rd generation member of a mid-western farm family. Over the past 40 years, Gary's sons, Joe and Jack, have worked closely together to maintain and build on their father's legacy. Typically, to brothers and family businesses, the brothers had fought over their business decisions, risk tolerance differences, and roles. They had always found a way to resolve their disagreements and conflicts, and they had been able to until now. The blow-up after Gary's violation seemed to set them on a path that could take down their family and their business.

Where Does It Begin? Generational Success and Family Patterns

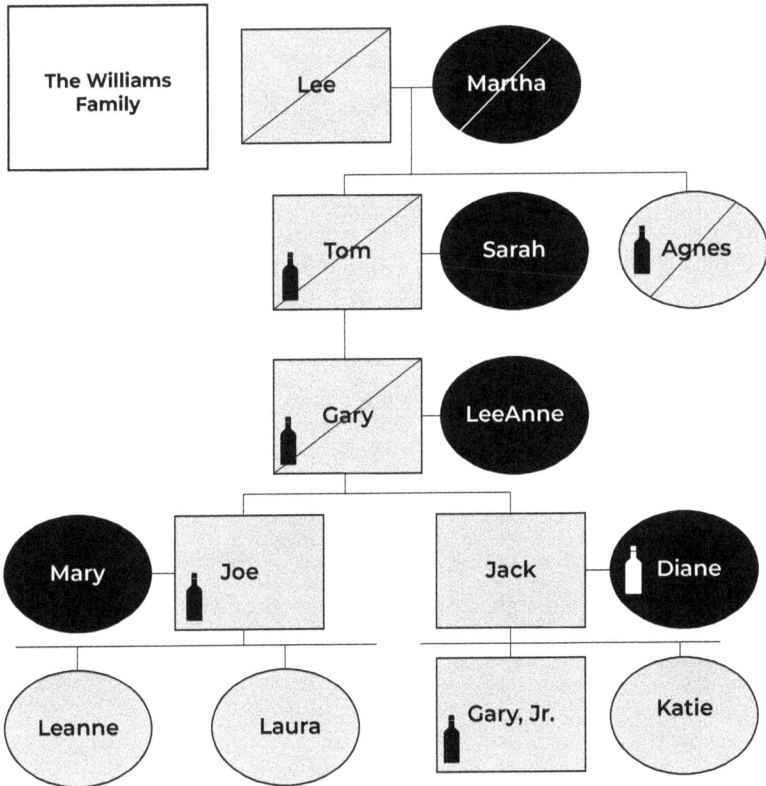

In the genogram figure on page 105, we observe a generational pattern of addiction and alcoholism in the Williams family. Generations had ignored, misunderstood, or denied the behaviors and consequences of addiction in the family. Addiction and Substance Use Disorder (SUD) was a problem for some but not all family members. Jack Williams appears to have dodged the cycle of addiction—but he may have arrested the cycle when a health condition forced him to stop drinking in his early 30s. Notably, applying self-control and discipline rarely succeeds in interrupting the addiction cycle because it isn't a disease that can be successfully treated with discipline, punishment, or inconsistency.

Like many other addicts, Gary had also tried and failed to quit drinking. He recognized that he had a problem when he drank. He'd tried abstinence and health regimes with good intentions to stay sober. But, the hijacked neurochemistry of an addicted brain consistently underestimates risk and overestimates reward, preventing an individual with an addiction from assessing their health risks. Addiction hinders the brain's ability to calculate value and probability correctly; it becomes severely biased. Even in early recovery, people have difficulty assessing the likelihood of future harm. Despite his best intentions, he relapsed.

Current research for effective treatment didn't exist when the Williams family began their farming business in the early 1900s. Without awareness of their genetic and environmental vulnerabilities, the family did their best. Shame, secrecy, and stigma helped create a family pattern of denial, enabling, and over-functioning. They could have misattributed the consequences of untreated addiction to stress, overwork, and business-family conflict.

We now know that addiction is a disorder of the value calculator in the brain. The belief that substance overuse and its attendant health impacts can be overcome with self-control indicates a lack of understanding of the nature of addiction.[49] Families may point to an individual with the self-discipline to stop drinking. While previous generations may have experienced a forced or chosen interruption in the pattern of drinking, intermittent measures that result in abstinence are not sufficient to arrest the disease.

Research and treatment for SUD have come a long way in the last 30 years. Previous generations may have passed down the genetic and behavioral markers of addiction that plague the family. But they also possessed and passed on strengths and characteristics that contributed to their own and the businesses' longevity and success. Both things can be true. The positive attributes of perseverance, loyalty, and resilience can be tapped to support recovery and a return to health for Gary and the whole family.

Gary Jr's crisis at work was a relapse that should also be viewed within the context of recovery. Relapse isn't inevitable, but it's often part of the chronic nature of the illness. Thanks to awareness and better treatment options, the family has an opportunity to change their response to addiction in their family while leveraging the strengths and tools they have developed as a successful family business.

Risks: Beyond Strained Relationships and Communication Breakdowns

Substance abuse and behavioral compulsions lead to strained relationships within the family, which can spill over into the business setting. Family members who struggle with addiction may exhibit erratic behavior, emotional instability, and impaired decision-making, causing conflicts and discord within the business. The relationships of parent and child, manager and employee, owner and family member get tangled in the aftermath of violations of company policies and family values. Trust between family members is eroded and, over time, can be irretrievably shattered.

---

49 Goldstein, R. Z., Craig, A., Bechara, A., Garavan, H., Childress, A. R., Paulus, M. P., & Volkow, N. D. (2009). The neurocircuitry of impaired insight in drug addiction. *Trends in Cognitive Sciences*, *13*(9), 372–380. https://doi.org/10.1016/j.tics.2009.06.004

Addiction brings with it risks and repercussions to the business, the family, and the individual. If the addiction problem becomes public knowledge, it may tarnish the individual's professional image and erode the trust of employees, customers, suppliers, and other stakeholders.

Risks to the business are often evident to outsiders despite the family's attempts to shield or hide the consequences of the addict's behavior. Overwhelmed or unable (due to lack of knowledge or acceptance), the family, board, or management team may not effectively address the risks to the business or the individual when:

- Negative publicity surrounding a family member's substance abuse undermines the business's credibility and integrity, making it difficult to attract new customers, retain employees, and maintain existing client relationships.

- The consequences of a damaged reputation become long-lasting and expensive. The business may become subject to burdensome terms for contracts, insurance, and access to sources of capital.

- Drug or alcohol overuse inside the family drives divorces, child custody fights, disputes over support, and ownership battles. All these can distract owners and managers from the business, causing negative repercussions for generations.

- SUD is "normalized" and ignored by the family.

The informed family, business leadership, and board should weigh and discuss the corresponding reputational and financial risks that come with a family member or employee with SUD. Candid and informed discussions at every level can be leveraged to incentivize adherence to treatment and a unified path forward toward recovery for the person with a substance use disorder.

Risk to the family comes in the form of a genetic predisposition combined with a family pattern of coping with stress. The family may tell heroic stories of hard-working predecessors who created businesses and wealth and died in their 60s. In truth, earlier generation's lives may have been cut short because of stress and addiction.

Typical health consequences and comorbidities of addiction include premature heart disease, hypertension, and strokes. Women may experience earlier and more severe health consequences as a result of the differential impact of alcohol on women.[50]

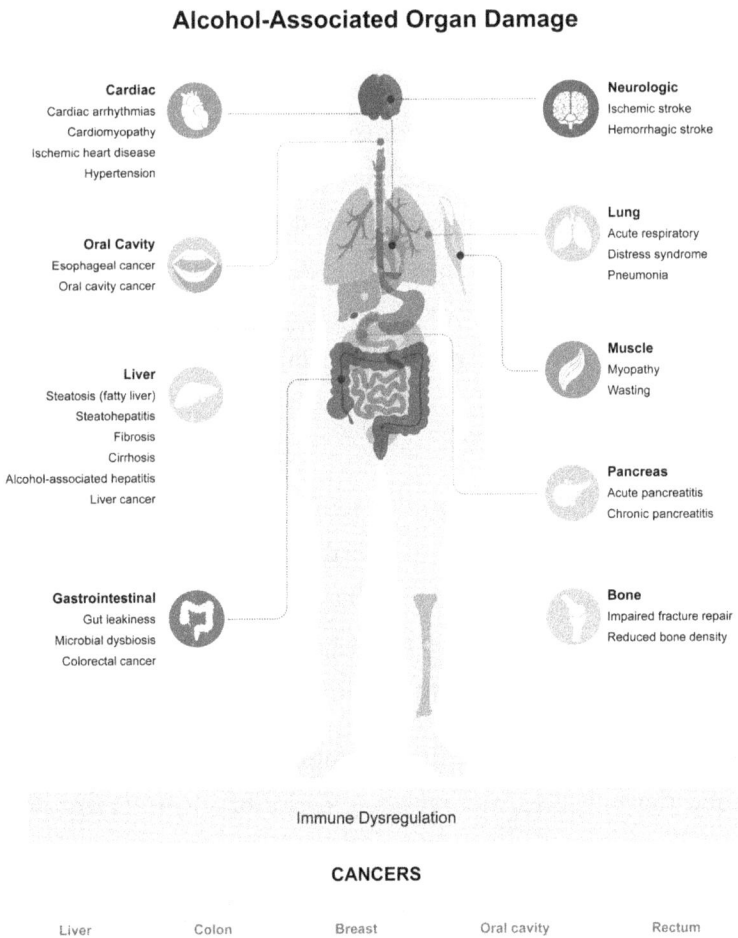

Alcohol-Associated Organ Damage

Cardiac
Cardiac arrhythmias
Cardiomyopathy
Ischemic heart disease
Hypertension

Neurologic
Ischemic stroke
Hemorrhagic stroke

Oral Cavity
Esophageal cancer
Oral cavity cancer

Lung
Acute respiratory
Distress syndrome
Pneumonia

Liver
Steatosis (fatty liver)
Steatohepatitis
Fibrosis
Cirrhosis
Alcohol-associated hepatitis
Liver cancer

Muscle
Myopathy
Wasting

Pancreas
Acute pancreatitis
Chronic pancreatitis

Gastrointestinal
Gut leakiness
Microbial dysbiosis
Colorectal cancer

Bone
Impaired fracture repair
Reduced bone density

Immune Dysregulation

CANCERS

Liver   Colon   Breast   Oral cavity   Rectum

---

50 *Alcohol's effects on the body | National Institute on Alcohol Abuse and Alcoholism (NIAAA).* (n.d.). https://www.niaaa.nih.gov/alcohols-effects-health/alcohols-effects-body

The most significant *preventable* mortality risk for men aged 50-64 is from "Deaths of despair," or deaths attributed to drug overdose, alcohol-related liver disease, and suicide[51] from untreated addiction. Premature death can result from cardiovascular complications, but the preceding cause that leads to them often comes from the abuse of one drug, alcohol.

Heart conditions in families can be a manageable health risk, but gravely under-controlled hypertension and cardiac arrhythmias are intensified by heavy drinking. Several drinks each night can exacerbate underlying obstructive sleep apnea and elevated blood pressure and facilitate the laying down of plaque (atherosclerosis), narrowing every artery.

Risk tolerance and exposure will vary in the business, the family, and the individual. The entrepreneur/founder may have needed a higher financial and operational risk tolerance. But succeeding generations must work to balance the risk/reward ratios in all the overlapping domains of family business. The (healthy) family and healthy business can learn to develop the ability to assess and respond to risks in the business and for their individual. To do so, we must open the conversation to influence the probabilities positively.

Conflict Sounds the Alarm

Families organize themselves around something. The enterprising family organizes their communications, financial well-being, careers, leisure, and sense of pride and identity around their business. The family experiencing the negative consequences of addiction learns to organize around and react to the addict's behaviors. When these two systems overlap, so does family conflict.

Common reactions to a loved one's untreated SUD are denial, offering second and third chances, and repeating cycles of anger, threats, and high

---

51   Beseran, E., Pericàs, J. M., Cash-Gibson, L., Ventura-Cots, M., Porter, K. M. P., & Benach, J. (2022). Deaths of Despair: A scoping review on the social determinants of drug overdose, Alcohol-Related liver disease and suicide. *International Journal of Environmental Research and Public Health/International Journal of Environmental Research and Public Health*, *19*(19), 12395. https://doi.org/10.3390/ijerph191912395

emotion. These maladaptive behaviors serve different purposes and contribute to a false sense of harmony. However, as the consequences of addiction mount, keeping peace at all costs becomes more challenging to maintain at home and work.

In the home and the workplace, standards of accountability erode to accommodate the person with an addiction. Disruptive behaviors follow, threatening the sustainability of the business and the family. At work, employee morale is sacrificed to damaging arguments and factionalism. Conflict is a normal part of the family business system. But unaddressed addiction fuels unhealthy conflict.

Without enacting measures to address and resolve it, the Williams family conflict will follow a predictable pattern of avoidance and eruption, causing continued stress for individuals and the business. Successfully addressing the conflict presents the family with the opportunity to prevent or interrupt the cycle of addiction in their family.

Generational Patterns: Nature Loads the Gun and the Environment Pulls the Trigger?

If willing, the Williams family can seek to understand the causes and conditions behind Gary Jr's behavior. We know genetics can set up landmines for families, but it's equally important to look at the environment in which the genes operate. Stressors faced by one generation may have an outsized influence on how a disease gets expressed in another generation. For example, their predecessors may have been hard-working entrepreneurs who also developed serious health risks that hadn't been attributed to the amount and frequency of their alcohol consumption.

The hallmark of addiction is denial. Lacking acceptance of SUD as an illness, the family may minimize or cover up the natural consequences of their actions, delaying or preventing the family member from getting appropriate help.

Increasing Financial and Emotional Tolls

Ignoring the cost of SUDs to the business can be perilous. Quantifying the cost to family relationships is difficult, but we can measure the prevalence and cost of untreated substance abuse to the business, even as it varies by industry.

The economic burden of SUD consists of health care costs, lost earnings and productivity, and premature morbidity. NIDA (National Institute on Drug Abuse) reports aggregate costs of SUD in the U.S. as more than 700 billion dollars yearly.[52] The cost of a single employee with an untreated SUD ranges annually from $2600 in agriculture to more than $13,000 in the information and communications sectors.[53] Preventative measures and treatment interventions significantly reduce the cost to businesses and families.

Family members may express concern and worry as their relationships with the addicted family member become more complicated. The consequences of their behavior become more difficult to deny or ignore. They either become convinced the addicted person is managing on their own, or they rescue, enable, and protect the family member with financial, emotional, and social support.

Unexpected Partners in Recovery

Running a family business is inherently challenging, requiring an ongoing balance and rebalancing of personal and professional dynamics. Grappling with dependence or addiction— the family and the business may lack an awareness and understanding of SUD and its corrosive impact. Identifying effective help for family members with SUD is often hampered by social stigmas and fear of reputational exposure. Adding to the complexity is the need to observe shareholders' and beneficiaries' legal rights and responsibilities.

---

52 NIDA. 2021, August 3. Introduction. Retrieved from https://nida.nih.gov/publications/drugs-brains-behavior-science-addiction/introduction on 2024, June 22

53 Fardone E, Montoya ID, Schackman BR, McCollister KE. Economic benefits of substance use disorder treatment: A systematic literature review of economic evaluation studies from 2003 to 2021. J Subst Use Addict Treat. 2023 Sep;152:209084. doi: 10.1016/j.josat.2023.209084. Epub 2023 Jun 9. PMID: 37302488; PMCID: PMC10530001.

Protecting underperforming family members from the inevitable consequences of untreated addiction can lead to its own set of complications. Co-workers may identify performance issues for family members with SUD but are ill-equipped to address the problem. They may also unconsciously enable or attempt to protect the family employee out of misplaced loyalty or fear of retribution. The emotional strain may lead to decreased motivation, burnout, and a decline in overall job satisfaction, impacting the business's productivity and success.

As family businesses grow, they begin to codify employment policies, performance measures, and healthcare benefits for all employees. Family leaders may find help from unexpected partners, such as their HR leads, board members, and benefit providers. Notably, allies inside the business, or even on the business board, can offer strategies that support family members and any employee with SUD. They can model candid confrontation, share resources, and create processes that balance accountability with dignity and compassion. By developing and supporting employee training and education policies that build awareness of addiction as a treatable illness and providing resources to access treatment, they can encourage treatment and accountability for the individual and help their families. As family businesses grow and professionalize, the family and the business systems can work together to leverage the *means* and incentive for the individual to seek treatment and succeed in managing their illness. The bi-directional benefits of this approach can serve the family, the business, and the individual.

Prevalence of Addiction

Nearly 48 million Americans live with an addiction, according to the 2023 Key Substance and Mental Health Indicators report by SAMHSA (Substance Abuse and Mental Health Services Administration).[54] Despite the economic and public health impacts of the illness on the individual, families, and the

---

54 *Addressing Excessive alcohol use: State fact sheets.* (n.d.). https://www.cdc.gov/alcohol/fact-sheets/states/excessive-alcohol-use-united-states.html

economy—addiction and effective treatment for it is misunderstood and undertreated. Finding the appropriate treatment and paying for effective treatment is challenging. In the US, insurance almost always dictates the level and effectiveness of care. Beyond paying for it, the language and terms of treatment can be confusing for families.

Finding Help: Wealth, Privacy, Lack of Knowledge, and Finding the Right Treatment

Addiction brings with it a sense of shame and stigma. Business-owning families have a double bind. They often have a public profile. Family businesses carry a public profile that can add a burden to their search for treatment and support for SUD. In the Williams family, each family member will have experienced a breach of privacy, been a subject of gossip or criticism, or had assumptions made about them that were not grounded in truth or deserved. The public nature of the business can transform a natural desire for privacy into a maladaptive pattern of isolation and secrecy. Their isolation can interfere with identifying early and effective treatment for the addicted family member.

Reacting to the crisis of the moment, daily relationships may be strained. Earlier and less troublesome behavior may have preceded the crisis, and the family denied the severity of the problem. When the Williams family seeks treatment for Gary Jr., they will have a dual purpose of sheltering their business and finding a "cure" for him.

The family faces real challenges in searching for confidential and effective help. Finding the right treatment for the individual and family isn't like finding the best lawyer for the firm. Asking for help or resources outside the small circle of known and trusted advisors is complex, and isolation makes them vulnerable to charlatans and luxury-designed programs lacking evidence-based outcomes. Their closest advisors (e.g., attorneys, wealth managers, personal physicians) may not know how to identify the correct and most effective resources because it is beyond their specialty.

As a result, families in business and families of wealth often do their "research" online — mistaking the best marketing and websites for those with the most effective treatment. A better calculator of effective treatment is to talk to a board-certified medical addiction specialist. Starting with a medical assessment can help determine the appropriate service, treatment, and provisions for the individual in your family. It can also be helpful to begin adopting a team and collaborative approach.

Families may be referred to a 30-day inpatient treatment facility, expecting it to cure their family member. Meeting the short-term crisis with a short-term solution is ineffective and insufficient. Everybody would like to see an "addiction-ectomy" performed, i.e., an imaginary surgery where we simply remove the diseased part. If we could, we would simply send the loved one to treatment, and they would come back "fixed." But the individual and the family's vulnerabilities will persist if we take that limited view of recovery. Success measures for long-term recovery must include the family's commitment to learning about the disease of addiction and adopting effective coping skills as a family.

It can be challenging for families in business—self-reliant and driven to succeed—to accept the necessity of long-term treatment. A long-term plan includes multiple tactics to improve outcomes. Finding a case manager or concierge substance abuse specialist can help navigate the early period of treatment and recovery for the individual and the family. They can continue to work collaboratively after treatment with the addicted family member, their family, and the addiction medicine specialist.

Families can't force a change in an individual's behavior, but they can influence it and change the behaviors that inadvertently contribute to the continuation of it. People in early recovery (up to two years) may still have difficulty self-assessing the likelihood of their risks of relapse and future harm. Successful treatment shares characteristics critical to successful family businesses: taking the long view, a team approach, and measuring success over time. Successfully treating addiction, like every chronic illness, requires taking a longitudinal focus and building and maintaining a support team with the ability to adapt as circumstances dictate.

Accommodation and Accountability: Influence and Unexpected Support

There may be missteps on the way to successful treatment and recovery, but effective business policies and supportive expertise inside the business can help. One option is to take a page from the best business leadership models —and lean into the internal business leaders with the right expertise. A quality HR partner, for example, can help the leadership team design and implement employee benefit policies that offer reasonable accommodations for employees with disabilities or chronic illnesses. Effective accountability and performance standards aren't arbitrary and can benefit all employees. Similarly, developing standards and clear guidelines for treatment referral and return to work for the family employee with an SUD or other mental health illness can help move them toward accepting treatment.

We find it helpful to remember that while not inevitable, relapse is common. Instead of reacting, business leadership can respond with awareness and acceptance of recovery as a desirable option for the addicted employee. Just as families' and individuals' business efforts sometimes fail, treating this chronic illness might include an initial ineffective attempt.

That is not a reason to throw in the towel on the concept of recovery. We accept that failure is a natural part of the business life cycle, yet it's challenging to accept that this might also be true in treatment. Like any chronic disease, SUD recovery is never linear, and there are times when people will need escalated treatment and testing.

Medicine is good for acute illnesses, like a broken leg or pneumonia. Beginning with simple causations and evolving rapidly, patients are usually cured with a single intense intervention. Addiction, however, is a chronic illness, and like diabetes, asthma, or hypertension, it has variable onsets and courses and requires a more comprehensive care strategy expressed over a lifetime.

Successful treatment requires a team approach and continuity of care relationships over a lifetime. Successful outcomes follow from lay and community support and the ability to incorporate new learning. Treatment strategies must be flexible enough to account for changes in behavioral and life circumstances.

Addiction is a disease affecting the whole family and thus requires a family orientation towards recovery. Outcomes improve when we combine the medical treatment model for SUD with a public health treatment model that extends over a lifetime and includes lay and professional supportive communities (health professionals, therapists, work partners, and family members) and the ability to adapt to changing life circumstances.[55] See the Public Health Model of Recovery below.[56]

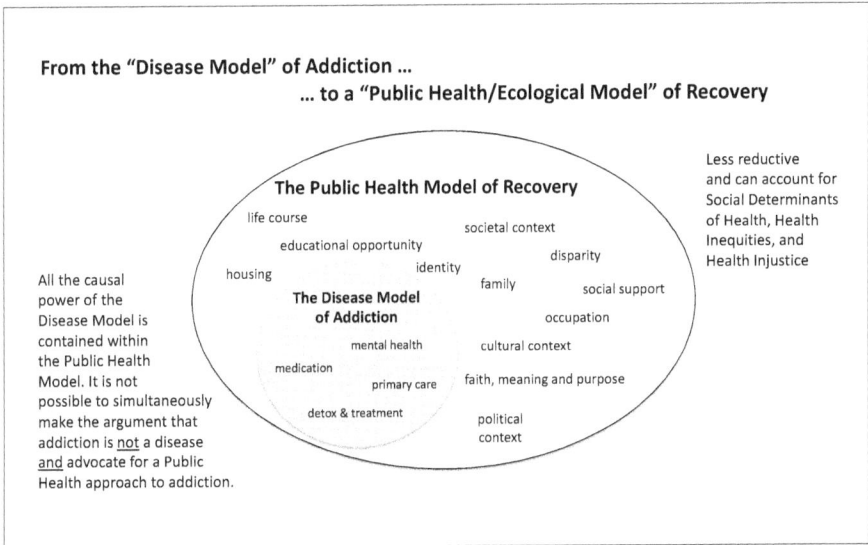

From the "Disease Model" of Addiction …

… to a "Public Health/Ecological Model" of Recovery

The Public Health Model of Recovery

life course
educational opportunity
societal context
identity
disparity
housing
family
social support
The Disease Model
of Addiction
occupation
mental health
cultural context
medication
primary care
faith, meaning and purpose
detox & treatment
political context

Less reductive and can account for Social Determinants of Health, Health Inequities, and Health Injustice

All the causal power of the Disease Model is contained within the Public Health Model. It is not possible to simultaneously make the argument that addiction is not a disease and advocate for a Public Health approach to addiction.

---

55 *Dr. Kevin McCauley*. (n.d.). Dr. Kevin McCauley. https://drkevinmccauley.com/

56 *Dr. Kevin McCauley*. (n.d.). Dr. Kevin McCauley. https://drkevinmccauley.com/

The chances for long-term sustainable recovery are vastly increased when treatment and recovery are measurable, evidenced-based, and rigorous. This blended treatment model also acknowledges the importance of community support (including business partners) and family involvement. Trying to treat or manage the isolated problem or person in the family or the business without addressing the family dynamic (the family reactions and responsibility) will result in adverse outcomes for the family and the patient.

Where to Begin and What to Expect

The best treatment centers include a careful medical and psychological assessment (including risk for accidental or intentional injury), drug testing (trust but verify), and medical detoxification, which might include a brief hospitalization.

Family members, business advisors, and the impaired individual are not diagnosticians. An assessment team, working with a skilled treatment team, should be able to address all co-morbidities and the family's needs. Ongoing substance testing, nutritional evaluation, and psychological and neuro-cognitive testing may be appropriate. Good programs have master's level prepared counselors with proper certifications (e.g., by SAMHSA[57] or JCAHO[58]) who can adapt or escalate a treatment plan when treatment isn't going well. Escalation of treatment or actions may mean pulling in more services or a higher level of care if necessary.

The importance of proper evaluation can't be overemphasized: e.g., alcohol use disorder assessment may also reveal an over-treatment of ADHD medications, resulting in psychostimulant dependence. Early cognitive impairment can also be the result of years of sedative use. As the brain clears from substances of abuse, other diagnoses may be revealed, like PTSD, a sexual compulsion, an eating disorder, or major depression. (See Chapter 5 on Depression.)

---

57 *SAMHSA - Substance Abuse and Mental Health Services Administration.* (n.d.). SAMHSA - the Substance Abuse Mental Health Services Administration. https://samhsa.gov/

58 The Joint Commission. (n.d.). *A trusted partner in patient care.* https://jointcommission.org/

Sharing candid collateral information from families and friends assists in comprehensive evaluation and treatment. These shared inputs may indicate an initial lack of disclosure about other areas of concern, such as gambling. It is all too common for stigmatized behavior to be underreported, and it's a feature of the disease to minimize embarrassing things. An expert team, which might include medical, legal, and psychological advisors, can incorporate newly discovered information, begin to mend interpersonal relationships, and provide ongoing resources for all.

Families are often surprised and disturbed to learn that people who are underdiagnosed or undiagnosed with mood disorders frequently mask or use substances. A different underlying disorder may reveal itself once the substance is removed and treatment is ongoing. Collaboration with family and other identified partners, during and after treatment, exponentially improves coordinated and integrated plans (or case management.") As in business, goals and plans are best managed when parties are aligned and open to the help of specialists. In this case, addiction medicine specialists.

If you are seeking treatment for a loved one in your family business, here are some suggestions for addressing medical needs and business needs.

Medical Needs

- Begin with a board-certified addiction medicine specialist working with a treatment center. Ask how long they follow their patients and how they track them in aftercare. What's the possibility of longer-term involvement with random testing?"

- When looking at treatment centers, don't be wowed by beautiful websites and marketing efforts that push their sites to the top of the Google search engine. Ask them to share data on their specific outcomes and how long are patients followed. The longer, the better once treatment is completed.

- Addiction is not a one-size-fits-all disease, and it is never a one-size-FIX-all treatment. Most treatment programs are attached to the insurance-designed, 28-day treatment programs in the United States. These programs treat all patients the same, for the same period, hoping that when they emerge, they will be "in recovery." No other system of care in the United States for any other illness approaches treatment with blind adherence to a set program without giving attention to the specific family and business needs. This is unfortunate. If treatment recommendations exceed the insurance structure, consider private pay options for a duration of treatment that is appropriate for your family member.

- Learn as much as possible about addiction and stay on top of current addiction research.

Business Needs

- Create a trusted team within the business that can assemble during a crisis and agree to communication, support, a tiered level of treatment and consequences, and privacy terms affecting the employee/family member for the long term. Much like a business risk committee, it can comprise the HR partner, legal advisor, essential family leadership, and family business advisor, who can develop policies that support the family and employees affected by an employee's SUD and respond to a crisis.

- The best people to protect an individual's medical privacy are their healthcare team. Respecting the individual's healthcare privacy within the work domain is also critical.

The Advisor

A gifted family business advisor with a background in marital and family therapy and organizational behavior can help. When a family is overwhelmed with the crisis, an advisor can help gather resources and support from the advisor's and family's network. They may have experience with other family businesses that have dealt with family addiction. The advisor can collaborate to help identify the steps necessary to support the family member while protecting and supporting the business. They might suggest a meeting with the risk team (the HR lead, legal, and direct reports) and even facilitate assessing the impact on the business and help the family leadership prioritize actions and decisions that affect the business and the family.

Most importantly, they can help calm the overlapping family and business systems and facilitate productive conversations about appropriate response and planning in each domain.

The family business advisor should know that:

- SUD is a chronic progressive and deadly disease from which recovery can be 100 percent, which is better than before the substances were started.

- In a misguided attempt to protect them, family and business stakeholders too often fail to move their loved ones toward recovery because they don't know how or who to ask for help.

- As hard as it is for the family to ask for help and as highly emotional as the situation might be, seeking the right help can make the difference between effective treatment and frustration.

- Referral to a board-certified Addiction Medicine specialist should be the first step to getting the addicted family member the appropriate assessment.

- Assessment should be reviewed for any medical concerns or psychiatric comorbidities that require management.

In collaboration with the Addiction Medicine physician, a good advisor can support the family and leadership as they move through a process to support their loved one. A medical stay for detoxification may follow assessment, then treatment that may include an inpatient and later outpatient recovery support plan. Medical treatment for the person with an SUD, set inside the context of their whole life, including the culture and conditions of the family business, can provide an integrated approach to successfully treating SUD as the chronic illness that it is.

What Happens to the Williams Family and Their Business?

The Walsh Resiliency framework supports one possible and positive ending to the Williams Family Business story. In our story, Joe and Jack used all available resources to help one another, their families, and Gary Jr.

With the help of their family business advisor, they identified the short and long-term priorities for themselves, their family, and their business. And even though they sometimes struggled, together they supported one another and learned as much as they could about addiction in their family and ways to support recovery.

Joe and Jack divided up responding to the short-term crisis in their family and business. Joe asked their HR lead to research and propose a best practice and employee protocol supporting clear guidelines and training when suspected of addiction and workplace impairment. An employee assistance plan was added to their insurance benefit that could provide short-term disability, referral for treatment, and a clear path to return to work.

Their family business advisor introduced Jack and Gary Jr. to an addiction medicine specialist affiliated with a well-regarded treatment center. Gary Jr. entered a 90-day treatment program and then an IOP program for another 90 days and attended 12-step meetings four times per week. After six months, he met with the HR lead and was offered a return-to-work plan and position that better matched his skills and health needs. He was required and agreed to submit to random drug and alcohol screening at work for two years. His family and his employer have supported Gary Jr.'s recovery.

He may want to avoid leading the company or being able to do so. Since Joe and Jack and their children don't want to sell their company, they are working on a succession plan that includes hiring a non-family CEO, establishing a high-performing board, and investing in comprehensive family education that provides for personal and professional development, family mental health learning and awareness, financial literacy, and governance training.

Despite these painful experiences, they believe that the adversity they experienced and their response to it has made them a stronger and healthier family and business. They have tackled some who also believe that the inherent shared strengths in their family, their culture, and their businesses were foundational to their ability to navigate their challenges as a family and business.

A Successful Model for Long-Term Recovery

Physicians, airline pilots, and some justice-involved communities use a distinctive management model reporting SUD's best long-term outcome data, documenting sobriety for 80% of participants at five years out. Key elements can be incorporated into a family business model of treatment, recovery, and accountability. These include:

- Early, confidential intervention in a respectful way. (Please see Chapter 12 "Raising Sensitive Subjects" for guidance.)

- An opportunity for thorough, cohort-specific evaluation by an addiction professional

- Treatment to reduce the negative impact of a disease on a family and a business

- Data-driven monitoring with quick response to concerning behavior

At the onset, as with diabetes or hypertension, substance use disorders require a lot of work to manage. Outside professionals are usually necessary to push all participants forward through the initial family conflict, denial, and ambivalence and to comply. The family and business leadership need to be aligned and committed, and all parties (the family, business team representatives, and external health partners) must understand their responsibilities and lines of communication. Attention must be paid to co-occurring conditions, personality issues, work/life balance, and family dynamics. The goal is to move all towards internalizing the diagnosis and treatment insights, personal commitments, and self-management.

Often, a third-party case manager is designated. The family business might consider creating its case management team, comprised of an HR person, family business advisor, attorney, and trusted family member, with regular involvement and access to sophisticated random substance abuse testing results. If the family member isn't working in the family business, private case managers can support the identification of and admission to appropriate treatment resources.

The successful process will include collecting easily trackable and communicated data for the individual and the family. Data might include adherence to individual and family therapy appointments, relapse prevention strategies, and work goals. Tracking this data can help identify emerging issues at the family, individual, and business levels.

Any indication that more treatment is needed when or if relapse occurs should be supported by a consistent, cohesive response in the overlapping systems. Taking a measured response to relapse is important. Firing the family member, ignoring behavior, or making threats will not help. To prevent rapidly escalating relapse cycles, support should be escalated during disease exacerbations. The care team should re-evaluate the care plan and, with the help of outside specialists, formulate a new disease containment strategy. Those can entail increased frequency of monitoring, escalated use of support groups, re-assessment of therapy for relapse prevention, and even protective housing with additional therapy.[59]

---

59   https://www.nytimes.com/2023/12/13/opinion/addiction-policy-treatment-opioid.html

One quantifiably successful treatment model to benchmark against is the PHP (Physicians Health Program[60]). In this model, success is determined by the routine measure of participant outcomes for at least five years. In collaboration with the HR lead and advisors, the family might consider adopting some, if not all, the Physicians Health Program measures as a guide to treating their family members and other employees inside and outside the business.

The Physicians Health Model recommends:

1. Zero tolerance for any use of alcohol and other drugs

2. Thorough evaluation and patient-focused (rather than program-focused) care

3. Prolonged, frequent random testing for both alcohol and other drugs

4. Interventions are conducted non-confrontationally with assistance lined up for the participant if they submit to a thorough evaluation to determine if there is indeed a problem.

5. Defining and managing relapses: swift and meaningful consequences for any substance use and non-compliance

6. A goal of lifelong recovery rooted in peer support groups and fellowships

7. Immediate response to relapse—and escalation of services

For the Family

The story of addiction in a family and a family business system doesn't have to end in the destruction of the family and or the business. Families in business can lean into their natural strengths and apply adaptive coping skills to

---

60 https://www.boardpreprecovery.com/rehab-blog/3-frequently-asked-questions-about-physician-health-programs/

support the family and the business. Both the successful family and business share an orientation towards collaboration.

Enterprising families often adopt a family charter that expresses their hopes for the future and a shared vision for the family. The Williams family crisis can be transformed into an opportunity—families who desire to change maladaptive patterns of behavior in their generational family story to explore areas for family development and a path toward a shared family vision of health.

One helpful framework that supports family orientation towards collaboration and comprehensive recovery is the Walsh Family Resilience Framework.[61] (Please see Chapter 2: Family Systems.) Tapping into the endemic strengths that are also part of the family business system, Walsh invites the family to remember their strengths and nurture the qualities often present in enterprising, multi-generational family businesses. She notes that resilient families:

- have beliefs and attitudes that facilitate coping.

- do their best to maintain routines and rituals but with flexibility.

- use effective communication about both information and feelings.

Conclusion

By writing about SUD in a family business, we hope to help remove the stigma and shame that prevents individuals and families from seeking effective treatment. There is hope in recovery. Families can learn to successfully address and care for families and employees with SUD and effectively run their businesses.

We've described family resistance as the result of shame and lack of knowledge, which create maladaptive responses. Perhaps more importantly, we've

---

61 Walsh, F. (2021). Family resilience. In *Oxford University Press eBooks* (pp. 255–270). https://doi.org/10.1093/oso/9780190095888.003.15

acknowledged the resilience endemic to enterprising families as resource families have drawn upon to overcome challenges throughout their shared family history. Stories abound of generations pulling together through business and financial reversals.

Treating addiction saves lives, and new advances in addiction medicine and family support offer breakthroughs in treatment. The family business system can be part of successful treatment for the individual and the family. Like most other successful sustainability practices, it will depend on an investment in the family.

Awareness and acceptance that substance use disorders are prevalent in many families can free a family from feeling isolated, ashamed, or overwhelmed, accepting that addiction affects the whole family and invites the entire family to participate in a return to health.

Summary of Key Points

- We want to eradicate the stigma and shame that comes with SUD. Addiction comes from and affects the whole family. Functional, effective responses must include the family, family business partners, vetted medical experts, and the individual.

- Emotional pain travels in families. If it's not transformed, it is transmitted. Families don't have to pass it on or poison the family system for future generations. By learning and modeling healthy coping strategies, we can stop perpetuating the maladaptive strategy of the past, transforming inevitable family business challenges into opportunities for the family and business to grow in cohesion and health.

- Addiction is a lifelong chronic condition. It is a brain disease that affects behavior choices, understanding, and awareness. Acceptance with focused and committed attention to treatment requires a thoughtful plan woven throughout the overlapping family business systems. This multilateral approach can also become a model to drive better communication, transparency, trust, and outcomes for the business, the family, and the individual.

- Enterprising families are not alone. Great support is available to families who act with courage and recommit in every generation to the shared values of learning, practicing, and teaching the skills present in resilient families.

- Treatment can get you out of a bad place, but it doesn't necessarily get the family and business into a good place. A broader, comprehensive family and business commitment to longitudinal care is required. The disease model of addiction, which emphasizes detox, treatment, medications, and mental health, can effectively be incorporated into the public health model and adapted for the benefit of the family and the business employees. After treatment, a public health recovery model includes work, meaning and purpose, social and workforce support, and education for the whole family.

- We have shared a model for treating addiction/substance use disorder, but this model also applies to behaviors such as gambling, sexual compulsivity, and other compulsive behaviors.

- The family, so greatly affected by SUD, can move toward developing resiliency and coping and managing behaviors associated with health and sustainability.

GLOSSARY OF TERMS

Comorbidity: the simultaneous presence of two or more diseases or medical conditions in a patient.

Internalization: the process of making attitudes or behavior part of one's nature by learning or unconscious assimilation.

Detoxification: Usually, but not always, in-patient. Medically supervised treatment from withdrawal of the substance. Patients who try to detox without medical supervision are at risk of seizure and death.

Treatment: Residential or Intensive Outpatient (IOP): treatment and patient education after detoxification. It should include behavioral counseling, group/peer discussion, education about addiction, observation, medical oversight, random drug and alcohol testing, nutritional and sleep support, and more.

Step-down treatment: Outpatient group support and behavioral counseling after treatment. Medical oversight and random testing should be offered.

Random drug and alcohol screening: testing of blood, hair, and urine levels for substances.

Addiction: The American Society of Addiction Medicine (ASAM) identifies addiction as a stress-induced, genetically mediated, primary, chronic, and relapsing behavior that alters motivational hierarchies such that addictive behaviors supplant healthy, self-care behaviors.[62]

Genetic vulnerability: This is dictated by several genes that can be passed through generations. "Epigenetic" changes to gene structure can also occur due to an individual's experience of physical, emotional, social, and cultural distress. Genes influence voluntary and involuntary behavior but do not solely determine our behaviors and choices.

Reward: refers to wanting something even more than liking it. It is mediated through the effects of one chemical, dopamine. Dopamine is the first chemical in the cascade of chemicals that generate a rewarding experience. It grabs our attention and zeros us in. All drugs of abuse and many compulsive behaviors (like gambling, spending, sex, overwork, internet addiction) release dopamine.

Memory: defined as habits and cues, and deep learning occurs as the brain is remodeled in addiction. It utilizes the same ancient neural pathways that helped us search for food and water millions of years ago.

---

62   News-Medical. (2020, May 13). *The biological mechanisms behind addiction.* https://www.news-medical.net/whitepaper/20190311/The-Biological-Mechanisms-Behind-Addiction.aspx

Remodeling of the brain: caused by an intense desire for drugs or alcohol (craving), strong cues to repeat, over-valuation of the experience provided by drugs and alcohol, and narrowing of focus.[63]

An overwhelming demand for available resources defines stress: When stressed, people engage in good and bad coping strategies. Alcohol, drugs, and compulsive behaviors briefly distract from stress, but they aren't a treatment. Motivation and insight are about prioritizing hierarchies, which get scrambled by addictive chemicals.

---

63 News-Medical. (2020, May 13). *The biological mechanisms behind addiction.* https://www.news-medical.net/whitepaper/20190311/The-Biological-Mechanisms-Behind-Addiction.aspx

CHAPTER SEVEN

The Role of ADD/ADHD in Family Business

by Gail Silverstein, PhD

"I thought she had finally grown out of that," lamented Peter Smith, CEO of the Smith family design business. Peter had just been told that his 25-year-old daughter, Jessica, had missed another deadline, causing the business to lose an important client.

Jessica was a mystery to her family. It took her six years to graduate from college, and she did so only by the skin of her teeth after attending three different universities and changing her major multiple times. It wasn't that she wasn't bright enough; she had always been an excellent student up until she started college. However, she struggled with the increased volume and complexity of college courses. Her parents had always closely supervised her schoolwork when she was younger, but there was no supervision in college, and she had to structure her own time. Nothing the family tried seemed to help, and everyone breathed a sigh of relief when she finally graduated.

After graduation, Jessica came to work at the family business. Company policy was that all new employees, including family members, started at entry-level positions and worked their way up, thereby gaining familiarity with the company as a whole. Jessica did very well at first. The entry-level positions tended to be fairly structured, with clear guidelines, expectations, and deadlines, and she could meet all of the benchmarks established for her. She also earned several promotions.

However, the most recent promotion put her into a more managerial and less structured position where she needed to work with many details. She was given less guidance and expected to work more independently. And Jessica was not able to handle it. She was extremely disorganized and often lost track of what she was supposed to be doing or where she was supposed to be. She neglected to return phone calls, emails, and texts. She missed or arrived late to several meetings. When she did attend them, she tended to be unfocused, distractible, and unprepared. When she fell too far behind, she became over-whelmed and reverted to the behavior she had engaged in in college. She stopped attending meetings and sometimes simply called in sick. Because she was very likable, co-workers and supervisors tried to cover for her. But finally, she lost that important client, and word of her failures got to her parents.

Not knowing what to do, her parents talked to their new family business consultant. He recommended neuropsychological testing for Jessica. I tested her, and I diagnosed her with ADHD, Predominantly Inattentive Type (what used to be known as ADD).

Family members who aren't as fortunate as Jessica to receive a diagnosis that helps them understand the problem behind her challenges often get labeled as a problem. Seeing problems of attention as a character flaw rather than seeking to understand and manage the symptoms of ADHD can be hugely detrimental to their self-confidence and potentially lead to depression. When a family gets curious and seeks to understand the realities around ADHD, they can unlock the untapped capabilities of that individual, helping both the individual and the family business.

What Exactly is ADHD?

People with Attention Deficit Disorder have difficulty regulating their attention and controlling their impulses. Currently, there are thought to be three different subtypes of ADHD: the predominantly inattentive type, the predominantly hyperactive/impulsive type, and the combined type. The most recent official diagnostic manual (DSM-V) refers to all three as ADHD rather than using the older term "ADD" to refer to the predominantly inattentive type. That format will be followed here. At one time, it was thought that people "grow out of" ADHD when they reach adolescence. Now, it is understood that while some people's symptoms do improve dramatically in adolescence, more often, ADHD is a lifelong disorder, although the symptoms may change somewhat over time. As people mature, they often learn ways to cope with and compensate for their ADHD symptoms effectively, so the ADHD can appear to improve over time.

On the other hand, as we get older, we usually have more responsibilities than we did when we were younger. As happened with Jessica, these new responsibilities put more of a burden on the person's (previously effective) coping strategies, so the strategies may no longer work as well. Therefore, the ADHD may appear to be worse. In other words, the impact of ADHD on a person's life is determined by a combination of biological limitations, the demands of the environment, and learned coping strategies.

People with ADHD often have difficulty sustaining attention and are easily distracted. They tend to be disorganized, forgetful, often late and frequently lose necessary things. They may make careless mistakes due to a lack of attention to detail. They may plunge right into a task without regard for the directions. They often don't follow through or finish things they have started or promised to do. They may not seem to listen when spoken to directly. Those with symptoms of hyperactivity/impulsivity tend to be fidgety and noisy and have trouble sitting still, relaxing, or waiting their turn. They may talk excessively, blurt things out, and interrupt other people. They seem to be constantly "on the go." In adults and older adolescents, some hyperactive symptoms may take the form of an internal feeling of restlessness.[64] ADHD behaviors are most often seen in situations in which the person is required to do something

---

64 `Diagnostic and Statistical Manual of Mental Disorders, 5th Edition (DSM-5). (2021). In *Springer eBooks* (p. 1401). https://doi.org/10.1007/978-3-319-91280-6_300515

they don't want to do, especially if the person perceives the task as boring or tedious. In addition to school and vocational problems, adults with untreated ADHD are at risk for substance abuse or other addictions (see Chapter 6 Substance Disorder), motor vehicle accidents, marital problems, financial problems, health problems, and other mental health issues.[65]

On the other hand, when people with ADHD are interested in what they are doing, they can often hyper-focus for long periods. Some people with ADHD are exceptionally creative, perhaps due to their divergent thinking (ability to generate multiple ideas from a starting point), impulsivity, willingness to take risks, and tendency to let the ideas flow freely with less emphasis on the practicalities.[66]

ADHD may look different in women than in men, not because of biology but because of differing cultural expectations for women and men. Men are given a lot of permission by our culture to be impulsive ("boys will be boys") and to be unconcerned about many of the petty details of everyday life (remembering to pick up their dry cleaning, scheduling children's doctor's appointments, etc.). Although things have changed to some extent, most working mothers are still expected to do most of the household chores and be the primary caretakers for the children. Women are generally the family organizer, managing schedules, appointments, events, etc. for the entire family, and being the primary social director, arranging play dates for children and outings for the couple. This is not only a heavier load than most men carry, but the ability to carry out many of these responsibilities depends on some of the very abilities that are weak or lacking in people with ADHD, such as time management and organization. People with ADHD may talk too much and interrupt other people. They may arrive late or not at all if they forget appointments or social engagements. Yet others (including other women)

---

65   Barkley, R. A., Murphy, K. R., & Fischer, M. (2008). *ADHD in adults: What the science says.* The Guilford Press.

66   White, H. (2024, February 20). The creativity of ADHD. *Scientific American.* https://www.scientificameri-can.com/article/the-creativity-of-adhd/

often expect women to be attentive to others even at the expense of their own needs and to be compliant and wait their turn. Therefore, women may feel more pressure to hide their ADHD behaviors. They hold themselves together to function at work but then fall apart at home. They are more likely than men to internalize all the many criticisms they have undoubtedly received over time and to suffer from reduced self-esteem, anxiety, and depression, as well as other mental health issues. When stressed, women are more likely to turn to relationships for comfort than men. Women generally "tend and befriend." Relationships are more central to women than men, so there is more need for social acceptance. Yet, many of the symptoms of ADHD interfere with the very relationships that women are naturally dependent on.[67]

Even for a professional, a diagnosis of ADHD is challenging. For some other mental health diagnoses, the criteria depend on the presence or absence of symptoms. You either have hallucinations, or you don't. It doesn't matter how often they occur; it is never normal to have them. By contrast, most of us have at least some of the above ADHD behaviors some of the time. Diagnosis depends on whether or not you have them *more than* other people the same age do, not simply on *whether* you have them. And who decides if you have "too many" of these behaviors or have them "too often"? People with ADHD are notoriously bad at insight into their behavior in this respect, so you can't necessarily take their word for it. The workaround is usually to get both the person who may have ADHD and others who know them well to provide information. However, this approach also has difficulties. If you know the person well enough to rate them on these characteristics, you probably also know them well enough to have your own biases in your perceptions of them. For example, if you are annoyed by the behavior, you may distort your reports of it negatively. A parent may feel responsible or guilty for not noticing a potential problem sooner, which may minimize the frequency or severity of the behaviors.

---

67 *Why ADHD is more challenging for women - CHADD*. (2023, July 24). CHADD. https://chadd.org/attention-article/why-adhd-is-more-challenging-for-women/

Another concern is that many other problems can look like ADHD. For example, people who are anxious or depressed may have trouble concentrating. People with language disorders may look inattentive because they have trouble following some complex language people use. People with bipolar disorder may be impulsive. People with ADHD may take a long time to do something because they are so disorganized. Anxious people may take a long time to do something because they are perfectionists and need to get it right. Depressed people may take a long time to do something because they are just not motivated to do anything. Low self-esteem may make them think they cannot do it anyway, so why even start? People who have had concussions often have many of the same difficulties that people with ADHD do.

For all these reasons, it is best not to try to self-diagnose ADHD but rather to consult a mental health professional if it is suspected. I believe the best way to diagnose ADHD is to combine understanding the person's life history, rating scales completed by the person and people who know them well, and neuropsychological testing to provide a more objective assessment of the behaviors and their severity.

What Causes ADHD?

Along with changes in the name of the disorder, there have been changes in the theories about what causes it. The most recent research indicates a chemical imbalance affecting frontal brain regions is the primary cause, and the basic result is a lack of inhibition of impulses. This leads to several types of difficulties. People with ADHD often seem to act without thinking or fail to profit from the experience. They can tell you what they should or should have done when asked directly. The problem is that they must refrain from inhibiting their impulse to speak or to act long enough to remember what they know. Most of us consult a mental timeline when considering whether to act in a certain way. We go to the past and remember what happened the last time we did this action. For example, "The last time I skipped this meeting, I missed hearing important information, so I made several mistakes in the project. Everyone was mad at me, and I lost my opportunity for a promotion." And we project into the future. For example, "If I don't attend this meeting, I may not hear important information, and then I might make mistakes in this new project and lose my opportunity for a promotion." If you have ADHD, you live in the present and attend to whatever is in front of you at any given time. "I don't feel like going to the meeting, so I won't go," and you don't.

People with ADHD are easily distracted by external stimuli (for example, a squirrel outside the window) and internal thought processes ("What should I have for dinner tonight?"). The person may start writing a report and then notice a paper on their desk, read it, and decide to Google something about its contents. Then an ad pops up, and they click on it, and they want to tell someone about the ad, so they get onto their email and see other interesting emails and follow up on those, and so on and so on. Then, all of a sudden, it's 5:00PM, and the desk is littered with tasks that were begun but never completed, and nothing has gotten done that day. Each task is perceived as equally important, and the person cannot inhibit the impulse to attend to each.

Executive functioning weaknesses are generally a part of ADHD. Executive functioning can be thought of as an executive's tasks—organizing, planning, prioritizing, directing the company's attention to specific areas rather than others, etc.

Some Frequently Asked Questions about ADHD

Q: Sometimes, I can pay attention very well. Doesn't that mean the diagnosis is wrong?

Jessica's mother initially disagreed with the ADHD diagnosis. She said, "Jessica doesn't have any trouble paying attention. She loves video games, and she can play for hours. Sometimes, you must say her name three or four times before she even realizes you are in the room." Many people who have just been diagnosed with ADHD or their family members make similar comments.

But actually, Jessica's mother's description of her behavior fits very well with ADHD. Having an attention deficit disorder doesn't mean you can't pay attention. It means you can't *regulate* your attention to pay attention to things you are not interested in. Video games tend to be fast paced, with bright colors and loud sounds, and they are designed to hold your attention. Most people can pay attention to that type of situation. Sometimes it's hard not to. But what about paying attention to a long, boring, tedious, but necessary task? Who enjoys doing their taxes or compiling statistics for an annual report? That's where people with ADHD run into trouble. It's easy to see this behavior as voluntary, just laziness, but it's biologically based and not under the person's control. With some discussion, the family could see how many of Jessica's new responsibilities fit into the latter category.

Q: Why didn't I know that I had ADHD before now?

"So, did she just develop this ADHD in college? Everything was fine until then," said Jessica's father.

People are born with ADHD. Jessica's parents told me that Jessica spent much time looking out the window or doodling in elementary school. She's very bright, her grades were good, and she did not show any behavior problems, so naturally, no one saw a problem. Bright girls often fall through the cracks like this. Hyperactive kids, more often boys than girls, usually cause other people trouble, so their problems are more likely to be noticed early. Squeaky wheels get the grease.

Also, like many parents, Jessica's parents intuitively provided her with compensation for her weaknesses without necessarily knowing why they were doing what they did. They gave her the structure she could not provide by ensuring that she studied and did her homework. They also helped her plan by breaking down large projects into smaller parts and making checklists and timelines for her to follow. Further, her school was a small private school with excellent teacher-to-student ratios so that the teachers could do the same thing. Then, when she got to college, there was no one there to do that for her, and she had no idea how to do it for herself, so she fell apart. And now, in a similar workplace situation, she was falling apart again.

ADD/ADHD and Family Business

Having an employee with undiagnosed and untreated ADHD can cause significant problems for any business. As in Jessica's case, the employee's lack of organization and time management skills can mean that important tasks may not get done or may not get done in a timely fashion. The employee may over-commit and then not follow through. Communication may be poor if they do not attend to or remember important information. They may make bad decisions impulsively without entirely thinking things through. Relationships with co-workers can suffer for all of the above reasons. All of these issues are magnified in a family business. If the employee is a family member, other family members may have an agenda regarding the success or failure of the person with ADHD. Succession plans may be rethought.

As with anxiety disorders, the impact of an individual with ADHD in a family business system is not just issues of performance. These challenges with concentration and distractibility can also significantly impact family dynamics. Often, when ADHD causes the individual to drop the ball on something, another family member adjusts and compensates for the impact of the ADHD behaviors, as Jessica's parents did when she was younger. Over time, the family system may adapt to minimize the impact of the behaviors. One family member may realize that a deadline will be missed and fill the performance gap. Over time, a pattern may emerge where the family moderates the work given to the individual with ADHD. These subtle adjustments can lead to resentment and tensions that can build up within the family relationships. So, identifying ADHD and implementing strategies to support the person with ADHD will ultimately reduce interpersonal tensions within the family.

Case Example

Jessica had an assignment on her desk, which her father gave her directly. It was a project she designed. She organized a team to help her execute the work over the next three months. In the interim, Jessica learned about two other projects her father oversaw. These were assigned to other non-family staff members. Even though Jessica's family and her non-family associates were aware of the potential of her dropping the ball on projects or initiatives in the business, they were also aware of her gifts of innovative thinking and her creative entrepreneurship inside the business. The problems showed up when she'd overcommitted. This happened after she learned about the other two projects her father was overseeing.

Her colleagues would refer to her desk as filled with "doom piles," documents that may or may not fall through the cracks and affect her, her associates, and her business performance. Jessica was also known to move from one "shiny object" to another in her personal life. This might be the men she dates, taking a piano class, then dropping it to take a class on astronomy, then spontaneously deciding to go to France with her girlfriends. Because she is affable and cherished by her friends and family, she is often given a pass, which enables the problems rather than resolving them. Her "time blindness," as a colleague put it, often causes Jessica and her family in the business, as well as the non-family members, breakdowns in execution, delays, and out-and-out failures.

Recommendations for Managing ADHD in the Family Business

Often, the most challenging part of making changes is understanding and admitting that you need to. Once you can do that and get some guidance about just what the problem is (and is not), the solutions come more easily.

One way to help with ADHD symptoms is to take medication. Medication can be beneficial for improving focus and concentration and helping control impulses. But medication is not the whole story. Not everyone can or wants to take medication. Medication for ADHD does not cure the problem in the way that antibiotics can cure an infection. Most ADHD medications work only as long as you are taking them, and they provide no help when they wear off or if you discontinue them. It is also important to know that taking medication for ADHD can make things worse if the person has some of the other mental health problems noted above instead of ADHD. Therefore, anyone who prescribes medication will probably require a formal diagnosis of ADHD. Medication alone is unlikely to solve the problem.

Other interventions are behavioral and require the individual to change how they function. For example, people with poor organizational skills will not learn better skills by taking medication. "Pills don't teach skills."[68] If you want to be better organized, you must learn new habits and strategies. For example, the person can be taught to use lists and reminders regularly and properly. There is a great deal of information about this in books, other publications, and online, and some people find this type of information helpful. However, the best way to learn these new skills is probably to work one-on-one with a coach, family business consultant, or therapist.

It can also help to change the environment. For example, if the person cannot sustain attention throughout long meetings, maybe shorter, more frequent meetings can be scheduled instead. Maybe an assistant can help with some tasks the individual has trouble remembering to do or help them manage their schedule. Perhaps they can have an office with a door that can be closed to reduce distractions rather than working in a cubicle. There are numerous possibilities. Knowing the person's weaknesses usually points to what kinds of changes will be helpful. People who have never been formally diagnosed but see some ADHD characteristics in themselves can also benefit from these behavioral and environmental strategies.

Especially important in the family business context is the fact that ADHD often causes problems in relationships. Others may be annoyed by the person with ADHD's tendency to interrupt others impulsively. If the person with

---

68   Tuckman, A. (2007). *Integrative Treatment for Adult ADHD*. New Harbinger Publications.

ADHD does not follow through on commitments they have made, it is easy to see how co-workers and family members (often the same people in this context) can take it personally. They may incorrectly assume that the person with ADHD does not care about them or their needs, rather than realizing that the person may have simply forgotten the commitment they made as soon as they finished making it. If this type of thing has been happening since childhood, the problem is only compounded.

On the other hand, relationships and teamwork are often part of the solution in family businesses. I have worked with several families in which one sibling was the visionary, and another sibling was not as creative but excelled at adapting the visionary's ideas to be more practical. As a team, the two could develop brilliant and innovative ideas that could be implemented in the real world. This kind of teamwork can work especially well if the two siblings have been interacting in some of the same ways since childhood. (One sibling may think of stealing cookies from the cookie jar, while the other sibling may figure out how to do it without getting caught.) Suppose there is not that type of complementarity among family members. In that case, another solution is to hire a non-family member as an assistant to the visionary who can translate the ideas into workable, pragmatic strategies.

Peter, Jessica's father, initially reacted to her ADHD diagnosis with skepticism, saying, "I don't believe in ADHD." He saw much of himself in Jessica (ADHD is often hereditary). However, he insisted that he had no difficulty managing these same issues and did not see why Jessica should be different. The family business consultant reminded Peter that Carmen had worked with him as his assistant since he started the company. Carmen is a very bright woman who intuitively understood what Peter needed and generally provided it without any discussion necessary. However, Jessica did not have a Carmen equivalent, so things were more of a struggle. Peter was still skeptical until the consultant arranged a meeting where Carmen described how she spent her time at work. This opened Peter's eyes a bit, and he began empathizing more with Jessica. He was then more willing to listen to suggestions that would benefit Jessica and reduce his criticism of her. Father and daughter greatly appreciated this change in their relationship on many levels.

So, If I Think I Have ADHD, What Should I Do?

The first step would be to have a neuropsychological evaluation to determine which aspects of ADHD are affecting you. Not everyone experiences ADHD in the same way. Or you may have some of the characteristics of ADHD without fully meeting the criteria for diagnosis. Then, you can work with the evaluator, a coach, or your family business consultant on which strategies might help you to compensate. Some options are:

To minimize distractions:

- Closing your office door and turning off your phone and email and text alerts when you need to concentrate

- Using noise-canceling headphones

- Keeping your desk organized and clear of anything except what you're working on at the time

To work with, instead of fighting a reduced attention span:

- The Pomodoro technique in which you work for 20–25 minutes at a time and then take a 5-minute break

- Use the break to walk around the office suite or outdoors before returning to work.

To help with organization:

- Learning how to use lists of things to do effectively and the best ways to use electronic reminders

- Learning to reward yourself when successfully implementing a strategy rather than condemning yourself when you see yourself as failing

- Hiring a high-level, talented person to be your assistant. It would be helpful for you, the family business consultant or coach, and the neuropsychologist to meet with you and your assistant to make the assistant aware of the issues. This meeting could also help you and your assistant develop strategies that would work for you, the assistant, and the company.

- The assistant can, for example, manage your schedule so you do not over-commit, remind you about upcoming deadlines, and proofread anything you write (because many people with ADHD are prone to making careless mistakes).

- Having an assistant may also allow you to delegate some of your responsibilities, leaving you free to concentrate on the most critical tasks only you can do.

- Recognize that a desire to avoid certain tasks or meetings may signal that you are overwhelmed and need help. The assistant can help you break large projects into smaller, more manageable components, setting realistic timelines for each element.

Memory

Many people with ADHD have a poor memory. To remember information, one needs first to attend to it. (People who think they have memory problems actually often have attention problems instead.) Then, one needs to organize the information in a way that helps one to remember it, a skill often lacking in people with ADHD but one that can be taught. You may need to learn to accept that when you and someone else have different recollections of what happened or was said in a meeting, the other person may be more likely to be correct.

Family Issues

When you have a young child with ADHD, there are many things you can do to help. For example, you can ensure they receive the appropriate school support. You can provide them with reminders and other types of structure at home. But when the person with ADHD is an adult, those options are no longer available to you. In my experience, the most helpful way for loved ones of people with ADHD to provide support is by learning more about ADHD and adjusting their expectations accordingly. It is common for family members of people with ADHD to see the person as not caring about them and their needs. These hurt feelings and resentments may be carried on for years. It may be life-changing for the family to meet with the neuropsychologist, the family business consultant, or a family therapist. In that way, the family can better understand what the person with ADHD has control over and what they do not. The person with ADHD can not only learn more about themselves but also more about their impact on other family members. Of course, since ADHD is often hereditary, there may be more than one family member who has it. This only complicates things. Nevertheless, better communication strategies and other strategies can also be learned through such meetings.

There is no cure for ADHD, and having undiagnosed ADHD carries a lot of risks, including risks for performance at work. However, once you know that you have it and how it affects you, there are many excellent strategies available to you for managing ADHD and its sequelae. The biggest obstacle is accepting that you have a problem and will be much better off addressing it than trying to hide or deny it. Getting evaluated by a professional rather than trying to self-diagnose is essential. The good news is that ADHD is well-known and well-researched, and there is no shortage of effective interventions for it.

CHAPTER EIGHT

Finding Strength in Family Unity: Addressing the Challenges of Dementia and Cognitive Decline

by Andrew Keyt

Sophie and Fredrick Schaefer entered the Munich offices of Schaefer Automotive Distribution with a sense of relief and excitement. This was the day they would finally put the details behind the plan that was started in 2019 for the two of them as 4th generation siblings to become CFO and COO of Schaefer Automotive. As both drove the company's growth over the past few years, Sophie and Frederick were becoming increasingly concerned about their father Reinhard's memory and decision-making. Just last month, their father had placed the same order with one of their key suppliers three times, which created a cash crunch for the company. Sophie and Frederick felt a responsibility for their 600 employees, their younger brother Torsten, and their 12 cousins, who also owned the company. It was time to take a greater leadership role to protect the business from what they saw as the increasing cognitive decline of their father.

As they entered the board room, Reinhard shouted,

"So, you think I have a screw coming loose?"

Frederick responded, "Dad, what do you mean?"

"I just found out that you told your mother that you thought my memory was a problem and that you weren't sure if I could still run this company. How can I trust the two of you to take on such senior roles when you don't even think I can run this company?"

Sophie immediately glared at her mother, Johanna, with a look of betrayal. Three weeks ago, Frederick and Sophie had cornered their mother and talked about their concerns about their father's ability to track the conversation in meetings and how he was making more and more financial decisions that cost the company money. While Johanna had seen some of these memory lapses, she refused to believe that her husband was anything but the same man who had grown the company from $200M to $800M over the past 20 years.

The story of the Schaefer family shows us the emotional and financial impact that cognitive decline can have on both a business and a family: a father who feels betrayed by his children, a mother who feels caught between a husband she loves and her children, and children who are both concerned for the health and well-being of their father and the financial health of Schaefer Automotive.

Breaking the silence about the cognitive decline that they witnessed must have felt overwhelming for Sophie and Frederick. Questioning the fathers' capabilities, which they loved and respected, challenged the structure and fabric that had sustained the Schaefer family for decades. For a child to challenge the authority and leadership of their parent turns the world upside down.

Cognitive decline and its impact create risk not just to business decision-making and the health of the business, as we see in the Schaefer's case, but it can also create stress and friction for the owning family and their relationships.

Cognitive Decline: Why We Need to Talk About It

We all know that physical and cognitive decline is a normal part of aging. As we age, we don't have the physical stamina we had at 25. When we were young, we could remember the lyrics to every song we loved as teenagers, but we can't remember the name of the sales representative we met for lunch last Thursday. While cognitive decline is something almost every human deals with, in a family business, the physical and cognitive decline of one of its leaders has dramatic implications for succession. The more control and influence the individual experiencing cognitive decline has, the greater the impact and risk. As we see in the Schaefer's case, it can tear apart the fabric of family relationships. We must understand that these family relationships are critical to sustaining a family business's succession across generations.[69] The individual and the family business are interdependent and always impact each other. The stresses on an individual in the system place stress on the family. The stress placed on the family results in stress on the family enterprise.

The research shows that 1 in 7 people over the age of 71 will develop some sort of dementia,[70] which is the most severe form of cognitive decline. Researchers project that these numbers will grow. They estimate that due to the combination of population growth and extended life expectancy (the number of Americans over the age of 65 is projected to more than double over the next 40 years)[71,72] the number of dementia cases will triple by 2050.[73] The implications of these statistics for leadership are also critical to understand. Eight of ten leaders of the most populous countries in the world are now over 70 years old.[74]

---

69   Astrachan, J. H., McMillan, K. S., & Pieper, T. M. (2012). *Family business.*

70   *One in seven Americans age 71 and older has some type of dementia,*. (2015, October 22). National Institutes of Health (NIH). https://www.nih.gov/news-events/news-releases/one-seven-americans-age-71-older-has-some-type-dementia-nih-funded-study-estimates

71   U.S. Census Bureau, U.S. Department of Commerce, & Economics and Statistics Administration. (2010). *THE NEXT FOUR DECADES: The older population in the United States: 2010 to 2050.* https://www.census.gov/content/dam/Census/library/publications/2010/demo/p25-1138.pdf

72   *GHE: Life expectancy and healthy life expectancy.* (n.d.). https://www.who.int/data/gho/data/themes/mortality-and-global-health-estimates/ghe-life-expectancy-and-healthy-life-expectancy

73   Nichols, E., Steinmetz, J. D., Vollset, S. E., Fukutaki, K., Chalek, J., Abd-Allah, F., Abdoli, A., Abualhasan, A., Abu-Gharbieh, E., Akram, T. T., Hamad, H. A., Alahdab, F., Alanezi, F. M., Alipour, V., Almustanyir, S., Amu, H., Ansari, I., Arabloo, J., Ashraf, T., . . . Vos, T. (2022). Estimation of the global prevalence of dementia in 2019 and forecasted prevalence in 2050: an analysis for the Global Burden of Disease Study 2019. *The Lancet. Public Health*, 7(2), e105–e125. https://doi.org/10.1016/s2468-2667(21)00249-8

74   Emont, J. (n.d.). *Old Leaders Run the World - and They're Not Going Anywhere.* The Wall Street Journal. Retrieved June 22, 2024, from https://www.wsj.com/world/for-world-leaders-70-is-the-new-50-290c1ba7

These data tell us that more and more family businesses will be encountering questions about the cognitive capabilities of our aging leaders. The impact of cognitive decline on leadership has never been on display as much as it has in high-profile cases such as Sumner Redstone and his company Viacom. The Viacom case included challenges to Sumner Redstone's competency, challenges to the estate, family estrangement, and multiple people in the system trying to manipulate Sumner's vulnerability for their gain. These stories show the real damage that legal fights, bad actors, and family tensions can have on a family and a business. We must end the silence around cognitive decline to avoid these soap opera scenarios in their own family businesses.

What is Normal?

Cognitive decline and dementia are perhaps the biggest hidden risk in the family business succession process. We talk about managing estate taxes, preparing successors, and creating strong governance, but we don't discuss and prepare for what we would do if our leader shows signs of cognitive decline. There has been insufficient discussion or study of these issues in family business despite the real legal, financial, and relational risks that cognitive decline creates for family business owners and their families. When a family business leader starts to experience problems with memory, processing speed, and conceptual reasoning, issues for the business can develop. The leader will struggle to understand complex financial matters, may be more open to manipulation by others, and may make decisions that hurt the company's reputation and finances.

We must first understand that it is a normal part of the aging process to identify the signs of cognitive decline when they arise. Normal signs of aging include forgetting when we started the new division of the company, forgetting that our children already own the business, and mixing up the names of family members or long-time employees. All those lapses fall into the realm of normal.

That normalcy makes it difficult to assess changes in cognitive functioning as problematic is difficult. Every person's intelligence shifts with aging. The

National Institute for Mental Health[75] highlights two types of intelligence that impact how we engage in daily life as we age:

1. Crystallized intelligence refers to the accumulation of knowledge, facts, and skills that a person gathers throughout life. It involves using and synthesizing previously learned information to solve problems, make decisions, and understand concepts. Examples include complex problem-solving, and comprehension of situations based on their years of experience and learning.

2. Fluid intelligence is the ability to solve problems in real time, independent of acquired knowledge. It involves reasoning, identifying patterns, and adapting to new information or circumstances. Fluid intelligence is like mental flexibility and problem-solving skills that allow us to tackle new challenges, adapt to change, and figure out solutions in unfamiliar situations.

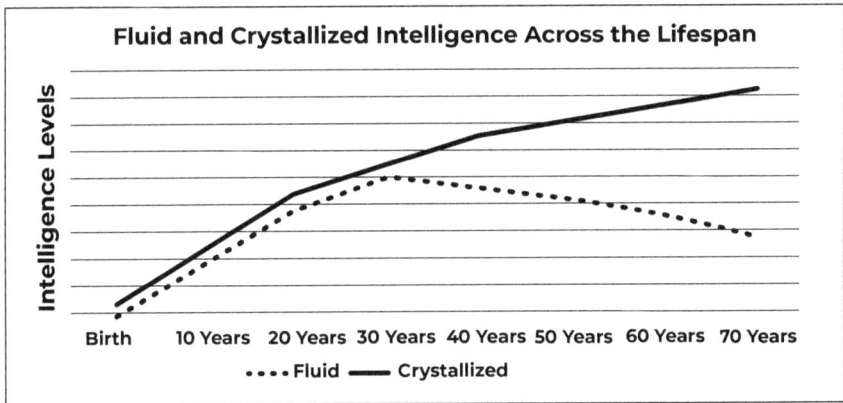

Fluid and Crystallized Intelligence Across the Lifespan

Interestingly, this research shows that crystallized intelligence remains relatively stable in normal aging until about 80; Fluid intelligence steadily declines from age 20 to 80. A decline in fluid intelligence may make it difficult for the older generation to adapt to new technologies or changes in the industry. This is why we see that innovation as more likely to come from

75 Murman, D. (2015b). The impact of age on cognition. *Seminars in Hearing*, *36*(03), 111–121. https://doi. org/10.1055/s-0035-1555115

younger family members.[76] This also has implications for assessing changes we see in a family member. Suppose the family member we are assessing is 75 years old and struggling to adapt to new technology in the industry. In that case, it may not be as big a concern as if they can't recall how to solve problems they are familiar with.

Another nuance in determining what is normal is that cognitive decline can vary significantly from person to person.[77] Each needs to be evaluated in comparison to how they have performed in the past rather than comparing them just to the performance of others. For instance, when we are assessing the cognitive decline of a parent, we should be comparing their performance to their past performance rather than comparing them to their peers.

How to Distinguish Dementia from Normal Aging

To move beyond the nuances that exist for a family to manage the risks effectively, they must work to understand the difference between normal aging and the more accelerated process of dementia. Frederick and Sophie Schaefer are faced with the challenge of determining if their father's struggles to follow a conversation or poor decision-making were just typical signs of cognitive decline or if there is a more serious cognitive problem happening. In a certain percentage of cases, cognitive decline is accelerated by dementia. According to the Alzheimer's Association[78]:

Dementia is a general term that describes a wide range of symptoms associated with a decline in memory or other thinking skills, including judgment, reasoning, and complex motor skills.

---

76 Brooks, A. (2021). *From Strength to Strength: Finding Success, Happiness, and Deep Purpose in the Second Half of Life*. Penguin.

77 Widera, E. (2022, February 1). *Samir Sinha: Redesigning health care systems to be elder friendly*. A Geriatrics and Palliative Care Podcast for Every Healthcare Professional. https://geripal.org/samir-sinha-redesigning-health-care-edler-friendly/

78 *What is Dementia?* (n.d.). Alzheimer's Disease and Dementia. https://www.alz.org/alzheimers-dementia/what-is-dementia

According to the Alzheimer's Association, a key aspect in the diagnosis of dementia is that the impairment is severe enough to interfere with daily life. There are several types of dementia, some of which include Alzheimer's disease (which accounts for 60-80% of all dementia cases), vascular dementia, Lewy Body disease, frontotemporal dementia, and alcohol-related dementia. Regardless of the type of dementia, the results can be devastating for both the business and the family.

The insidious part of this disease is found in its progressive nature. Its severity exists on a spectrum and does not have a simple diagnosis. While we associate dementia with aging, it is important to understand that age isn't the only factor. There are many 80- or 90-year-olds who hold on to many of their cognitive capabilities, whereas there may be 65- or 70-year-olds who decline quickly. It is also important to mention that other medical issues can create dementia-like symptoms. Families should first rule out other medical problems that can produce symptoms that look like dementia. Some of these include medication interactions/side effects, respiratory infections, urinary tract infections, sleep disorders, dehydration, and normal pressure hydrocephalus.[79]

This leads to the vexing question, "When is cognitive decline a problem?" Barry Reisberg, Professor of Psychiatry from the NYU Grossman School of Medicine, put forth a seven-stage model (see Table 1) to illustrate the progression of the disease. It helps define the progression of symptoms of the disease over time.

As we look at the seven stages of dementia and examine the indicators that go along with each stage, we can posit that family businesses are most likely to struggle to deal with the risks and challenges of dementia during phases 3 and 4. In these early stages, the symptoms can often be explained away or hidden by the individual and sometimes those around them. A next-generation member may attribute memory problems to fatigue because they want to

---

79   Crouch, M. (2023, April 25). *These problems can mimic dementia*. AARP. https://www.aarp.org/health/conditions-treatments/info-2022/medical-problems-mimic-dementia.html

maintain a belief in their father's strength. A CEO's assistant and senior leadership team may maneuver to limit a declining CEO's exposure to the outside world by taking up some of their responsibilities. Typically, by stage 5, the symptoms will be so pronounced that we have already had to start to address the issues. During phases 3 and 4, there may not yet be a diagnosis, and the family will struggle with issues of the individual's competency and capacity.

Some of the struggles that clients have shared with me over the years include:

- *My father forgot an email agreement that he had made with our tenant via email.*

- *My mother is getting lost in the plant and forgetting the names of long-time employees.*

- *My dad is missing sales meetings that are clearly on his calendar.*

- *My mom can't remember the name of someone she met at our industry conference last week.*

These symptoms leave people questioning whether it is this normal aging or the early signs of dementia. The defining difference between normal cognitive decline and that associated with dementia is the degree to which the decline impacts everyday activities. Does the person recognize their memory lapse, and can they jump back into the conversation quickly, or does it take a long time to realize that they aren't following the conversation? Are they finding their lost keys in a logical place such as a pocket or on their dresser, or are they finding lost keys in illogical places like the refrigerator?

It's Not Just Normal Aging: Now What?

Given the subtleties of the early stages, it's not unusual to be reluctant to raise concerns. It can seem intrusive and disrespectful to suggest that something is wrong. So, how can it be diagnosed? And what hope is there once there is a diagnosis?

Perhaps the most challenging part of the process of determining whether a family member has some form of cognitive impairment is opening up the conversation both with the individual and, when appropriate, with the family as a whole. Later in this book, in the chapter "Raising Sensitive Subjects," Diana Clark takes a deeper dive into how to start a conversation about a mental health issue such as dementia, but we will offer a few initial thoughts here:

- Seek advice and support from professionals who have experience guiding these conversations. You don't have to do this alone. Experts can help guide families through some of these challenges.

- Gather data and information about what you are seeing and its impact on the individual, the family, and the business. Having real examples of the behaviors and lapses and their impact will help to make the discussion more concrete.

- Work to develop empathy for how hard this will be for your family member to hear and prepare for resistance. It can be very scary to realize that you may be losing the ability to reason, make decisions, and recognize people, and your family members may become very emotional.

- Have a group of people the individual trusts be a part of the conversation. One person's opinion is more easily dismissed than the observations of many people that someone trusts.

- Do any assessments of the individual late in the day. Individuals with dementia often experience "sunsetting." This is when an individual's memory is best in the morning and weakest towards sunset. Thus, an individual can seem almost normal in the morning and have significant symptoms around sunset.

- Choose a lens that offers support to help them deal with the issues.

Consider the Schaefer family's story, which opened the chapter. Sophie and Frederick's recent confrontation with their father highlighted the need to address his cognitive decline more deliberately. Rather than talking with their mother behind the scenes and making their father feel like people were talking behind his back, it may have been more productive for Sophie and Frederick to involve professionals, gather information, or have a broader group engaged in the conversation.

Seeking a Diagnosis

There is no definitive test that will screen for dementia. Your physician may enlist the help of other specialists, including geriatricians, neuropsychologists, and psychiatrists. In most cases, if behaviors are observed or concerns are raised, there are a variety of methods that these doctors will use to determine a diagnosis, including[80] cognitive and neurological tests (Mini-cog[81], Montreal Cognitive Assessment[82]), brain scans, genetic tests, psychiatric evaluations, blood tests, and brain imaging.

Treatment and Progression

The unfortunate reality is currently, there is no cure for dementia. There are many promising studies on the horizon[83] but today, the best we can do is understand the disease's progression and use treatment to slow it. An individual's coherence, competency, and decision-making capabilities will change significantly as the disease progresses. Sometimes, family members may see variations in their abilities throughout the day. Witnessing the decline of a family member will stir difficult emotions, and their behaviors will create real stress and strain in your relationships.

---

80 *What is dementia? Symptoms, types, and diagnosis.* (2022, December 8). National Institute on Aging. https://www.nia.nih.gov/health/alzheimers-and-dementia/what-dementia-symptoms-types-and-diagnosis

81 *Mini-COG© – Quick Screening for Early Dementia Detection.* (n.d.). https://www.mini-cog.com/

82 The Montreal Cognitive Assessment, MoCA: a brief screening tool for mild cognitive impairment. *Journal of the American Geriatrics Society, 53*(4), 695-699.

83 *Alzheimer's treatments: What's on the horizon?* (n.d.). Mayo Clinic. https://www.mayoclinic.org/diseases-conditions/alzheimers-disease/in-depth/alzheimers-treatments/art-20047780

One family shared that their father, who was struggling with moderate dementia, at the end of the day, would become agitated and upset with his son, who was running the day-to-day aspects of the business. Eventually, he fired his son. When he woke up the next day, rested and more coherent, he didn't remember the conflict and continued working with his son as if he had never been fired. And this pattern would repeat itself again and again. While logically, we can see that this behavior is connected to the father's dementia, the emotional impact of the son having his father yelling at him and firing him creates an emotional aftermath that is hard to recover from.

For this reason, a family must understand how dementia typically progresses. If we can understand how this disease progresses, we can be more mentally and emotionally prepared to deal with our loved ones' decline and put together a more detailed and effective care plan.

Facing Reality: The Family Implications of Dementia for a Family Business

In examining dementia's challenges and risks for family business owners, it is essential to address the emotional risks, explore the impact of dementia on the decision-making of the dementia patient, and address the implications for the business.

Emotional Risks

Taking care of someone with dementia is both physically and emotionally stressful for a family. When the family doesn't understand the reality of dementia, when they don't communicate and coordinate, it can result in resentment, depression, and unnecessary conflict within the family. One family that I worked with ended up in a deep conflict where the two siblings who were living closest to their father, who had dementia, felt that they were doing all the work to care for their father, with no acknowledgment from their siblings who lived across the country. As we see in this case, the stress and strain of dealing with the disease can threaten the family unity and cohesion essential to family success.

The first step in addressing the family's emotions is acknowledging the loss. The slow and insidious decline of a family member with dementia is truly a loss. When a person dies, we experience that loss all at once. With dementia, we are gradually losing the person that we know. With each month and each year, it seems that the one we loved is fading away. We must mourn the loss of the person we know and take what joy we can from our relationship with the person in front of us. We must mourn the loss of the relationship that we used to have with that individual and find support in our relationships with family and friends to support us through the difficult times.

The second step is that we need to take care of the individual with dementia, but also the family that is caring for them. The added responsibilities of taking care of a family member with dementia, coupled with losing the person you once knew, make dealing with dementia one of the most stressful life events someone can face. If you work to face this together as a family, you will create a support system and lessen the burden on each individual.

Consistency and communication will carry you through. Hold regular family meetings. These meetings should address both the logistics of care and the emotions and struggles that family members are experiencing in delivering that care. In the best of all worlds, these meetings can help people understand what's happening and tighten the bonds between family members.

A crucial part of such meetings is developing a caregiving plan. In many families, one or a small group of family members take on the brunt of the caregiving responsibilities. Creating and communicating a caregiving plan can create clarity and reduce stress on family members. We've included some resources to help you with this in the appendix of this chapter.

The stress of managing the complex issues around dementia will exacerbate any existing fissures in the family (and may create new ones). Be compassionate with yourself and seek support. Building a support system will help alleviate the stressors that strain family unity. A support system can include psychologists, MDs, Attorneys, friends, or a church network.

To effectively manage these emotional risks, we must also understand the behaviors contributing to the emotions.

Masking. In Chapter Two, we explored the interdependency of the family system, and we discussed how a family seeks to maintain the stability of homeostasis. A family member(s) may seek to mask the actual level of dysfunction of the individual with dementia. This may distort the family's understanding of the full extent of the symptoms and the individual's impairment level. This leads to the family seeking to consciously or unconsciously hide the decline. We need to recognize that hiding the disease will lead to behaviors that will stress and strain our family relationships.

The individual doesn't recognize their decline. While most individuals will understand that there is something wrong, there comes a point where they don't understand their impairment or the broader implications of their decisions on the family and the business. So, we will need to understand that when we are conversing and trying to make decisions, the family members may not be aware of their impairment.

Paranoia and Delusions. It is common for individuals struggling with dementia to experience delusions (firmly held false beliefs) and paranoia.[84] As we see in the Schaefer Automotive case, Reinhard became paranoid that he was being pushed out, which complicated the business discussions and had a considerable family impact. The volatility and anger this can create need to be understood and managed.

Dementia's impact on decision-making. Dementia causes a gradual decline in an individual's ability to make sensible decisions in everyday

---

84 *Delusions, paranoia and dementia.* (2021, February 26). Alzheimer's Society. https://www.alzheimers.org.uk/about-dementia/symptoms-and-diagnosis/delusions

situations. This can range from making basic decisions about what to say in social situations, what to wear, or how to plan their day to the more complex decisions related to business.

An added risk to the decline in decision-making is that the challenges of memory and decision-making make the patient vulnerable to manipulation by others in the system. People in the system (family or non-family) may seek to use the individual's cognitive deficits to advance their interests. That may include pushing to have the patient give them money, sign over shares, adjust the estate plan, or do other things.

As the cognitive decline progresses, the family member becomes more and more susceptible to this manipulation and sometimes fraud. I have seen these bad actors come from within the family and also from outside the family. In some situations, spouses or other family members start to restrict access to the impaired family member and seek to influence the person to change documents and existing estate plans. In other situations, non-family employees have shielded the family from knowing the extent of the issues and have gotten approval for big pay raises and bonuses. We need to be prepared to prevent this.

Implications for the Business: Determining Capacity and Competency

Dealing with the emotions of the situation is challenging, but often, one of the more difficult aspects of dealing with the disease is the issue of decision-making. This is the dilemma that every family faces after receiving a diagnosis of dementia. And we continually need to ask this question as the disease progresses. As we seek to answer this question, we need to look through three different lenses:

1. Practical Assessment: What is our practical assessment of what they are capable of and what support they need to live? These are the real challenges that we, as family members, face every day to manage and take care of our loved ones. This includes the practical judgments that family members make every day in their interactions with the patient.

2. Medical Assessment of Capacity: The medical community assesses the individual's capacity to make decisions about their health and well-being.[85] This involves assessing the individual's ability to understand the "benefits, risks and alternatives to proposed health care" and make and communicate their decisions. Capacity is a medical construct and is determined by doctors.

3. Legal Assessment of Competency: Legal competency is determined by the court system. Legal competency looks at an individual's capability to make certain decisions. Chapter 11 will explore the complexity of the issues around competency in greater depth, including:

   • Competency to sign or change a will

   • Competency to vote on a slate of directors for the board

   • Competency to make day-to-day business decisions.

   • Competency to gift money or property to people

Key Questions to Consider

It is critical for an individual and, ideally, the family to think carefully about a few key questions as they prepare for the possibility of dealing with a diagnosis of dementia. These questions all orient around the dementia patient's ability to make decisions.

Who Should I Name as My Power of Attorney (POA) and When?

When you give someone your Power of Attorney, you are giving them the right to make decisions on your behalf if you cannot make those decisions for yourself. Suppose you provide a power of attorney to one person. In that case, there is a risk of them acting in their self-interest or being driven by family

---

85   *The New Uniform Health Care Decisions Act: An Overview.* (2023, September 19). https://www.americanbar.org/. Retrieved June 22, 2024, from https://www.americanbar.org/groups/law_aging/publications/bifocal/vol45/vol45issue1/new-health-care-decisions-act/

dynamics, so when choosing someone to serve as your Power of Attorney, you need to assess their knowledge and character. You may have one POA for your healthcare decisions and another for legal, financial, and business matters. Any individuals being entrusted with this power should be people who:

- care about the health of the affected individual, the family, and the business and be able to balance the needs of those stakeholders.

- have the capability to understand the legal issues involved.

It's not always clear when a power of attorney should be invoked. The decline caused by dementia often progresses slowly. It can be hard to assess whether the person can still make their own decisions. The thought of legally moving to take away someone's decision-making authority, whether for health care or financial and legal decisions, can seem like the nuclear option. Because this is such a difficult decision, a family should consider developing a competency panel to make the process as objective as possible.

How Can We Objectively Assess Competency?

As we have outlined in this chapter, diagnosing dementia and determining an individual's capacity and competency to make decisions isn't easy. Asking one person to make this determination is onerous for that individual and opens the possibility that one person can manipulate the process. In one family I worked with, the next-generation successor took on the process of having her father declared incompetent. The stress of the process led to a huge rift between her and her siblings and led her into a deep depression. Assessing an individual's competency to make decisions has such an impact that we recommend that the family establish an objective process using qualified experts well before any signs of dementia occur. One way to do this is to establish a competency panel that is given the responsibility for determining when decision-making capabilities are taken away from someone with dementia.

A competency panel should be composed of a group of individuals (we recommend 3–7 people) who collectively have experience with the medical and legal issues of competency, the family business, and the family itself. This ideally should include a psychiatrist, a gerontologist, and a dementia specialist in addition to 1–2 board members or business leaders. This panel is created far in advance (ideally before there are any concerns about dementia) with the buy-in of all family stakeholders if possible. There should also be a clear process for naming replacements and a clear process for seeking a decree of incompetency.

How a competency panel is documented is critical to its enforceability. You should work closely with your attorneys to ensure that the language will hold up in any jurisdiction if litigated. It is important that the people who are subjecting themselves to the judgment of this panel sign documentation to that effect. The language should specify the confidentiality of the process and the outcome and can specify the intent of any public messaging following a finding of incompetency. This may include how the findings will be made known to the shareholders, the board, and family members.

Sample Panel Framework

Goal of Panel:

To provide an objective assessment of a family member's decision-making capacities.

Principles:

This panel should, when possible, use objective medical data and testing, as well as information gathered from family members and the business regarding the individual's behavior and performance in making their determination. The panel will keep the proceedings private to protect the individual, the family and the company.

Membership:

- Neurologist who specializes in Dementia

- Gerontologist

- Psychiatrist with experience in assessing decision-making

- One or two independent members of our board of directors

- A member of the family council

Process for seeking a decree of incompetency:

1. Who can convene the panel (individuals or groups), and what indicators must they prove before convening the panel?

2. Who will be interviewed to provide testimony about the individual's capabilities, how will we select them, and how many will be interviewed?

3. What information must be provided by these individuals?

4. What information/testimony can the individual being evaluated submit to support their case?

5. Can the board compel tests?

6. To what degree do the board and senior management need to provide information? [This needs to be discussed because of the impact it can have on credibility and dynamics once a decision on competency is made.]

7. How long is the panel allowed to reach a decision?

8. How many votes will be required to declare the individual incompetent?

9. What is the process once a decree of incompetency is made?

Having a competency panel doesn't mean there won't be any family tensions, conflicts, or disagreements, but it will provide a clear and objective process that will hopefully help manage the emotions that will inevitably surface.

Navigating the Path Forward Together

As we saw through the challenges of Frederick and Sophie Schaefer, raising the topic of a family member's cognitive decline is not easy. Throughout this chapter, we have sought to unveil cognitive decline's challenges for a family and a business. The stressors we have explored can potentially threaten the family unity important to your family business's long-term success. Unaddressed conflicts make it harder to work together to solve problems and care for your family members. The stronger your relationships as a family, the better your communication, and the higher the trust, the more prepared you will be to deal with the challenges of dealing with dementia. Dementia stresses the entire family system and can tear the family apart if the family doesn't work together to understand and plan for the challenges that dementia presents.

The investments that you make in the health and well-being of your family and business will create a foundation to help you deal with the shock of a diagnosis of dementia. Many of the activities you commit to build a healthy family business will also serve you well when addressing the challenges of dementia. Here are a few of the activities that we have found helpful over time:

1. **Commit to strong governance.** By actively committing to good business and family governance, you establish processes and procedures to help make important business and family decisions. The board of directors should ensure a clear succession plan and be a source of objective input (if outsiders are on the board) to help determine when a competency evaluation is needed. Regular family meetings and a family council can help the family communicate and stay aligned through stressful times.

2. **Build your family communication skills.** The foundation of a strong family business is how well we communicate, deal with conflict, and work together. These skills are equally important when dealing with the real challenges of navigating a family member's gradual cognitive decline.

3. **Educate the family about dementia.** When we don't understand something, emotions are more likely to drive the conversations.

   - Know your family medical history. **Dementia has** a strong genetic component, and knowing your risk factors can help you prepare.

   - Understand the early warning signs.

   - Understand the medical and legal issues involved. (Understand the legal rights and protections for people with dementia.)

Dealing with cognitive decline is not easy for anyone involved. The stress and strain can have real emotional, legal, and financial impacts on the lives of our families and businesses. But if you educate yourself and your family, understand the issues involved, and work together to develop a plan, you can preserve the family unity and connection that will sustain your family business over time.

For Family Working in the Business	For Family Owners	For Advisors
When you have a concern about cognitive decline, gather concrete examples.	When you receive a diagnosis of dementia, work together to develop a care team and a care plan so that no one individual bears all of the burden of care.	Understand the importance of involving the family in the planning process for how to deal with dementia where possible.
Work collaboratively with the board when you are concerned about problems.	Mourn the loss of your relationship with the individual, and deal with the grief together as a family.	Think about how you can help the family find objective support to deal with these challenges.
	Create a competency panel to help make assessing the competency of the family member more objective.	Look for ways that the family may be masking the symptoms or hiding the impacts of cognitive decline.

Table 3-Implications

Appendix/Addendum

It can be helpful for a family to discuss scenarios that might arise about dementia. Identifying these scenarios can help people air questions and concerns that can be explored before putting any legal documentation together.

1. **Observing symptoms:** A family member is showing some symptoms of cognitive decline. Multiple family members and some non-family employees are observing these symptoms.

    a. How do we raise these concerns?

    b. Who do we raise these concerns with?

    c. How will we assess the observations?

2. **Legal and Financial Implications:** A family member has been diagnosed with dementia and is seeking treatment. They are in the early stages and can still handle basic self-care, but they are easily confused and repeat themselves often.

   a. When should they resign from any leadership positions?

   b. What needs to be done to protect their financial well-being? Who should be involved?

   c. When should health care and legal POAs be invoked?

3. **Implications for Family Support:** A family member has been diagnosed with dementia for over a year. They have expressed a desire to stay in their home, but their spouse is having more and more difficulty with care. Physically, the spouse must help the individual dress. Once or twice a week, the individual leaves the house—unannounced and wandering around the neighborhood, requiring the family to enlist the help of neighbors and sometimes the authorities to help find them.

   a. How would we as a family mobilize and organize to provide support in this situation?

   b. How would we honor the person's request to stay home without moving into a memory care facility?

   c. How would we communicate the person's situation with family employees, customers, and the community?

Other Resources

- Alz.org

- Dementia.org

- Stanford Center on Longevity (www.longevity.stanford.edu)

Stage	Level of functioning
No cognitive decline	· No obvious signs of cognitive deficits
	· Still able to function independently
	· Has no memory loss
	· Is mentally healthy
Age-related **forgetfulness**	· May experience normal forgetfulness, such as names
	· Misplacing items
	No evidence of issues with work or social situations
Mild cognitive **impairment**	· Impaired concentration
	· Able to get up, use the bathroom, get dressed
	· Increased forgetfulness
	· Difficulty with work tasks
	· Difficulty finding the right words
	· May get lost more frequently
	· Some denial about deficits
	Typically, when family begins to notice
Moderate cognitive decline: **Mild dementia**	· Difficulty concentrating
	· Forgetting recent events and personal history
	· Difficulty managing finances or traveling alone to new locations
	· Reduced expression of emotions
	· Withdrawal from situations that are challenging (Social situations)
	A physician can detect clear cognitive problems
Moderately severe cognitive decline: **Moderate dementia**	· Has major memory deficiencies
	· Needs some assistance to complete daily living tasks
	· Significant memory loss
	Lack of orientation to time, place, or date

Table 1. Reisberg Stages of Dementia   *(Continued next page)*

Stage	Level of functioning
Severe cognitive decline: **Moderately severe dementia**	· Needs significant help with daily activities · Forgets the names of close family members · Little memory of recent events. · Incontinence · Sleep disturbances · Changes in personality and emotional regulation **May exhibit anxiety, agitation, obsessive behaviors, hallucinations**
Very severe cognitive decline	· Little to no ability to communicate · Requires assistance with most activities **Loss in motor skills such as walking**

Table 1. Reisberg Stages of Dementia

Resources to Help Create a Caregiving Plan

https://www.nia.nih.gov/health/advance-care-planning

- https://www.nia.nih.gov/health/alzheimers-caregiving

- https://www.alz.org/media/Documents/alzheimers-dementia-caregiver-stress-ts.pdf

- https://www.alz.org/media/Documents/alzheimers-dementia-behaviors-ts.pdf

Alzheimer's Disease Continuum 2020 Alzheimer's Disease Facts and Figures – Alzheimer's Association Report[86]

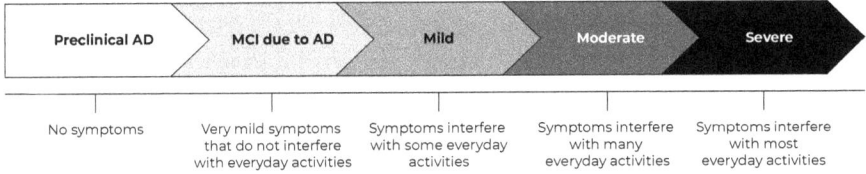

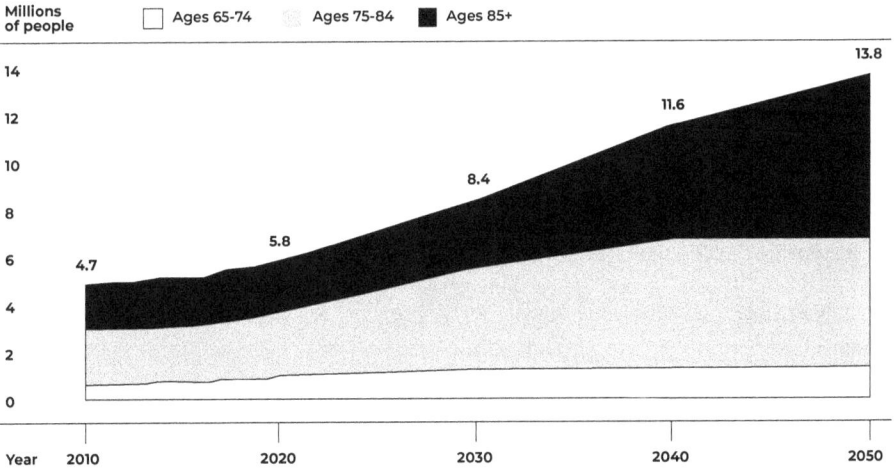

Figure 1

---

86   2020 Alzheimer's disease facts and figures. (2020). Alzheimer's & Dementia : The Journal of the Alzheimer's Association, 10.1002/alz.12068. Advance online publication. https://doi.org/10.1002/alz.12068

Signs of Alzheimer's or Other Dementias	Typical Age-Related Changes
Memory loss that disrupts daily life: One of the most common signs of Alzheimer's is memory loss, especially forgetting recently learned information. Others include forgetting important dates or events, asking for the same information over and over, and increasingly needing to rely on memory aids (for example, reminder notes or electronic devices) or family members for things that used to be handled on one's own.	Sometimes forgetting names or appointments but remembering them later.
Challenges in planning or solving problems: Some people experience changes in their ability to develop and follow a plan or work with numbers. They may have trouble following a familiar recipe, keeping track of monthly bills or counting change. They may have difficulty concentrating and take much longer to do things than they did before.	Making occasional errors when balancing a checkbook.
Difficulty completing familiar tasks at home, at work or at leisure: People with Alzheimer's often find it hard to complete daily tasks. Sometimes, people have trouble driving to a familiar location, managing a budget at work or remembering the rules of a favorite game.	Occasionally needing help to use the settings on a microwave or record a television show.
Confusion with time or place: People with Alzheimer's can lose track of dates, seasons and the passage of time. They may have trouble understanding something if it is not happening immediately. Sometimes they forget where they are or how they got there.	Getting confused about the day of the week but figuring it out later.
Trouble understanding visual images and spatial relationships: For some people, having vision problems is a sign of Alzheimer's. They may have difficulty reading, judging distance, and determining color or contrast, which may cause problems with driving.	Vision changes related to cataracts, glaucoma or age- related macular degeneration.

Table 1: Memory and Aging

Signs of Alzheimer's or Other Dementias	Typical Age-Related Changes
New problems with words in speaking or writing: People with Alzheimer's may have trouble following or joining a conversation. They may stop in the middle of a conversation and have no idea how to continue or they may repeat themselves. They may struggle with vocabulary, have problems finding the right word or call things by the wrong name (e.g., calling a watch a "hand clock").	Sometimes having trouble finding the right word.
Misplacing things and losing the ability to retrace steps: People with Alzheimer's may put things in unusual places and lose things and be unable to go back over their steps to find them again. Sometimes, they accuse others of stealing. This may occur more frequently over time.	Misplacing things from time to time and retracing steps to find them.
Decreased or poor judgment: People with Alzheimer's may experience changes in judgment or decision-making. For example, they may use poor judgment when dealing with money, giving large amounts to telemarketers. They may pay less attention to grooming or keeping themselves clean.	Making a bad decision once in a while.
Withdrawal from work or social activities: People with Alzheimer's may start to remove themselves from hobbies, social activities, work projects or sports. They may have trouble keeping up with a favorite sports team or remembering how to complete a favorite hobby. They may also avoid being social because of the changes they have experienced.	Sometimes feeling weary of work, family and social obligations.
Changes in mood and personality: The mood and personalities of people with Alzheimer's can change. They can become confused, suspicious, depressed, fearful or anxious. They may be easily upset at home, at work, with friends or in places where they are out of their comfort zones.	Developing very specific ways of doing things and becoming irritable when a routine is disrupted.

Table 1: Memory and Aging

Declines with Age	Remains Stable with Age
Delayed free recall: spontaneous retrieval of information from memory without a cue[87,88] Example: Recalling a list of items to purchase at the grocery store without a cue	Recognition memory: ability to retrieve information when given a cue Example: Correctly giving the details of a story when given yes/no questions
Source memory: knowing the source of the learned information Example: Remembering if you learned a fact because you saw it on television, read it in the newspaper, or heard it from a friend	Temporal order memory: memory for the correct time or sequence of past events Example: Remembering that last Saturday you went to the grocery store after you ate lunch with your friends
Prospective memory: remembering to perform intended actions in the future[89] Example: Remembering to take medicine before going to bed	Procedural memory: memory of how to do things Example: Remembering how to ride a bike

Table 2: Decline vs. Stability with Age[90]

87   Price L, Said K, Haaland KY. Age-associated memory impairment of Logical Memory and Visual Repro-
     duction. *Journal of clinical and experimental neuropsychology.* 2004;26:531–8.

88   Cargin JW, Maruff P, Collie A, Shafiq-Antonacci R, Masters C. Decline in verbal memory in non-demented
     older adults. *Journal of clinical and experimental neuropsychology.* 2007;29:706–18.

89   Schnitzspahn KM, Stahl C, Zeintl M, Kaller CP, Kliegel M. The Role of Shifting, Updating, and Inhibition
     in Prospective Memory Performance in Young and Older Adults. *Developmental psychology.* 2012

90   Harada, C. N., Love, M. C. N., & Triebel, K. L. (2013). Normal cognitive aging. *Clinics in Geriatric Medicine*,
     29(4), 737–752. https://doi.org/10.1016/j.cger.2013.07.002

	Crystallized vs. Fluid	Declines with age?
Processing speed	Fluid	Yes
Attention	Fluid	Simple tasks — no Complex tasks — yes
Memory	Fluid	Mixed
Language	Crystallized > Fluid	In general — no Visual confrontation naming, verbal fluency — yes
Visuospatial	Mixed	Simple tasks — no Complex tasks — yes
Executive Function	Fluid	Mixed

Table 3: Summary of Neurocognitive Changes with Age

PART THREE

ADDRESSING MENTAL HEALTH ISSUES IN THE FAMILY BUSINESS

CHAPTER NINE

Knowledge is Power—Contributions of Neuropsychological Testing to Optimize Performance in Family Business

by Gail Silverstein, PhD and Edward P. Monte, PhD

After graduating from college two years ago, Jack began to work at Gide Industries, his family's business. His father, the current CEO, wanted to groom Jack to take over the company someday. He felt that Jack should start at the bottom and work his way up, gaining experience with different company divisions along the way. Mr. Gide had always seen Jack as lazy, irresponsible, immature, and too complacent about the family's wealth and his future inheritance to put any real effort into anything. He hoped that at age 30, Jack would have finally grown up. At first, Jack did well, excelling in relationship-building with co-workers, customers, and vendors. But then he got promoted to a position with greater responsibility, a higher volume of work, and many more details to keep track of, and he began to struggle. He became anxious and depressed, and his self-esteem plummeted, and he began to drink too much. He started missing deadlines, often did not show up for meetings, and sometimes did not come to work at all. Mr. Gide was disappointed and frustrated and asked for help from his new family business consultant.

The business consultant suspected that Jack's issues had little to do with laziness or being a spoiled next-generation family business member. She recommended neuropsychological testing to explore how Jack thinks and experiences the world around him. The goal was to discover both Jack's strengths and challenges to help him better cope and find his rightful place in the organization. Testing revealed that Jack is much brighter than anyone had given him credit for, but he has ADHD and is dyslexic. Several of the recommendations made by the neuropsychologist proved to be helpful. Part of the problem is a mismatch between Jack's capabilities and the role he is in. Although having him try out different positions in the company is a good idea in theory, none of us can do every task, and it backfired for Jack. After appropriate changes were made in his position in the company and support staff with capabilities to compensate for his deficits were hired, Jack was not only able to get back on track in the company but flourished.

With the improved self-esteem that the results of the testing and his newfound success gave him, Jack was less depressed and anxious. He was able to greatly reduce his substance abuse, which had been serving not only as a way to escape but also as self-medication for his ADHD. In line with the recommendations, Jack also sought out a physician who could help him with appropriate medication for his ADHD. Both he and his family came to see him differently. Family relationships were greatly improved, especially between Jack and his father. Due to heredity, family members often exhibit many of the same patterns in testing. However, this family was surprised by how much Jack's father identified with some of the findings for his son and realized that he had had many similar struggles himself.

It also became clear that Mr. Gide had set up the company so that he was most comfortable with how it worked. It fit him. Unfortunately, some ways the company has always operated make things more difficult for many employees. With the new understanding brought about by the testing, Mr. Gide and the family business consultant made company-wide changes that positively impacted the bottom line while concretely addressing differing cognitive styles, needs, and issues.

Decision-Making in Family Business

Many factors create a successful business: a solid and needed product, an essential service, state-of-the-art production and supply chains, and clear and essential policies and procedures to help guide the company's running. When discussing what is essential for a successful business, owners and their executive teams discuss the fundamentals of their decision-making. And, consistently, they cite research and preparation as key components. Decisions should be made thoughtfully and aligned with strategy and goals, hopefully after careful information gathering and analysis. This certainly is true when hiring top-level individuals. Batteries of personality tests are given to assess their leadership style, ability to work well with others, and fit in with the culture and work ethic of the organization. Credentials and work experience are also reviewed carefully to ensure candidates have the skills and abilities to do the job. These invaluable research tools yield a great deal of essential information and, very often, a successful hire, particularly from an extensive pool of strangers where hiring the most qualified person for the particular position is the only goal.

But what happens when the process of hiring for a position is narrowed in a succession plan to one, two, or three family members? The reality is in most family businesses, if the family insists on family leadership, the selection options are, in fact, very restricted. Often, the saving grace is that despite this limited selection, family members work tirelessly and have above-average intelligence so that they can do the job on some level. However, a few questions emerge: Will diligence, endless hard work, and basic ability make for a successful and thriving business? In such a selection process, do you have the best person for a particular job? Is that family member surrounded by a staff who can complement his or her cognitive style? And what personal cost is there to the individual when they are expected to succeed if what they are doing doesn't come naturally to them?

This last statement may be the most impactful. With above-average intelligence, one can usually struggle through most anything. But if what is demanded doesn't naturally fit how one thinks or perceives, the emotional cost over time can be enormous even though the family member can muddle through the process. The assumption is that a solid family business doesn't need its leadership struggling through any process that doesn't fit them, which will greatly increase the risks to their mental health (i.e., anxiety, depression, low sense of self-esteem), not to mention eventual burnout. The impact on the business is that it may survive but definitely will not thrive. Additionally, with a stressed and unhappy family leadership, the message to the next generation is that working in the family business is not exciting or self-fulfilling. Parents will then discourage their children from pursuing the business as a career alternative, or the next generation will decide that living unhappily as their parents have is not what they are going to choose for their lives. Many fine legacy family businesses have disappeared because of this singular dynamic.

There is another factor to consider, particularly in the "bigger than life" world of family business. Children are often raised being told that they can, in fact, achieve anything they put their minds to. As family members in a family business, they believe they are shining examples of success, and there are no limits to their potential and achievement. But what if it's not entirely true? Despite learning the rudimentary aspects of anything, no matter how hard one tries, things like math skills, emotional IQ, strategic thinking and problem-solving, etc., cannot be mastered if a person doesn't have the basic cognitive ability to grasp and use that skill.

Not only is it a myth that one can do anything they put their mind to, but it is also a fallacy to promote the notion that if you can't do something, it's only a matter of hard work to master it completely. Neuropsychology challenges that myth and hopes to direct individuals to pursue what comes naturally and to hold their expectations about mastery of something they don't do naturally at a realistic level. It's important to remember that the legacy against which the next generation is often compared contains a great deal of stunning truth and achievement mixed with a good dose of family myth and ancestral aggrandizement.

It can be miserable to be trapped in a job for which one is not suited by a feeling of family obligation. People in such positions are at risk for suffering from any of the mental health issues discussed elsewhere in this book. What is exciting is discovering what one does wonderfully well at the base, so any effort in mastering that skill will not be wasted. Once one's natural aptitudes are discovered, not only is the path forward clearer, but the facility to learn and grow in that area can be remarkable.

One example was a young man known to be very mechanical and assigned to the maintenance department of his family's business. Whatever mechanical problem was presented, he figured it out with solid research and his "common sense." What was discovered with his testing was that his skill was not about mechanical issues alone but in the area of general problem-solving and reasoning, aided by an astounding memory. No matter if the issue was how to fix a machine, how taxes work, or what strategy is best in closing a deal, this young man was discovered to be most likely the most capable of the sibling group to ultimately run the business. Once freed from the maintenance yard, he excelled in acquiring broader knowledge, and his value to the family business was remarkable.

Again, we emphasize here that there is a real dilemma in many family businesses. Some families decide to have the bulk of their company's leadership and operations provided by outside managers. Others, miraculously, may have several highly gifted siblings and cousins who fit into their roles naturally and are very passionately committed to the workings of the business, and, therefore, succession moves smoothly from there. For many family businesses, their succession plan ends up focusing on a few family members in the next generation who are presently working in the business, and this can become a major problem. The selection process often does not have the privilege of choosing from the best and the brightest for any leadership position but must build leadership from those family members who happen to be present.

The right person for a job is typically someone with natural and relevant talents and instincts and the ability to achieve great things in that position. The person should have a core of solid ability, know her strengths and challenges, and frankly, be smart enough to know the complexity of her responsibilities. She should surround herself with individuals who can do aspects of the job that she can't or that don't come naturally to her. Knowing what comes naturally and what doesn't can free large amounts of mental energy for the working family member that can be used to improve performance in the areas that are more important and for which they have innate ability.

When the older generation is ready to pass the business to the next generation, it can be difficult to decide which role each younger person will thrive in. The few next-gen working family members are loved ones known intimately by the upper generation who have certain perceptions of who they are and where they might fit best in the business. It would appear choosing which one for what position would be immediately successful after a lifetime of watching them move through the world. These individuals would also be expected to be given the same scrutiny as any stranger walking in for a job. That's what one would expect.

Certainly, the reality is that most have some experience, credentialing, and expertise in the area in which they are to work. But perhaps not. Often, many other factors, mainly relational and emotional, come into play in the decision-making and replace detailed research to arrive at this family placement. Gender and birth order may underpin the choices of role. Other subjective considerations may be who feels more like Dad or Mom or Granddad who passed last year, who is the favorite, who is most compliant, who is most ruthless in a familiar way, who behaves more in line with how we raised him or her, who is more in step, and who is most loyal?

Often, in a family business, people's positions replicate their role in the family. The caregiving sister heads HR, the domineering older brother becomes CEO, and the younger brother, who no one takes seriously but is handsome and personable, finds himself in sales. That may work well if that family is lucky, but are they the optimal positions for individuals or the family business based on their abilities? And, even if these positions are spot-on for that family member, what support might they need to do the best possible job? Who should they surround themselves with to succeed and fill in some of the gaps in their abilities that everyone has so that success is much more likely?

Neuropsychological assessment can go a long way to answering these and many other questions by providing objective input for this decision. Learning how one functions cognitively and neuropsychologically is very powerful and can be life changing. Comparing and contrasting the test results of several family members can help the consultant and senior family members to see who would function best in which role and with what responsibilities. Sharing the information with the family (with permission) allows everyone to understand why certain decisions are being made. This is likely to reduce conflict and hurt feelings. Guilt often plagues high-achieving people who delegate their disliked responsibilities to others. However, if there is an objective reason for delegating based on the science of testing, it can be easier to overcome this guilt and improve performance and production. All of this is done without judgment or shaming but with the intent to highlight each person's natural strengths and challenges for better performance, cohesion, and complementarity.

Neuropsychology—A Different Perspective

Neuropsychology studies the brain through its behavior rather than through brain scans, medical tests, etc. The focus is on basic building blocks of behavior, which most people, including most therapists, never consider. Some tests used in business focus on personality. Those tests help to understand things like whether a person is extroverted or introverted, how they respond to things emotionally, how dominant a person is, etc. By contrast, neuropsychology focuses on thinking and brain functions, which underlie not only healthy behavior and feelings but often also the types of mental health issues discussed elsewhere in this book. For example, neuropsychological testing can shed light on one's ability to sustain attention over time, remember what one hears or reads, fully and quickly comprehend language and express oneself in words, pick up on and accurately process nonverbal communication, understand math and apply it as needed, understand spatial relationships, process information rapidly, problem-solve, etc.

Sometimes anxiety and depression or other mental health issues are due primarily to situational causes, such as marital problems, illness or death of loved ones, or stress at work. Sometimes, there is a biological component. Sometimes, the primary source of the problem is longstanding family dynamics —for example, never being able to gain a parent's approval, merciless teasing or bullying by a sibling, or physical or sexual abuse. But sometimes, anxiety and depression or other mental health concerns can be at least partially attributed to some of the underlying building blocks revealed by neuropsychological testing. Is a person anxious or depressed because they never get things done because they are so disorganized? Is it because they have a short attention span and often "zone out" and miss much of what goes on around them? Do they worry because they have trouble remembering things? Is it because they can't always process language fast enough to keep up with a conversation? Do they have trouble seeing patterns and "connecting the dots"? Do they process information more slowly than most people? These are the kinds of things that can be assessed via neuropsychological testing.

For example, one of the authors of this chapter was once in a seminar with several therapists. The instructor was showing a videotape of a session with a client he was seeing (with the client's permission) because therapy was not progressing well. The instructor pointed out the client's speech patterns. He was slow to respond to questions asked by the therapist, and when he did, his responses often were full of "um" and "like," and his sentences were long and convoluted and ultimately didn't say much. The instructor interpreted these speech patterns as being indicative of anxiety, and all the therapists nodded in agreement. The neuropsychologist spoke up and pointed out that the client's speech patterns may also be an indication of a language disability. The instructor followed up with the client and learned that the client had been in speech therapy as a child and that he had had difficulty learning to read in elementary school; both issues are red flags for language disabilities. Testing was done (by a different neuropsychologist) and did indeed reveal a language disability. The client needed more time than most people to process language, had trouble understanding lengthy utterances, and had trouble finding the words to express what he wanted to say. No wonder he was so anxious! The client, a college student, was given some accommodations in school. The therapist understood that he would have to talk more in bullet points and less in paragraphs for the client to understand what he said. He would also have to give the client additional time to respond rather than reacting to silence with a barrage of more questions.

A similar example often shows up in couples therapy, where one couple member—usually a male—is chastised for not being communicative. It is seen as a prime example of simply not caring enough to share thoughts and feelings. A simple test to discover the origins of this behavior is to share something with that client and then ask him to repeat what you have just said. Time and again, the client gets very nervous and can't readily tell you what you just said. Not being able to follow conversations or process them makes having long, meaningful talks near impossible.

Neuropsychological testing sets realistic expectations. The ability of testing to alter the family process is often amazing. Discovering how one encounters the world neuropsychologically, cognitively, and behaviorally opens up a world of understanding that will create appropriate expectations between people. Chronic conflict between family members working together often stems from the expectation that "what I find easy to understand or do is what you should find easy to understand or do."

A sister and brother in a business constantly argued about things such as what occurred in their last meeting or if or when a particular meeting took place. Being very competitive, the opposing memories would be the source of often emotionally violent arguments. To make matters worse, actions were sometimes taken by the brother based on what he thought was said or decided, which was flawed. Through testing, it was discovered that the sister had a remarkable, almost flawless long and short-term memory, while memory was one of her older brother's deficits.

This simple fact, once realized, morphed into a new dynamic between them where he learned to trust her memory over his own and now consistently doesn't announce what he thinks happened but asks her what she knows happened. Along with her realization that he was a far better manager of people and possibly had a much more solid emotional IQ, she learned to rely on his perceptions of the people portion of their family business over time. Their emotional competition, which was multi-layered, has significantly reduced, and the conflict level between them has dramatically lessened. Both know themselves better, have made peace with it, and have learned that life is easier if you rely on someone you trust who has complementary skills.

Knowledge is Power—So What is Neuropsychological Testing?

Clients approached about considering going through testing rarely have any idea what neuropsychological testing is. Neuropsychological testing is a tool that has many applications. It is used in medical settings to better understand the effects of traumatic brain injuries or strokes and to diagnose dementia. It is used in educational settings to help understand why a child is struggling to read or whether a high school student should have extra time on standardized tests such as the SAT.

Again, it can also have many uses in business. As discussed above, it can help to ensure that the right person is in the right position for optimal success. It can help that person enhance and optimize their performance. It can help to improve communication in the workplace. It can help people to understand what behavior of co-workers or family members is intentional and what behavior is a result of their biologically-based limitations. All these factors will affect the smooth functioning of the business and how successful it ultimately is.

It takes many years to develop neuropsychological tests and many years of training to learn how to use them. Validity research is done to ensure that the tests are actually measuring what they should be measuring. "Norms" are developed by administering the tests to thousands of people and averaging their scores to make statistical comparisons. For example, if your score on a given test is 10, we don't know what that means unless we can compare your score to a norm. If the average person your age scores five on the test, your performance was above average. If the average person scores 15, then your performance is below average. This is a bit of an oversimplification, and interpretations are never made based on one test. Several tests are administered, and the neuropsychologist looks for consistencies, inconsistencies, and patterns.

Statistical comparisons are also made between the person's performance on different types of tasks. The neuropsychologist can determine the person's cognitive strengths and weaknesses by looking at the patterns revealed by these statistics. Examining the client's process to arrive at their responses can provide much information about how the person thinks, solves problems, and figures things out.

One of the benefits of neuropsychological testing is that it can provide objective information—numbers that are hard to argue with. Our self-perceptions are not always accurate. Sometimes, we make mistakes we don't notice. Sometimes, we exhibit tendencies we are not aware of. The neuropsychologist may be able to say something like, "Your score on this test was much better than your score on that test. That means that you are good at X but not as good at Y. These are the things that made the task more difficult for you, and these are the things that made it easier." It can also counter a belief about oneself. Often, people pride themselves on their ability to multi-task. Testing may reveal that while juggling several things at once may be possible for someone —particularly if holding attention to one task for any length of time is difficult —their clear understanding of each topic or task suffers with the addition of extra focus items. Once they learn to pare down their focus to fewer items or to move more sequentially in their day, their understanding and production increase greatly.

And often, the numbers are validating. "I knew I wasn't good at that," someone might say. "Maybe I'd be better off delegating tasks like that to others." Or maybe strengths you were not aware of become clear. "Everyone always told me that I was dumb and lazy," someone else might say, "but wow, these numbers say that I have a high IQ and excel in a particular area. Now I have the self-confidence to do things I was afraid to try." In any case, the information gleaned from testing leads naturally to recommendations about how things can improve, both by focusing on one's strengths and by knowing one's limitations.

The Testing Process

It may be helpful at this point to describe the testing process in more detail so families and advisors know what it entails, practically and logistically. Different professionals work in different ways, of course. The following describes the model used by Dr. Monte and me (GS). I function basically as a consultant. When Dr. Monte is working with a family, and he thinks testing would be beneficial, he contacts me, and we discuss in detail his impressions of the individual or individuals, the family, and the business, and the questions he is hoping to answer by testing. This gives me invaluable context and allows me to make sure that testing can answer the questions and decide which tests are needed. Once he has spoken to the family about testing, answered questions, and made sure they are on board, then I talk to the people involved and schedule the testing. It is important to know that, unlike a test like the SAT, no preparation is needed, or even possible, for this testing. It is also important to know that the information gained from the testing is the property of the individual being tested, no matter who pays for the testing. People I test are usually encouraged to share at least some of the results with relevant family members, consultants, etc., but the ultimate decision is up to them.

Neuropsychological testing is like a physical for your brain. Various brain functions are examined to see which are working well and which are not. Neuropsychological tests consist of a variety of tasks that the client is asked to do. Some of these tasks may be familiar, such as being asked to read a paragraph and answer questions about it. Some will likely be things the client has not done before, such as drawing certain designs or solving brain-teaser-type puzzles. Conclusions of a neuropsychological evaluation are based not only on the test results but also on a combination of background information, input from spouses or other family members, friends, or co-workers, and the neuropsychologist's observations during the evaluation.

Testing generally takes about 7–8 hours to complete. This time is broken up into three Zoom appointments. In addition to the formal testing, the person being tested provides me with a great deal of detailed background information and rates themselves on several rating scales. Someone who knows them well also rates them on the same scale. Once the testing is complete, my job is to score the tests, analyze the information, and look for patterns. During this process, I usually have another consultation with Dr. Monte to integrate the context he has about the family and the business to better round out and individualize the findings. This also allows him the opportunity to familiarize himself with the results completely. Then, we schedule a fairly lengthy initial feedback session. This initial session usually includes the person being tested, myself, Dr. Monte, and anyone else the person being tested wants to have present (which sometimes includes a spouse). In the feedback session, I walk them through my initial report.

It is crucial to present the results in a way that is clear and honest but also makes it easier for the person to hear, understand, and accept them without feeling judged. The emphasis is on the description of functioning, including both strengths and weaknesses, rather than categorizing or diagnosing. We discuss how this new information fits into what the person already knows about themselves, how it may validate that knowledge, and how it may be different from ideas the person has had about themselves. Often, the new information provides a different perspective on what was previously known, and some testees have described it as life changing. We also broaden the perspective to include how the new information affects family functioning and, particularly, functioning within a family business.

After the initial session, I finalize my report and send it to the testee. The report is quite lengthy and includes all the results of the various tests as well as integration and discussion of the results and their implications, and concrete and actionable recommendations for the individual, family, and business. Testees are told that they are welcome to contact me with any additional questions after they get the report or at any time in the future.

Once the testee has had the chance to digest the results and ask any questions they may have, there are usually additional meetings. Again, the testee is not required to share any of the information, and Dr. Monte and I cannot legally divulge it without their written permission. However, usually, at this point in the process, the testee can see the value in sharing the results with certain other people. We then may conduct additional meetings, which include those other people, to be sure that they, too, understand the results, are on the same page, and have an opportunity to ask questions. Together, Dr. Monte and I can provide perspective on how the family and the business can benefit from the new information, how and whether the business can incorporate the recommendations made in the report, and if there are other ways to improve things.

If multiple family members are tested, as often happens when working with family businesses, we go through the same process with each family member. It is then often extremely useful to have one or more meetings with multiple family members to share how the test results are the same and how they are different, so that they can learn more about each other. Much of the discussion in these meetings focuses on how their new understanding of each other can be applied.

Remember that family business members are brought up to feel that they can and should do everything, and it may be hard to let go of this idea. Benefitting from testing requires letting go of this notion because, in reality, no one can do everything, and we all have strengths and weaknesses. Not all weaknesses can be "fixed" or "cured". The important thing is not whether you have weaknesses but whether you know what they are and how to work around them. This is exactly what testing can supply.

It is rare that someone is not a candidate for testing. Certainly, if a person is struggling with intense anxiety, depression, or low self-esteem where the thought of testing seems threatening, they would not be a candidate. Another possible obstacle is when we are told that if we are going to test a next-generation family member, the person being tested should not know what his or her deficits are because it will cause them to quit every time they face an obstacle. You have read enough in this chapter to know our response. This is a family whose myth is that everything can be overcome with endless work and perseverance, and we know too well how, tragically, such a belief can impact the mental health of the individual and, ultimately, the success and survival of the business.

What Are Some Examples of the Changes Recommended After Testing with Jack and Gide Industries?

The following are examples of the types of recommendations that may be made as a result of neuropsychological testing. Some of them may be useful in other businesses as well, and some may not. The benefit of testing is that recommendations can be specifically tailored to the person and business in question.

1. Gide Industries has always had monthly three-hour staff meetings with multiple agenda items. After the testing, the meeting schedule was reorganized and is now in the form of three one-hour sessions with a short break in the middle, with fewer agenda items, in different weeks. This schedule was especially helpful for Jack and other employees with ADHD. This restructured schedule also reinforces the basic learning theory that most people, even those without ADHD, learn more when the intense learning time is limited, or breaks are built into the schedule.

2. A skilled support person was designated to take minutes of meetings and provide the minutes to all attendees. This meant that no one had to worry about taking comprehensive notes. Many people can either take notes or listen but cannot do both simultaneously. Taking notes is actually much more complex than most people realize. One must simultaneously listen to the speaker and process the information at the speaker's pace, quickly extract which information is important and which is not, organize the important information, put the important information into words, remember how to spell the words, and physically write the information down, all while the speaker continues to talk. Thus, a lot of multi-tasking is involved, and most of us are not as good at multitasking as we think we are.

3. Gide Industries had a culture that included many valuable exchanges of ideas in the hallway or "water cooler" conversations. The problem was that many of those outstanding ideas were lost at the end of the conversation. Everyone was now encouraged to follow up on these conversations with emails summarizing what had been said.

4. Because of Jack's dyslexia, he can read perfectly well, but he reads more slowly than most other people. Because of his ADHD, he sometimes zones out while reading long documents and has to reread multiple times to comprehend what he is reading. Jack's current role in the company involved researching and evaluating various options by reading long documents. After the testing, he was given a different role, in which he primarily talked ideas through with a working group rather than relying on reading for information. He proved to be able to produce several excellent and highly creative ideas in this format. People were asked to communicate with him by voicemail rather than by email or text. Again, the idea is to change the expectations of others to maximize their performance and the comfort of the team working together. With this change, Jack became a much more valued member of the team and

frustrations with his failure to comprehend or finish a long document ended while the essential and pertinent information was grasped.

5. The company culture called for managers to be totally available to their staff. Managers were encouraged to leave their office doors open, and people often popped in (at their convenience) to ask questions or to discuss an issue. This generally worked well for the staff but less well for the managers, who were often interrupted during a task. After the testing and consultation with the neuropsychologist, what was essential for Jack also turned out to be highly applicable to many of the managers. They were encouraged to shut their doors when they needed to get things done and to keep them open when they were less busy or working on something that required less concentration. The staff was told not to knock on the door unless it was an emergency. Similarly, managers were encouraged to turn off phone and email alerts at times. That way, they could check their devices when they were at a stopping point in their work rather than when it was convenient for other people. Each manager established "office hours" in which they were always available to staff.

Relationships

While most jobs involve relationships to some extent, this is even more true in family businesses. Your annoying co-worker may also be sitting across from you at Thanksgiving dinner, and you will see them outside of work on family occasions whether you want to or not. In addition, you may have been annoyed at your co-workers since the age of eight when they tormented you in various ways. Your boss could also be a parent whose approval you could never get. It will be much more difficult to complete projects and freely share ideas with someone with whom you have a problematic relationship, especially when the problems are long-term and mixed with other feelings like love and loyalty. In non-family businesses, these dynamics between bosses and employees and between employees are metaphorical. One's boss can represent one's mother or other authority figures in one's life. In family business, the obvious burden, or blessing, is that your boss *is* your mother.

Information gleaned through neuropsychological testing can be used to improve relationships. Testing multiple family members and comparing and contrasting the results can be particularly revealing. Suppose two family members, John and Mary, are working on a project together. Suppose Mary has always felt that John never listens to her. What if it turns out that John has attention problems and cannot listen to *anyone* for more than a few minutes? Mary is right; John is not listening to her, but for different reasons than she had originally thought. If Mary is made aware of John's attention problems (with John's permission to share the testing results), she may be able to take things less personally. It's not that John doesn't care about her needs, doesn't think she has anything useful to say, or sees her as insignificant. John is struggling with a biological limitation that is not under his control.

And maybe Mary's testing reveals that she has issues of her own. Perhaps she never did well in school and has always felt "dumb." John's apparent lack of interest in what she has to say triggers her feeling that she is not worth listening to anyway. If she is also tested, maybe she will learn the reasons for her academic struggles and better put them into context. In other words, maybe she is not globally "dumb"; maybe she just can't do math. If John and Mary can discuss the results of their testing together, with the help of a family business consultant, they can come to see each other in a different light, improve their communication, alter their expectations, reduce the longstanding anger and resentment between them, and therefore be able to work together more smoothly—a win-win situation.

As with Mary in the last example, one major obstacle to someone's happiness and self-esteem is, and ultimately, to their creativity and productivity is the sense that they are not "smart". As with Mary, this will affect everything they do and every relationship they have. What is remarkable about neuropsychological testing is that it seeks to fully understand the individual—their strengths, talents, and gifts and what is challenging. Certainly, there are some who have very high IQs and some (of us) who are more on the average scale. The notions of "smart" and "dumb" are replaced in this testing with what is actual and what is possible. One's challenges must be accepted and, when appropriate, delegated. However, once one's strengths are highlighted, it is possible to compensate somewhat through the use of one's strengths. A math deficit in a highly visual or language-based person can be better handled by visualizing the problem or by talking it through. Using what is learned in the testing to increase self-acceptance and ease one's sense of insecurity is the basic point.

Simply put, neuropsychological testing can be an extremely valuable tool for family businesses because it provides accurate, objective, and scientifically based information. Not only can this information enhance the performance of individuals, but it can also change the individual, along with the family and business relationships, thereby improving the performance of the business as a whole. The results of testing can help the company to make better decisions about succession and other important matters. When the basis for decisions is seen as objective and normalized, people are generally more accepting of them; thus, conflict and hurt feelings can be reduced or avoided entirely. We encourage consultants and family members to explore the use of neuropsychological testing to assure further true and lasting success in their family business.

CHAPTER TEN

The Biological Basis of Emotion and Why it Matters to the Family Enterprise

by Ellen Astrachan-Fletcher, PhD, FAED, CEDS-S
and R. Trent Codd, III, EdS, LCMHC

Following several recent employee departures, which occurred rapidly, Erica, the CEO of a family-owned enterprise, was concerned about further staff attrition. Part of her solution to this difficulty was interviewing her staff to learn their current employment satisfaction levels and to elicit any significant areas of concern. Though she was not surprised to learn that many individuals were feeling stressed because the company had recently experienced several operational changes, she was surprised to receive comments from staff suggesting the company was causing them to wrestle with several "moral dilemmas." Distressed by this information, she probed for specific areas of "moral" concern but could only elicit examples of concerns of substantially lower magnitude. It seemed the only expressed concern was that her nephew, a recent Harvard graduate, was given the new position of Director of Operations, and people were worried about his level of experience. Erica concluded the expressed areas of concern were being substantially mischaracterized, and she struggled to understand how her employees' perceptions could be so discordant with hers.

Like Erica, Brandon, the manager of his family's retail business, was similarly concerned about employee retention. Therefore, he was proactive and regularly checked in with his cousins and other employees regarding their levels of employment satisfaction. All reports he received suggested no areas of significant concern and relatively strong levels of satisfaction. Consequently, he was surprised by two recent employee resignations, one of which was his cousin. Even his cousin indicated he was pleased with work when feedback was last solicited, and neither exiting employee had ever expressed unhappiness or appeared unhappy. Brandon was at a loss to explain this turn of events.

Erica and Brandon's difficulty comprehending their respective circumstances with staff resignations likely resulted from not understanding the role their family and employees' biotemperaments played in their perceptions of the workplace environment and their communication regarding their satisfaction levels. They are not unique in failing to consider this important factor as it is typically not well understood outside the mental health professions. In this chapter, we will introduce you to biotemperament, including why business professionals need to understand what that is, how to classify your temperamental tendencies, a description of important subtypes of the two predominant temperamental styles, and strategies for managing employees more effectively based on biotemperamental factors.

What is Biotemperament?

Biotemperament exerts a powerful influence on one's experience of and response to the world. Biotemperament refers to the biological basis of emotion that impacts two things: 1) how we perceive the world and 2) how we regulate emotions. Consider a few questions. Do you perceive the world as safe and fun, or do you experience it as threatening? As a child, when you were in a park, were you more likely to notice the flowers or the thorns and bugs? When you felt upset, would you mask or hide your feelings or scream and cry? Your biotemperament largely influences your answers to these questions. Biotemperament also robustly influences how the world responds to you. It is powerful, in part, because it exerts its influence rapidly before you even have the possibility of being aware it is operating. The rapid onset makes it impossible to think yourself into different ways of reacting. Though we can learn effective ways of working with our biotemperaments, we cannot change them.

When understanding mental illness and biotemperament, clear patterns can be seen. While this is not 100% of the time, there are specific biotemperaments that typically underlie specific mental illnesses (see the Self-Control Dialectic below). For example, it takes a considerable amount of self-control to be able to not give in to the natural urge to eat, like in the case of anorexia nervosa. Given this idea that biotemperament underlies mental illness, there is currently a study being conducted to see if one can intervene with significant emotional overcontrol to prevent mental illness later in life.

The Self-Control Dialectic	
Undercontrolled (UC)	**Overcontrolled (OC)**
Emotionally Dysregulated and Impulsive	**Emotionally Constricted and Risk-Averse**
· Borderline PD	· Obsessive Compulsive PD
· Antisocial PD	· Paranoid PD
· Narcissistic PD	· Avoidant PD
· Histrionic PD	· Schizoid PD
· Binge-Purging Eating Disorders	· Anorexia Nervosa
· Conduct Disorders Bipolar Disorder	· Chronic Depression
· Externalizing Disorders	· Autism Spectrum Disorders
	· Treatment Resistant Anxiety-OCD
	· Internalizing Disorders

The Self-Control Dialectic[91]

Please remember that this is not a pure black-and-white picture but more of a significant pattern. There are plenty of people with bulimia who are overcontrolled, and there are people with anorexia who are undercontrolled. However, understanding biotemperament can enable us to be more aware of risks for certain disorders, attentiveness to certain symptoms, and then the ability to address the concerns both for the sake of the individual as well as for the sake of

---

91 Lynch, T. R. (2018a). *Radically open dialectical behavior therapy: Theory and practice for treating disorders of overcontrol.* New Harbinger Publications.; T. Lynch, personal communication, May 2017.

the system. Across cultures, two primary biotemperament types have been identified and described: undercontrolled and overcontrolled.[92] Three primary features characterize undercontrol. First is the ability to experience excitement more readily, or what is known as *high reward sensitivity*. Events that may be emotionally neutral for many overcontrolled persons may be experienced as rewarding or even highly rewarding to undercontrolled individuals. The second characteristic is *global-focused processing*, or the tendency to see the big picture while missing the finer and often essential details. The final feature is *low inhibitory control*. People with low inhibitory control may open a box of cookies only to eat a few but the entire box. In addition to these features, their behavior tends to be mood-driven (e.g., doing things when they feel like it). Many people with low inhibitory control also tend to be poor planners.

Overcontrolled individuals, by contrast, are *low in reward sensitivity*, *high in detail-focused processing*, *high in threat sensitivity*, and *high in inhibitory control*. In simpler terms, because their brains are wired differently than those with undercontrolled biotemperaments, they react to the world differently across these dimensions. It takes much more for them to experience rewards from events; things must be really exciting to them before they experience pleasure. They often find the expression of reward activation uncomfortable, and they typically use their inhibitory control to block expressing any excitement they feel. Their attention is more readily drawn to the details of situations, often resulting in their missing the general picture. As one person with an emotionally overcontrolled biotemperament once said, "If I go to a presentation and they have an editorial mistake in their PowerPoint, I am out. If they do not

---

92   Chapman, B. P., & Goldberg, L. R. (2011). Replicability and 40-year predictive power of childhood ARC types. *Journal of personality and social psychology*, *101*(3), 593-606.; Eisenberg, N., Guthrie, I. K., Fabes, R. A., Shepard, S., Losoya, S., Murphy, B., ... & Reiser, M. (2000). Prediction of elementary school children's externalizing problem behaviors from attentional and behavioral regulation and negative emotionality. *Child development*, *71*(5), 1367-1382.; Kendler, K. S., Prescott, C. A., Myers, J., & Neale, M. C. (2003). The structure of genetic and environmental risk factors for common psychiatric and substance use disorders in men and women. *Archives of General Psychiatry*, *60*(9), 929-937.; Krueger, R. F. (1999). The structure of common mental disorders. *Archives of general psychiatry*, *56*(10), 921-926.

care enough about their PowerPoint to edit it, why should I care enough to pay attention?" People with emotional overcontrol may also often feel anxious because they quickly see things that are threatening while simultaneously screening out benign features of situations. Finally, they tend to exercise high degrees of self-control skillfully.

Why is Biotemperament Important to Understand?

Biotemperament is vital to understand because it powerfully influences your experience of the world and the world's experience of you. It is a fundamental part of who you are, unalterable, traveling with you into every relationship and circumstance. Understanding your temperament and how it operates in your life will increase your effectiveness in living because you will have greater insight into your perceptions and behavior. With this knowledge, you can understand and govern your tendencies as you pursue essential goals.

Dominic, being in the third generation of the textiles family enterprise with a position on the board, often felt powerless after the unexpected passing of his father, which led to the quick decision to put his domineering younger stepbrother Damian as CEO. While Dominic and other family members began to notice discrepancies in what Damian was saying and, in the numbers, Dominic, being emotionally overcontrolled, was very uncomfortable confronting Damian. After extensive investigation and discovering many concerns, it was clear the discrepancies had to be addressed. Dominic became overwhelmed with guilt, to the point of losing sleep. All he could talk about was what a "bad brother" he was to Damian. He could sleep again when he realized that his overcontrolled temperament made him feel guilty for being so angry, and his anger was valid.

Understanding other people's temperamental biases is also important. It will increase your empathy towards them because you will be able to make sense of their responses to you and others and understand what is and isn't within their ability to control. It will help you know how to communicate with them more effectively, and it will help you understand how your temperament interacts with theirs (e.g., whether there's a mismatch or a congruency). For example, Erica, whom we introduced earlier, could have made sense of the moral indignation reported by her employees if she understood this might have been driven by undercontrolled temperamental biases, likely having a short-term, strong, emotional reaction to the hiring of her nephew. This understanding might have also assisted her in responding to these concerns more effectively by letting people know individually and giving them space for a potential emotional reaction, knowing that it will blow over when they have a minute to process and calm down.

Similarly, Brandon might have been more successful in eliciting actionable employee satisfaction feedback if he understood that overcontrolled employees, even if they are family, are likely to understate their displeasure, often resulting in miscommunication. He might have followed his inquiries with, "Would you tell me if you were unhappy?" These biologically based factors substantially affect employee social skills, influencing the quality of workplace relationships. This is even more important for the family businessperson to understand because the condition of workplace relationships matter even more. Since human behavior is a central component of business operations and temperament strongly influences behavior, the successful family business executive learns to work with temperament effectively.

Five Domains of Overcontrol and Undercontrol

In the table on the next page, we briefly summarize how individuals with overcontrolled and undercontrolled biotemperaments vary across five primary domains, which we then follow with several real-life examples to illustrate these concepts further. However, please note that these examples are not universally applicable since everyone is unique and at different places on the bell curve of overcontrol to undercontrol (which will be explained on the next page).

OVERCONTROL	UNDERCONTROL
High Threat Sensitivity	**Low** Threat Sensitivity
Low Reward Sensitivity	**High** Reward Sensitivity
High Detail Focused Processing	Globally Focused Processing
High Inhibitory Control	**Low** Inhibitory Control
Low in Novelty Seeking	**High** in Novelty Seeking

Threat sensitivity – Imagine passing your cousin in the hallway at work one day. You see them every day, and you politely smile and nod. You always say hello. One day, they pass you with a flat expression on their face. What is your first thought? Was it, "Huh, I wonder what is happening with them. It looks like they are having a bad day?" (This would be an example of low threat sensitivity.) Or perhaps was it, "Oh no! What did I do wrong? It looks like they are mad at me, so I have to figure out what I did wrong!" (This would be an example of high threat sensitivity, often connected to emotional overcontrol.)

Reward Sensitivity – This is how easily you feel excited about things. Do you get super excited about things that you like or things that you want? Are you motivated by reward, or does it take a ton of reward to feel rewarded? Do you often say things like, "I can't wait!!!" Imagine that the board of your family enterprise approves a special bonus for all the siblings. Would you be super excited about this reward with extravagant plans on how you will spend it? (This would be an example of high reward sensitivity, being excited that you are getting extra money.) Or would you be unimpressed because ALL the siblings got the bonus, so it is not considered a big deal? (This would be an example of low reward sensitivity, often connected with emotional overcontrol.)

Detail Focus versus Global Focus in one's processing. Someone who is overcontrolled will tend to see every vein, on every leaf, on every tree. They might not notice the forest, but they will notice all the details. Someone undercontrolled might run smack into the tree because they are looking at the beautiful forest. They do not even see the tree, let alone the leaves. While undercontrolled people can be great at the big picture but do not have them doing the bookkeeping!

Inhibitory Control refers to one's ability to not act on one's urges. We all have urges, but how effectively we stop ourselves from acting on those urges differs. People who are undercontrolled tend to have a difficult time not acting on their urges. They can be impulsive (in positive and negative ways), and it can take great, purposeful effort not to act on urges. In contrast, those who are overcontrolled, because they have superior inhibitory control, generally only act on their urges if they believe they *should* act on their urges.

Novelty Seeking – How much do you like new things and new experiences? If you had the opportunity to go to dinner one night, would you go to the place you always go, where you know just what you will order because that meal is always delicious and never lets you down, or a new restaurant that is getting a lot of buzz? An overcontrolled person will likely choose the old favorite restaurant because, as they might say, "Why would I risk getting a bad meal when I know I can get a good meal at the restaurant that I know?" Those who are undercontrolled are more likely to take risks with the business, and those who are overcontrolled are much more likely to be uncomfortable with that risk.

It is important to note that different biotemperamental patterns, unless they represent the extremes of the continuum, are not good or bad. These tendencies represent one of the many ways that humans vary. Understanding one's biotemperament is beneficial so that we can have compassion for ourselves and others and be more understanding of what motivates action in ourselves and others.

Do You Lean Undercontrolled or Overcontrolled?

It can be helpful to understand which way you lean biotemperamentally to deepen your understanding of the biologically based biases that you bring to every situation, including your work environment. This can also help you recognize these tendencies in your employees. No one test can definitively tell you which way you lean, overcontrolled or undercontrolled, nor is overcontrol or undercontrol a diagnosis, but the following self-assessment is useful in identifying your general disposition.

Styles of Coping Word Pairs[93]

Read each word pair in each row and place a checkmark next to the word that best describes you. Make sure you pick only *one* word or phrase in each row. If you are unsure which word best describes you, imagine what your friends or family might say about you. If neither of the words describes you, pick the one closest to how you would describe yourself. Make sure you choose one word from each row.

A		B	
Impulsive	☐	Deliberate	☐
Impractical	☐	Practical	☐
Naïve	☐	Worldly	☐
Vulnerable	☐	Aloof	☐
Risky	☐	Prudent	☐
Talkative	☐	Quiet	☐
Disobedient	☐	Dutiful	☐
Fanciful	☐	Realistic	☐
Fickle	☐	Constant	☐
Act without thinking	☐	Think before acting	☐
Animated	☐	Restrained	☐
Changeable Mood	☐	Stable Mood	☐
Haphazard	☐	Orderly	☐

---

93 Lynch, T. R. (2018a). *Radically open dialectical behavior therapy: Theory and practice for treating disorders of overcontrol.* New Harbinger Publications.

A	
Wasteful	☐
Affable	☐
Impressionable	☐
Erratic	☐
Complaining	☐
Reactive	☐
Careless	☐
Playful	☐
Intoxicated	☐
Self-indulgent	☐
Laid-back	☐
Unconventional	☐
Dramatic	☐
Brash	☐
Obvious	☐
Vacillating	☐
Unrealistic	☐
Gullible	☐
Unpredictable	☐
Dependent	☐
Improper	☐
Chaotic	☐
Susceptible	☐
Unstable	☐
Volatile	☐
Excitable	☐
Lax	☐
Unsystematic	☐
Thoughtless	☐

B	
Frugal	☐
Reserved	☐
Not easily Impressed	☐
Predictable	☐
Uncomplaining	☐
Unreactive	☐
Fastidious	☐
Earnest	☐
Clear-headed	☐
Self-controlled	☐
Hard-working	☐
Conventional	☐
Modest	☐
Unobtrusive	☐
Discreet	☐
Determined	☐
Sensible	☐
Shrewd	☐
Dependable	☐
Independent	☐
Proper	☐
Organized	☐
Impervious	☐
Steadfast	☐
Undemonstrative	☐
Stoical	☐
Precise	☐
Structured	☐
Thoughtful	☐

A		B	
Inattentive	☐	Attentive	☐
Short-lived	☐	Enduring	☐
Perky	☐	Despondent	☐
Passionate	☐	Indifferent	☐
Immediate gratification	☐	Delay gratification	☐
TOTAL score A		TOTAL score B	

Styles of Coping Word-Pairs Scoring Instructions

Tally up the number of checks in each column—the column with the greatest number represents your overall personality style.*

If you have a higher score for column A, this indicates you tend to be more under-controlled.

If you have a higher score for column B, this indicates you tend to be more over-controlled.

Note: This scale measures overall personality styles. A high score on either sub-scale does not necessarily indicate maladaptive over-controlled or maladaptive under-controlled coping.

We Are Not All in One Camp

While this might sound overly simplistic, humans are much more complicated than being one thing (overcontrolled) or another (undercontrolled). The Self-Control Tendencies bell curve continuum, from overcontrol to undercontrol, demonstrates that we have flexible control in the middle of the bell curve. Even though we still lean one way or the other, we can flexibly engage when we are more oriented toward the middle, and therefore we are more psychologically well.

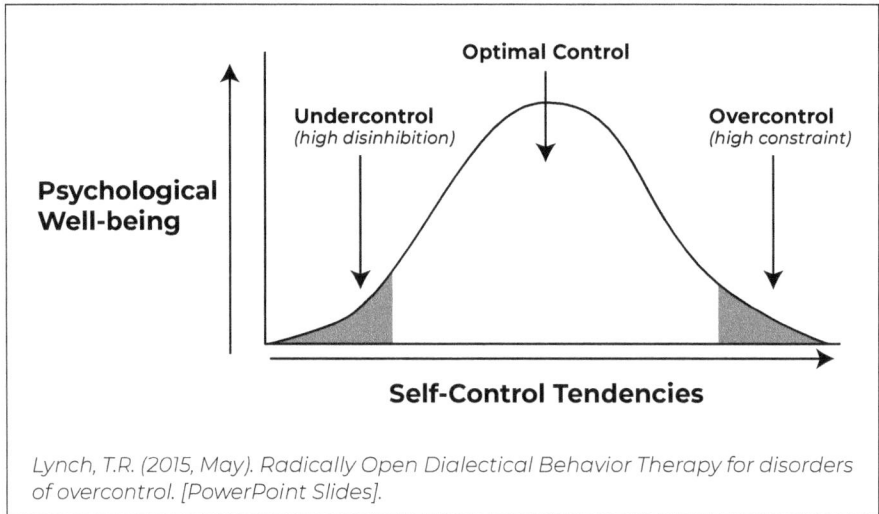

Lynch, T.R. (2015, May). Radically Open Dialectical Behavior Therapy for disorders of overcontrol. [PowerPoint Slides].

When learning about the idea of emotional overcontrol and emotional undercontrol, people tend to imagine that those who are undercontrolled always experience emotion and those who are overcontrolled never experience emotion. Overcontrolled-leaning people have emotions like anyone else. They use their superior inhibitory control to not act on urges to cry, scream, yell, or express their feelings. However, eventually, some emotion must come out. This is referred to as "emotional leakage." Emotional leakage can be small or large, and when it happens often, it can look like the behavior of someone undercontrolled. Whereas someone who is undercontrolled is likely to show emotions anywhere, anytime, with anyone, someone who is overcontrolled will emotionally leak. An overcontrolled person might hold in their emotions for hours, days, or weeks, and something just pushes them over the edge. They get home, walk past their family in the living room, and go straight into the bathroom, lock the door, sit on the toilet, and burst into tears. Or they get in the shower and scream or go for a drive alone and burst into tears. Sometimes, people with emotional overcontrol will emotionally leak with trusted friends and family. It is much rarer for an overcontrolled person to leak in public, and when they do, it typically stems from a strong sense of moral certainty, meaning "I need to teach you a lesson." Let's look at Bob's emotional leakage to see how emotions can get misdirected when ignored emotions burst out.

> Bob heard his older brother would be positioned to take over the Chief Executive Officer role. While he understood that his brother was older, he thought he was better educated for that position due to his MBA from Wharton, his experience in the company overseas, and his general intelligence. He viewed his brother as an entitled dolt. All that day, Bob stewed about this. Later that evening, he was out to dinner with a couple of friends from Wharton, and the waiter did not immediately bring the bread, olive oil, and cheese. When the waiter returned to the table, Bob emotionally leaked, yelling at the waiter, "There is one simple job for you to do, and that is to bring us the bread and oil when we are seated! How long have you been a waiter? Maybe you need some more training!" Everyone looked at Bob, who slowly quieted down as he sank into his chair, deeply regretting the emotional outburst.

Sometimes, emotional leakage can surface as displaced anger in public. At other times, anger can be expressed privately (like kicking the dog or only screaming at close family members). At still other times, it can be expressed anger at oneself (like non-suicidal self-injury). Regardless of how emotional leakage shows up, if one is told to "grin and bear it" or to "suck it up," they will likely have more leakage, more often and more severely. When a person is overcontrolled, they need to learn to let their emotions out more slowly with trusted loved ones.

Biotemperament in the Family Enterprise

Now that you understand biotemperament and its importance let's look at how it might appear in the family business. Below, we describe how Sasha's undercontrolled biotemperament positively and negatively impacts her leadership effectiveness.

> Sasha was a beloved leader of her small family business. Making others happy brought her lots of joy. However, when her father pressured her, she would throw anyone under the bus to protect his positive view of her. As the business grew, making everyone happy was more challenging than it used to be because what made one person happy might upset another. Although she had no ill will, she was focused on only the person in front of her, and she began to have more and more conversations in which she contradicted what she had said in previous discussions. As the conflict grew on-site, Sasha got the reputation of changing her mind on a dime, and her team began to lose respect and trust in her.

In contrast to the undercontrolled coping subtype, the overcontrolled person who must appear competent at all costs is likely what we see most often in the family business. Appearing competent is most important to this person. They are frequently closed-minded perfectionists who appear aloof in relationships and are driven to be right, no matter what. Their close-mindedness protects their perfectionism, so they do not take feedback seriously or get enraged in response to feedback. They often socially signal to others that they are superior, that others are incompetent, and that they do not trust others. While in typical systems, this type of person might not have many relationships, in the successful family business, they might have many relationships they feel they control yet do not feel close to or connected with anyone. See below for how Tommy's biotemperamental approach impacts his nephews in the family enterprise.

> When Rick passed away, and Tommy was the last of the four brothers running their father's business, Tommy announced that while he still

had three sisters who were never allowed in the business because they were female, the entire family business was now going to be run by him, with his sons and his nephews under him. He often disrespected his nephews on-site to the laughter of the employees. When one sister tried to give him feedback, he coldly commented that he disrespects his nephews because "they are idiots, and if they develop half a brain, I will be more respectful." When she tried to explain that they needed support, not criticism, he insisted that he would not baby anyone because he knew tough love was the best way. One of his nephews had depression and attempted suicide several years later.

As you can see in the above example, Tommy's biotemperament was not the same as his nephew's. Yet, most of us are unaware of these differences, and as human beings, we tend to believe that everyone's experience is similar to ours. With the understanding of biotemperament, Tommy could have recognized that instead of "tough love," his nephew would have likely benefited from more encouragement and support.

Ryan provides an excellent example of someone who is overly agreeable and whose coping has impacted his emotional and professional functioning.

At 20 years old, Ryan was the youngest in the family, and he needed to decide if he would pursue a more active leadership role in the family business. He told his family he was very interested because he knew that was expected of him. He would express insecurities, and his family would reassure him, conveying that they thought he would be great. The more reassurance he received, the more pressure he felt. This, in turn, led him to increase his expression of his insecurities, further escalating the reassurance he received into a vicious cycle. His anxiety became incapacitating with the inclusion of regular panic attacks, and much to his relief, he was told he could not become a leader in the family business.

Understanding the biotemperaments of others can help us communicate more effectively. In the example above, if Ryan's family understood his biotemperament, they could have understood that Ryan's search for reassurance was his way of communicating that he did not want the job. Yet the more reassurance they gave, the more fearful of the job he became.

I Understand Biotemperament. What Now?

Humans differ in many ways, yet patterns become apparent when we look closely at human nature. Focusing on biotemperamental traits helps us see patterns that develop as different traits hang together. As we learn to recognize and understand these patterns, we can develop compassion for the various areas of struggle in ourselves and others. Do we tend to process information as someone who is overcontrolled or undercontrolled? What about our loved ones? Is it possible that differences can cause conflict if not understood? How might biotemperament influence position in the family enterprise? Consider the undercontrolled high reward sensitivity and global focused processing and how that tendency might change their experiences versus operating with the overcontrolled high threat sensitivity and great detail focus. If a family member is put in a position needing detail focus but is undercontrolled, could they unintentionally set that person up to fail? How might you look at people with a different biotemperament from your own? If you are overcontrolled, do you view your undercontrolled loved ones as being erratic, inconsistent, and unmotivated? If you are undercontrolled, do you view your overcontrolled loved ones as rigid, uptight, and aloof?

It is important to recognize that brains process information differently. Someone who is overcontrolled might view their undercontrolled loved one as lazy and having low standards because their desk is such a mess. Meanwhile, the undercontrolled person does not even see the mess because of their propensity toward global-focused processing, and they might view the overcontrolled loved one as being judgmental and controlling for bringing it up. This difference in processing information is not good or bad in an absolute sense because we need global-focused and detail-focused processing in life. However, interpersonal conflict is more likely to arise when we do not understand, accept, and respect the differences in how people process information.

In addition, because appearing competent is very important to people with overcontrolled coping, they do not like being told about themselves. Often, even when feedback is accurate, an overcontrolled person is likely to reject it as it can feel threatening that others see their vulnerabilities.

Principles and Hints for the Family Enterprise

When interacting with people who are overcontrolled:

1. Get curious, really curious, and approach them from a place of questions (though don't pepper them with questions!). For example, if you want to give feedback that not responding to emails promptly is a problem, you might ask, "What do you think it might signal to others when you do not respond to their emails? Is that what you want to signal to them? Is that in line with your values?"

2. When asking questions, it can be helpful to understand and be aware of your social signaling.

   - Are your eyebrows up expressing curiosity and openness, or are your eyebrows down, possibly expressing concern that might be interpreted as judgment or disapproval by the overcontrolled person? Eyebrows up is referred to as an "eyebrow wag."[94] Having one's eyebrows gently up can help you engage your social safety system and help the person you are talking with to engage theirs. To feel this, look in the mirror with your eyebrows flat and ask, "Do you know where the bathroom is?" Make a note of how this feels and how this sounds. Then

---

94 Lynch, T. R. (2018b). *The skills training manual for radically open dialectical behavior therapy: a Clinician's guide for treating disorders of Overcontrol.* New Harbinger Publications.

look in the mirror, raise your eyebrows (this might not be as easy if you have Botox), and ask, "Do you know where the bathroom is?"

Similarly, make a note of how this feels and how you sound. Next, ask yourself: What differences do I notice? Did I see a change in my voice? Did I notice a change in how I felt? Did I feel more curious? Is there something for me to learn about myself and how I signal to others? The opposite of growth is remaining stagnant. While growth can be painful, stagnation is often worse.[95]

3. When people are emotionally undercontrolled, they love direct eye contact, which can help them feel heard and seen. Undercontrolled's love to feel understood, and direct eye contact with expressions of concern helps them feel that way.

4. Direct eye contact can activate the overcontrolled's threat system. While they might maintain eye contact when forced, they are often not hearing what the other person is saying, instead wishing the person would stop talking and stop with the eye contact.

5. People who are overcontrolled prefer to be recognized for their hard work and accomplishments. They do not expect to feel understood, as they often believe no one can understand them.

6. When people want to avoid conflict at all costs, they are likely to lie or not be honest about their thoughts and feelings when asked if they think their thoughts and feelings do not go along with the majority or could displease someone else.

   • When interacting with someone and there is a chance the person is not being honest, you can ask, "Would you tell me if you did not

---

95   For fun, take a look at YouTube BBC. (2010, September 22). *Talking Eyebrows - Michael McIntyre's comedy Roadshow Series 2 EP 2 Sunderland preview - BBC One* [Video]. YouTube. https://www.youtube.com/watch?v=ZaO-llc_E64

agree?" or "Would you be honest with me if you did not feel that way?" Sometimes, being allowed to realize that dishonesty is against their values makes people make a different decision.

7. Consider having a conversation as a family about everyone's biotemperaments and how they impact communication and dynamics at home and the office. Discuss ways to understand better, empathize with, and manage these tendencies for better family interactions.

Conclusion

Managing relationships in business and with families can be complicated, and doing this skillfully is of central importance to those in the family enterprise because the nature and strength of workplace relationships are associated with several principal business performance indicators. As discussed in this chapter, an important factor influencing these relationships is biotemperament. The effective business leader understands the role of biotemperament in relationship development and work performance and considers its effects when understanding family dynamics and making crucial decisions.

Summary of Key Points

In this chapter, we made the following points:

- Biotemperament is the biological basis for perceiving the world and regulating emotions.

- Understanding biotemperament can help us know vulnerabilities to mental health issues, and it can influence recommendations for mental health treatment.

- The effects of biotemperament are powerful and cannot be directly controlled.

- Undercontrol and overcontrol are two overarching biotemperamental types that show up in different behavior patterns. Identifying and understanding the nature of these patterns further increases our effectiveness in relating to and managing people.

• Identifying our family and employees' biotemperamental predispositions and our own can help us make sense of and more effectively understand, have compassion for, interact with, and even manage, when necessary, the behavior of ourselves and others.

CHAPTER ELEVEN

Navigating Legal Mental Health Issues and Family Businesses

by Domingo P. Such III, JD

Approximately one in four U.S. adults experienced a mental health condition, and one in three U.S. adults experienced both a mental health condition and substance abuse, according to a recent survey.[96] When working with a global family business, it is increasingly common that advisors and family members will have to deal with addiction or mental capacity issues.[97] Understanding the underpinnings of U.S. law and the mental capacity necessary to lawfully interact with one another is fundamental to our commerce-based society driven by family businesses. To promote family harmony, business succession, and continuity, family members must plan and sign estate planning documents memorializing their wishes. Should there be a dispute about capacity, the law determines decision-making, whether planned or in an emergency, which may or may not involve court proceedings. This chapter examines these topics, and through proactive global planning, the authors believe efficient

---

96   Daniel, M., Richesson, D., Magas, I., Brown, S., Hoenig, J. M., & Substance Abuse and Mental Health Services Administration. (2023). Key Substance Use and Mental Health Indicators in the United States: Results from the 2022 National Survey on Drug Use and Health. In Center for Behavioral Health Statistics and Quality, *Substance Abuse and Mental Health Services Administration* [Report]. https://www.samhsa.gov/data/sites/default/files/reports/rpt42731/2022-nsduh-nnr.pdf

97   While the author has a U.S. based practice, subject to national and local law principles, the subject matter of mental health issues has universal application. In the realm of global planning, the author regularly collaborates with counsel for the country where business interests are held to ensure cohesive international planning across countries recognizing treaties between countries and applicable laws that continue to evolve. Engaging with counsel in a particular country is the only way to ensure that a specific country's law is complied with and then the international plan is cohesively integrated among the counterpart countries. The Society of Trust and Estate Practitioners is global professional body, comprising lawyers, accountants, trustees and other practitioners that help families plan internationally. https://www.step.org

and harmonious succession may occur. Notably, according to Caring.com's 2024 Wills Survey, six out of ten U.S. adults don't have a will.[98] The survey found that even less than four out of ten made healthcare decisions related to incapacity or end-of-life decisions, leaving much work to be done to navigate successfully the legal mental health issues attendant with family businesses.

Family Businesses and U.S. Law

Benjamin Franklin said, "In this world, nothing is certain but death and taxes." Despite their certainty, we resist legal and medical planning for incapacity, death, and dying; perhaps this is because there is so much daily complexity with living, we feel as if we have no control. Daily complexity is compounded by a need for advisors and lawyers. If issues are avoided, simple problems can morph into bigger issues. Proactivity in dealing with one's affairs is a good general rule, and lawyers will cease to exist when there are no clients in need of advice as to legal rights and obligations.

In family businesses, the rights and obligations of family members and the operating business intersect and multiply with each interaction. The individual characteristics and interactions of individual family members who own a business venture, some with control and others without, some employed and involved in the business, and others who are not involved, when viewed in the aggregate, present some of the most fertile soil for success or failure. Tragically, the two are not mutually exclusive.

The news cycle and tabloids capture the economic success and failures with family strife in those business operations that are family-owned and governed. For example, unprecedented success in the cosmetics, communications, and hoteling industries has been accompanied by intrigue about the families that own the successful companies. Family struggles are being written

---

98   *2024 Wills and Estate Planning study - Caring.com.* (2024, January 16). Caring.com. https://www.caring.com/caregivers/estate-planning/wills-survey/

about at the Estée Lauder companies,[99] the Viacom companies controlled by the Redstones[100] and in the recent past, the Hyatt companies controlled by the Pritzkers[101] just to name a few. The glitz and glamour of Hollywood is cashing in on the compelling family stories that hit the airwaves during the COVID-19 pandemic, with the rise of live streaming capturing the reality of family dynamics. From television reality shows to record-breaking popular series including *Billions, Succession,* and *Game of Thrones,* family dysfunction combined with power, money, and politics portray "success" in a compelling drama drawing inspiration from real-life events and people. The growing world economy does not temper the demand for advice on legal rights and obligations. On the contrary, our legal system has only grown in response to developing economies and technologies for interpreting and enforcing the law, with new laws passed every year.

At its most basic, our legal system is based on justice as a fundamental concept. Justice is, in turn, based on ethics in legal and political philosophy that form a cornerstone of modern society. Often equated to fairness, justice is the principle that equal persons should be treated equally, and those who are not equal should be treated unequally. If two cases are viewed as substantially similar, justice dictates treating like cases similarly. This is referred to as precedent or precedential.

Distinguishing seemingly similar cases is an art that is taught in law school using a Socratic method of questioning regarding court cases and statutes to

---

99 Glazer, E., & Ojea, S. (2023, November 17). *The Estée Lauder Family Built a Beauty Empire. A Succession Rift Threatens It Succession planning. Business mistakes: Inside an American dynasty that has lost $15 billion in wealth this year.* The Wall Street Journal. Retrieved June 22, 2024, from https://www.wsj.com/business/retail/the-estee-lauder-family-built-a-beauty-empire-a-succession-rift-threatens-it-2eb2515f

100 Mullin, B. (2023, December 21). *Why Is Shari Redstone, Ruler of a Vast Media Kingdom, Weighing a Sale?* The New York Times. Retrieved June 22, 2024, from https://www.nytimes.com/2023/12/21/business/media/shari-redstone-paramount-sale.html; *Judge sets trial on mogul Sumner Redstone's mental capacity | AP News.* (2016, February 29). AP News. https://apnews.com/article/4ceb724c0058432d9b5e3d2d4467ea3a

101 Fitch, S. (2013, June 19). Pritzker vs. Pritzker. *Forbes.* https://www.forbes.com/forbes/2003/1124/142a.html?sh=6d73c29b4cf2

learn the law and its application.[102] Applying principles of justice to cases was first defined over two thousand years ago in Greece as recorded by Plato, a student of Socrates. Today, justice is applied to reduce conflict and promote social harmony, most visibly in commerce; think of the convenience of ordering food through your phone and having it delivered to your door. Countless agreements and exchanges are going on behind the scenes through binding legal contracts to make that transaction happen, finalized at your door with the delivery of goods. Reliance on the contracting, that is, the lawful nature of obligations as fair and just, is necessary, and in fact, commerce has defined and redefined norms. Most recently, with new technologies, a new body of law has emerged for electronic commerce known as "e-commerce." Commerce has also influenced the development of the law and the framework for punishment and compensation when injustice occurs. It is justice through the legal system that helps to ensure that everyone has equal opportunities to succeed in America, and it has been the case that family businesses drive the growth and success of the U.S. economy; family businesses account for 64 percent of U.S. gross domestic product, generate 62 percent of the country's employment, and account for 78 percent of all new job creation.[103]

When we consider our everyday dealings, we may struggle to believe that our society is fair and just. This is not a reflection of the legal system as much as it is that people can act unjustly and not be prosecuted or found guilty. As a billboard ad for the law office of Larry L. Archie[104] observes: "Just because you did it doesn't mean you're guilty."

We know that people can be influenced by power, money, and politics. It strikes closer to home when justice in a familial setting is examined, and equality issues are weighed against equity. How often have we heard from a

---

102   *What to Expect from the Socratic Method.* (n.d.). The Princeton Review. https://www.princetonreview.com/law-school-advice/socratic-method

103   Astrachan, J. H., & Shanker, M. C. (2003). Family Businesses' contribution to the U.S. Economy: A closer look. *Family Business Review, 16*(3), 211–219. https://doi.org/10.1177/08944865030160030601

104   *Funny or die.* (n.d.). Funny or Die. https://funnyordie.com/

parent that each child was raised and treated equally, while the children say the opposite, noting that one sibling has been favored? There are no easy answers where the dynamics of a family are taken into account. The starting point in the law is that parents will presumably treat their children to an equal inheritance.[105] Preference and inheritance of assets that cannot be divided present the opportunity for apparent unequal treatment, but this is not typically the parent's view. Looking generationally at inheritance, the "shirt sleeves to shirt sleeves in three generations" axiom is shown to be statistically accurate and by some is viewed as a curse.[106] In the first generation, an entrepreneurial founder of a family company rolling up her sleeves to work hard finds success. The next generation reaping the benefits of the prior generation's hard work may not be inclined to work hard like their parents. Perhaps they are content to spend and enjoy the spoils of the prior generation's hard work. Spending down the wealth can often be seen as easy, and the result is the next generation of children will not have the same economic advantage as their parents and will once again have to roll up their sleeves and work to make ends meet.[107]

Comedian Russell Peters: *Often working two jobs to make ends meet with a dual-income spousal family, putting their children through high school with extra tutoring and sports activities to get into a prestigious college, the immigrant parents proudly state that they work hard so our children will not have to!*

Punchline: *Welcome to your American dream turned into a nightmare. You are a success, and your children are lazy!*

---

105   Unlike many other countries, U.S law provides that individuals may customize inheritance, including disinheritance of a descendant, at one's own discretion. Unlike the U.S., many countries have forced heirship rules which is common among civil law countries (France, Germany, Spain most of South America, China, Japan and Muslim countries) where forced heirship rules determine which heirs receive assets of a deceased person without discretion or input of the deceased.

106   Jaffe, D. (2021, June 30). The "Shirtsleeves-To-Shirtsleeves" curse: How family wealth can survive it. *Forbes.* https://www.forbes.com/sites/dennisjaffe/2019/01/28/the-shirtsleeves-to-shirtsleeves-curse-how-family-wealth-can-survive-it/?sh=47b67b7c6c8d

107   To prove the curse, many turn to the statistics, according to the Family Business Institute, only 30 percent of family businesses survive beyond the founder's generation. From there the odds of survival only get worse: only 12 percent make it to the third generation, and a paltry 3 percent persevere into the fourth.

Comedy is often a parody of real-life situations. In this case, what may not be noticed is the irony of the parent working so hard for the family, and the result of that work is a child who never "grows up." The successful founder of a company or the founder's widow or widower who happens to be singularly obsessed with business success may be an egomaniac, a person vexed with impostor syndrome, or a successful person with a type A personality. Many examples of business owners with differing degrees of success are afflicted by hubris and self-doubt. Martin Luther King Jr. observed that "There is a violent civil war raging within each and every person: between our good and bad impulses, between our ambition and our principles, between what we can be and how hard it is actually to get there."[108]

As we have read in Chapter 6 about Substance Disorder, the biological disease of addiction is a compulsive need for and use of habit-forming substances and is a recognized mental illness. Not restricted to biology, addiction can be an obsession with a thing or activity that blossoms into personality disorders. One can become obsessed with one's own self and the primacy of one's urges and thoughts to the point of diagnosed mental illness.

As we learn more about mental illness, it appears that the disease is not discriminatory in who it affects or why it affects some and not others. Chances are, in working with families, be it addiction or aging, it is increasingly common that advisors and family members will have to deal with addiction or mental capacity issues when working with family businesses. The question then is how do you lawfully plan? Are there instances when we are not allowed to plan? How is it best to plan? To answer these questions, a legal understanding of mental capacity is necessary.

---

108   Holiday, R. (2019). *Stillness is the Key*. Penguin.

Mental Capacity Drives Commerce

The mental capacity of individual action is fundamental to a successful economy. There is a societal presumption of capacity[109] until proven otherwise. Incapacity, or mental illness, is the exception and, as such, is commonly stigmatized in society. By presuming capacity, the law respects individual's right to decide for themselves. The presumption of capacity is important because it ensures due respect for personal autonomy by requiring any determination of "a lack of capacity" based on evidence and due process.

In mental health, capacity refers to a person's ability to make decisions regarding their own treatment or care. It is the ability to understand, retain, weigh information, and then communicate a decision. A person's principal physician or a court may assess a person's decision-making abilities to make health care decisions; the choice can be our own or foisted upon us. If a person is deemed to lack capacity, they may be unable to make decisions about their treatment or care, and they may complain about such circumstances for years.

There are four types of legal capacities[110]: (1) Legal capacity, which is a subject's ability to bear rights and duties acquired at birth; (2) Capacity to act, in which the subject's capacity to perform legal acts, dependent on age, mental capacity, and insolvency; (3) Criminal capacity, in which the ability to be held liable for crimes; and (4) Capacity to litigate, in which the ability to sue or be sued in a court of law.

This chapter explores the capacity to act in contracting/marriage, writing a last will and testament, and healthcare decisions. Family businesses will, by

---

109   Astrachan, I. M., Keene, A. R., & Kim, S. Y. H. (2023). Questioning our presumptions about the presumption of capacity. *Journal of Medical Ethics*, jme-109199. https://doi.org/10.1136/jme-2023-109199

110   For the mentally ill who lack capacity, there are statutes for involuntary commitment that is beyond the scope of this chapter. Involuntary commitment has been determined to be a U.S. Constitutional issue and is subject to the due process clause of the 14th Amendment because it severely infringes on a person's right to be free from governmental restraint. Courts have ruled that involuntary commitment statutes must bear some reasonable relation to the purpose for which the individual is committed. In addition, the criminal justice system address issues of responsibility, appropriateness of trial and treatment in the light of mental health considerations based on capacity.

necessity, address the legal capacity to act daily, although most of the time, it will be assumed; that is, until a family member does not have the capacity. And then what happens?

Capacity to Contract and to Marry

Since the mental capacity of individual action is fundamental to the economy, we need to examine individual action more closely. Freedom to contract is a concept that individuals possess a general freedom to choose with whom to contract, whether to contract or not, and on which terms to contract. The right to make and enforce contracts is embedded in the United States Code Title 42, dealing with public health, social welfare, and civil rights. The term "make and enforce contracts" includes "the making, performance, modification, and termination of contracts, and the enjoyment of all benefits, privileges, terms, and conditions of the contractual relationship.

The law regarding contractual capacity is full of fine distinctions and can be burdensome well beyond the scope of this chapter and book. From commerce to marriage to inheritance, it may be surprising to see that these fine distinctions have significant consequences. In day-to-day business dealings, a person must have the capacity, meaning the individual is of sound mind and understands the contract's terms, benefits, and obligations. Some people do not have the capacity to contract, such as the underage, mentally ill, or intoxicated people. Contracts made with people who do not have legal capacity are voidable. If the contract comes before a court, the court may opt to void or rescind a contract if one of the parties lacked legal capacity when the contract was executed. If the court voids the contract, it will attempt to put all parties back in their position before the agreement, which may involve reversing the exchange of property or money.

In all 50 states, the ability to enter into marriage focuses on age and capacity. At the core, marriage is a civil contract between two individuals, and the "capacity" in this contract is based on the ability of the parties to provide consent. "Consent" is paramount to marriage validity, and consent may not be valid in instances where one or both of the parties are underage, lack mental capacity, or are intoxicated. Furthermore, the law is replete with examples where one party is deemed to have forced or coerced the other party to marry (the old-time "shotgun wedding," which is invalid today). Fraud or deception are also factors that cancel out "consent." Fraud may be as simple as one party pretending to have more money than is true or promising to get your spouse (or their family) citizenship in exchange for marriage. Fraud invalidates a marriage and may also open the individual to criminal charges.

Family businesses tend to be excellent creators of generational wealth. When two independent families of means combine, there can be a higher chance for succession to be successful across multiple generations. While the medieval times, where marriage was for economic reasons and arranged marriages were common, have passed, it is certainly the case that the succession of family business as part of an inheritance continues. We need to explore capacity with respect to inheritance.

Testamentary Capacity to Execute a Will

Surprisingly, the capacity test to execute a will is lower than the capacity to contract. Sufficient mental capacity to execute (or to revoke) a will or a will-substitute requires the testator to understand that when signing, (1) the testator is making official the document that will control the distribution of all or part of their assets after their death, (2) the testator knows the nature and extent of their wealth, and (3) the testator remembers who are the natural objects of his/her bounty. The law tells us that a will may be valid if the testator merely experiences a "lucid interval" when a person meets all three of the foregoing requirements, even if only for a few minutes.

Applying this "testamentary" capacity test to degenerative decline provokes interesting discussion and planning situations. First, the best practice is for there to be a common understanding among a testator's family, physician, and lawyer of the debilitating and progressively degenerative disorder affecting a growing number of the elderly. In some cases, the degenerative decline in capacity is hereditary.

As we learned in Chapter 8, dementia is not a static disease impacting an isolated area of the brain but rather is a general term that describes a group of dynamic symptoms affecting memory, thinking, and social abilities that interfere with everyday activities. Of the elderly population in the United States, estimates suggest that 10% of U.S. adults ages 65 and older have dementia, while another 22% have mild cognitive impairment. Rates of dementia and mild cognitive impairment rise sharply with age: 3% of people between 65 and 69 have dementia, rising to 35% for people aged 90 and over.[111] Family business members can't be unaffected; consider Sumner Redstone's story reference above.

Coordinating a meeting among a person with early-stage dementia, her spouse, her lawyer, and her doctor to specifically address health care needs, both current and future, is the best way to make sure one's wishes will be identified and respected. Should a person's condition progress to later stage dementia with a loss of mental capacity, actions based on expressed and documented wishes in various legal documents, such as powers of attorneys, living wills, and an estate plan, will allow those involved with the person's care to confidently proceed in carrying out her wishes. Rather than in an unanticipated emergency, assisted living care or other services can be secured in the normal course. This simple proactive step to have a will and powers of attorney for health care in place avoids conflicts with different family members and is vital to preserving harmony in a family business.[112] The failure to provide a coordinated plan should be avoided; loved ones and professional advisors

---

111   *One in 10 older Americans has dementia.* (2022, October 26). Columbia University Irving Medical Center. https://www.cuimc.columbia.edu/news/one-10-older-americans-has-dementia

112   Consider the famous case of Terri Schiavo, a 41-year-old Florida woman, who died fifteen years after an anoxic incident related to cardiac arrest that started in 1998 until her death in 2005. Her husband and her parents engaged in a 7-year legal battle over what care she would or would not have wanted, her proper diagnosis and prognosis, who should be given authority to act for her, and the appropriate legal procedures to determine the answers to questions. The battle raged through state courts, federal courts, the state legislature, and even the U.S. Congress. Ms. Schiavo's death was a tragedy. The legal battles surrounding her death were another kind of tragedy. Little about her case shed any light on the legal issues involved in end-of-life decision-making. Her case was not unique or even all that uncommon. The legal principles involved were actually quite well developed, since Florida already had some of the most extensive case law on "right to die" issues even before Ms. Schiavo's heart attack but she never reduced her wishes down to writing.

serve the valuable role of prompting action that proactively avoids confusion and controversy.

Capacity to Make Health Care Decisions

It is important to note that mental capacity is not static. It may fluctuate and can change over time. More precisely, capacity to act refers to the capability and power under the law of a person to occupy a particular status or relationship with another or to engage in a particular undertaking or transaction. Let's look at an actual client situation where a former family business-owning executive who has retired successfully, having transitioned control of a business to her children, is now concerned with her next stage of life. There is a family history of dementia, and with enough resources to afford in-home care from the success of the business, the issue will not be one of the affordability of care but rather how and when care will be accessed and who will make those care-related decisions when one cannot decide for oneself.

The following letter, taken from an actual case, is an example of how a collaborative undertaking between medical care providers, an experienced estate planning attorney, and a client can all work together to provide peace of mind and care today and in the future for some of the most challenging of situations:

> *Dear Nancy:*
>
> *I would be happy to meet with you, your spouse, and your lawyer in my office. I am sure that your lawyer has probably talked to you both about the issues involved, as there are a lot of components to your question at hand.*
>
> *I believe we are still in the middle of your evaluation, Nancy, to determine a diagnosis of dementia. I know you are very concerned about this due to your family history. As far as I can tell, we have not had a formal neuropsychological evaluation yet. We have completed all the precursor steps, including the MRI. The key will be to complete the neuropsychologic and dementia evaluation so that we can have a concrete*

assessment and diagnosis, which may also help us with prognosis for the future and future planning.

Please bring any official documents pertaining to medical power of attorney, but Nancy, you still have input and control over your decisions.

We can meet and discuss this further in person, but we will have limited ability to make any strong determinations until further neuropsychological evaluation is performed.

Making Decisions When You Are Unable to Make Decisions for Yourself

A loss of capacity can come about immediately, for instance, as a result of an accident, an acute health issue, such as a stroke or heart attack, or another cause resulting in unconsciousness, a coma, or a persistent vegetative state. The sudden accident is unexpected and can result in panic if the "fire drill" to address the situation has not been reviewed in advance. Let's contrast Nancy's proactive approach with a difficult, sudden situation.

Guardianship

We need a video conference ASAP. The Crisis Team is being called to mobilize. We briefly discussed guardianship for Ronnie on our recent calls recently. We are very close to pursuing guardianship and would like to know if this is something you could handle for us. We would appreciate it if you could let us know at your earliest convenience.

The above message is taken from an actual case and highlights concerns that could have been prevented with proactive planning. Failing to plan for a person with an addiction issue left the family in a situation where they had to weigh an involuntary guardianship or another bout at a rehabilitation facility. The guardianship proceedings that followed were public and contentious.

When a person's ability to act autonomously becomes impaired, public policy justifies the court system stepping in to make choices on the person's behalf to promote the person's best interests and to protect the person from personal and financial harm. The court proceeding in this situation is a guardianship petition that can be contested in an involuntary or voluntary proceeding if the person in question is asking for a guardian, which is rarely the case.

In a guardianship proceeding, the court assesses a person's decision-making capacities. After a judicial hearing, decision-making rights may be removed from the alleged disabled person (the ward) and reassigned to another person approved and appointed by the court (the guardian). Guardianship orders are individualized. A ward may retain rights to make certain decisions, and other decision-making rights may be assigned to the guardian. The specific guardianship order must be reviewed to determine which decision-making powers the court assign to the guardian. Medical decision-making may or may not be one of the decision-making powers removed from a ward and assigned to a guardian.

The guardian of the ward's estate may also be appointed to manage the ward's financial affairs if wealth is involved. Guardianship may trigger a sense of traumatic loss of personal autonomy for the ward and the family. Consequently, legal safeguards are of great importance, and court proceedings should be viewed as a last resort, to be exercised only after the failure of all alternatives, such as interventions, rehabilitation centers, and assisted living facilities. Unfortunately, the lack of planning by the elderly population and by those who are mentally or physically impaired is causing there to be a greater need to resort to the courts to make decisions. The author has participated in contested guardianship and conservatorship proceedings, which are undoubtedly inconvenient, unpleasant, and undignified. Several of the problems inherent in using the courts to provide care and supervision are evident.

Most states impose some limitations on the powers of a guardian, including, for example, limiting the guardian's power to involuntarily commit her ward to a mental health treatment facility or rehabilitation center. In addition, there are practical limits on the ability of a guardian to affect care decisions in the best interests of her ward; imposition of guardianship does not usually create additional care resources, and even with the legal authority to do so, it may not be possible to compel the ward to stay in a given facility, receive specified care, or participate in a treatment regimen.

Of course, the problem of surrogate decision-makers attempting to eliminate (rather than merely control) risk is not unique to guardianship and conservatorship proceedings–it regularly occurs in management by agents (under general or health care powers of attorney) and family members exercising authority under state surrogacy statutes. However, reviewing and signing powers of attorneys will avoid guardianship court proceedings because the document specifies what is to happen should there be a loss of legal capacity. This simple proactive step to review and sign powers of attorney avoids the Terry Schiavo scenario that many people fear.[113]

Durable Power of Attorney

When you execute a power of attorney as part of an estate plan to promote family harmony and avoid conflict in a family business, you nominate and authorize someone else to handle certain matters, such as dealing with a family office or family business, real estate closings, finances or health care, on your behalf for a stated period of time. It can be very specific and is regularly used in commerce, with real estate and commercial closings being among the most commonly known use of a power of attorney. In the family office/ family business setting, powers of attorney are commonly utilized to address various complex and numerous financial matters. If the power of attorney is durable, it remains in effect if the principal becomes incapacitated for any reason, including illness and accidents. It can also have a condition that only takes effect in the event of an illness or accident. Accordingly, the durable power of attorney helps you plan for the future, appointing someone to

---

113   Keyt, A. (2016). *Myths and Mortals: Family Business Leadership and Succession Planning.* Wiley.

handle finances and make medical decisions if you become unable to do so for yourself. Notably, the law governing powers of attorney differs from state to state. Guardianships, conservatorships, and durable powers of attorney are "legal substitutes" for the ability to manage one's affairs when the individual in question lacks capacity. Harkening back to Aristotle, in this situation, family members, doctors, and lawyers must be sufficiently perceptive to anticipate debilitating events and sufficiently experienced to implement flexibility and structure during an otherwise unpredictable emergent situation.

As the law of surrogate health care decision-making has developed, it has become increasingly common for a "substituted judgment" approach rather than simply handling to the agent's unfettered discretion. There is a growing school of thought that even though state statutes prescribe the use by the agent of a "best interests" analysis, the agent's approach should first be to try to ascertain what the principal's actual wishes might have been (or, sometimes, what they might now be). The principal can anticipate and express their desires in writing before an incapacity event by pre-planning and executing a durable power of attorney. Only when the principal's wishes cannot be determined or inferred should the agent make decisions in accordance with a "best interests" analysis.

Financial wishes are best expressed through an estate plan, including integrated, durable powers of attorney, a will, and a living trust. These plan documents should reflect related family business plans, any history of gifts, management of assets, or desired support of family members or charities. Topics like continuing payments for in-home care, 24-hour nursing assistance, etc., may be addressed under a durable financial power of attorney.

It is important to address the possibility that the principal's assets will dwindle and the person making the financial decision may have a conflict of interest. For instance, it is not uncommon to see a child act as an agent for a parent. That child is legally required to spend the parent's funds on the parent's care, thereby dwindling the child's inheritance. The conflict is clearly seen in considering if the answers of a parent and the child differ in considering the care of a 77-year-old parent who has been declining after a stroke, falls, and breaks a hip. Should the parent get hip surgery after a fall? Should your parent, who is 73 and fighting late-stage cancer, benefit from an experimental drug that could have serious side effects at large out-of-pocket expense? For 40% of U.S. households, medical bills in the five years before death will exceed the financial assets.[114] As a result, these are conflicted and gut-wrenching decisions that can pit family members against each other. These scenarios will raise significant ethical concerns and quality of life considerations that are best addressed by the parent with full faculties well before this financial crisis emerges.

Advance Directives (Living Wills and Durable Power of Attorney for Health Care)

The law on advance directives started at least a century ago. It starts with the premise that something is much better than nothing. Oral exchanges are better than silence, letters are better than conversations, living wills are better than letters, and living wills combined with a durable power of attorney for health care are better than mere living wills. What the legally valid document (or documents) do is give leverage to the doctor who is trying to give voice to the patient's loved ones when the patient has suffered a catastrophic injury or a massive decline in organic function.

To put the matter slightly differently, a valid living will, or a valid living will in conjunction with a valid durable power of attorney for health care, permits the doctor to start the conversation with the loved ones in such a way that it is very likely to lead to consensus among the relevant parties as to the patient's

---

114   One out of every four Medicare dollars, more than $125 billion, is spent on services for the 5% of beneficiaries in their last year of life. Out-of-pocket expenses for Medicare recipients during the five years before their death averaged about $39,000 for individuals, $51,000 for couples, and up to $66,000 for people with long-term illnesses like Alzheimer's. "Many people are shocked by the high out-of-pocket health care costs near the end of life." Wang, P. (2012, December 12). *Cutting the high cost of End-of-Life care*. Money. https://money.com/cutting-the-high-cost-of-end-of-life-care/

care, and to do so soon. Most end-of-life decisions are made by doctors and agreed to by loved ones without the involvement of lawyers or judges. The proactive approach makes us look back to Nancy to address issues before they arise. To facilitate peaceful and appropriate end-of-life events, clients should address the issue in advance to equip the doctors and loved ones to act with valid legal documents that will, along with the client's medical condition at the time of the conversation, be the focal point of the decision-making process conversation.

One practical problem with advance directives is that they assume we can know how our loved ones or we would feel under life-ending circumstances, unlike our current circumstances. This problem suggests that we should give very careful thought to the selection of a suitable surrogate.

Although living wills, health care powers of attorney, or both are specifically authorized by statute in nearly every state, a few interstate pointers should be kept in mind:

- Not all states permit broad language in either document. Some states restrict the operation of advance directives to circumstances where the principal is terminally ill, for example, or purport to limit the agent's authority to remove life-sustaining treatment.

- Statutory form documents are almost always more restrictive than needed, even when the statutory authority is broad. Although the statutory forms may be useful in providing a bare minimum practice (mostly for those who choose not to seek legal advice), a more detailed, personalized document is almost certainly preferable.

- The statutory authority for advance directives should not be considered the only available authority. Indeed, if, for some reason, a state legislature should attempt to invalidate all advance directives, federal and state Constitutional principles, and the common law probably would prohibit such state action.

- The generic "living will" form (for example, the "Five Wishes" document widely promoted by a Florida-based non-profit, Aging with Dignity) can also be part of a client's estate plan. There are two schools of thought: on the one hand, using a document that is not state-specific and that might even conflict with lawyer-prepared advance directives creates an opportunity for confusion. On the other hand, it is undeniably true that tens of thousands of patients have completed the "Five Wishes" documents, and if this is a case of something is better than nothing, the fact the Five Wishes documents have been used in thousands of cases with effect could suffice in the most basic circumstance.

"Surrogacy" Statutes

This chapter espouses comprehensive, proactive planning involving loved ones and a clear plan for addressing succession questions if a family business is involved.[115] However, the reality is most people are not planning for health care decisions through legal documents, so it is worth mentioning that in many states, legislatures have grappled with the reality that most adult patients have not signed advance directives. For those patients no longer able to make decisions, state law may authorize someone, typically on a priority list based on degree of kinship, to make some or all health care decisions for a person no longer capable of making decisions for himself or herself, but who also lack a guardianship or signed advance directive.[116]

---

115   Binz Astrachan C., Waldkirch, M., Michiels, A., Pieper, T., & Bernhard, F. (2020). Professionalizing the Business Family: The Five Pillars of Competent, Committed, and Sustainable Ownership | What characterizes a professional — think capable of making informed decisions that benefit the family and the business — ownership group, and how can your family become one?

116   For example, in Illinois under 755 Illinois Compiled Statutes §40 a surrogacy for a patient is established. It applies to patients, including those who are in a "terminal condition," "permanent unconsciousness" or an "incurable or irreversible condition." It allows someone on the following list (in order) to make health care decisions (for those with one of the three above conditions, specifically including a decision to forego life-sustaining treatment) in an appropriate case: (1) The patient's guardian of the person; (2) The patient's spouse; (3) Any adult son or daughter of the patient; (4) Either parent of the patient; (5) Any adult brother or sister of the patient; (6) Any adult grandchild of the patient; (7) A close friend of the patient; and (8) The patient's guardian of the estate.

Developing an Estate Plan

With the ideal client, family members, and advisors will proactively address the changing and developing needs of the family and the business. For example, just like clothes that must be tailored to fit, the estate plan must be modified, amended, and adjusted to changing circumstances. Here is a simple checklist for consideration.

- Have a business transition plan.

- Develop the next generation.

- Decide who should inherit your assets and in what proportions.

- Decide who should care for your minor children, if you have any.

- Decide how much is needed for your children's care and education.

- Decide who should manage your financial affairs if you become incapacitated.

- Decide who should make health care decisions for you if you become incapacitated.

- Decide who should be responsible for distributing your assets.

- Develop your estate plan by meeting with an advisory team, including a lawyer, and put your estate plan into action.

- If you have an estate plan in place, review and update the plan as your situation changes or as current laws change.[117]

---

117   In 2024 families of wealth with a business or family office with investment management for their benefit are faced with unprecedented opportunities in transferring wealth and modifying plans to meet objectives. The *Inside the Minds: Best Practices for Structuring Trusts and Estates*, Aspatore Books, A Thomson Reuters business 2016 ed., provides a high level review on the foundation of estate planning comprised of a powers of attorney for property and health care, pour over Will and revocable living trust, using increased exemption amounts, portability of gift and estate exemption that was enacted into law and investment driven estate planning that provides powerful and unique opportunities for the transfer of wealth. Investment-driven estate planning is an especially powerful tool when the business is growing and expanding. For more basic checklists see https://www.ncoa.org/adviser/estate-planning/estate-planning-guide-checklist/ or https://www.kiplinger.com/retirement/estate-planning/602219/estate-planning-checklist-5-tasks-to-do-now-while-youre-still

A Cautionary Tale

A senior client reflects on the past and bemoans her and her husband's generosity, prompted by their attorney to give away the stock of the family business to their children when they were young. Today, as adults, the client says she gave away too much too soon to their progeny. Reflecting on what went wrong, she recounts how she had to fire her son from the family business. Each child had an equal opportunity to join the business with her, and while two washed out, one stayed away while one did join her to become the successor. Years later, after successfully transferring ownership in full to the children (even the one she fired), she sees her children, the sole owners of the business, sue each other in court; one child claims shareholder oppression against his older sibling who controls the business.

This was not a failure to plan. By many measures, it was a tremendously successful transition that avoided the maxim of "shirtsleeves to shirtsleeves." If we interviewed the estate planning lawyer, he would undoubtedly note the tremendous success of avoiding estate and gift taxes that was accomplished. While successful in various measures such as taxes, timing, and leadership succession, the transition was accompanied by unfortunate incidents of mental health lapses among the siblings. One child is an egomaniac. Another child is a substance abuser. There is another child who exhibits narcissistic tendencies. An egomaniac is obsessed with their own importance and believes they are superior to others. Narcissism, on the other hand, refers to a personality disorder characterized by a sense of entitlement, a lack of empathy, and an excessive need for admiration. (See Chapter 3 on Narcissism.) It is astonishing that these diverse personalities cooperated, functioned, and survived under one roof as they grew up. As adults, when they all converged in a legal entanglement, it typified why the need for legal counsel in America is not in decline. The fact is a tsunami of wealth is being transferred in the next few decades[118], and much of the wealth will involve ownership in a family business. This trend is fueling

---

118 York, D. R. (2022, June 28). *The coming $60 trillion wealth tsunami*. CEOWORLD Magazine. https://ceoworld.biz/2022/06/28/the-coming-60-trillion-wealth-tsunami

intra-family conflict, and those afflicted by a mental health condition and/or substance abuse will be involved.

Conclusion

This chapter began with the observation that "nothing is certain but death and taxes." Given their certainty, it is easy to understand that best practices plan for medical care in illness, incapacity, and dying. Because death and dying can be contentious and public, the mental deterioration that often precedes death for many people will be sad, inconvenient, undignified, adversarial, and in the public eye. But it does not have to be so. We can maximize efforts to keep our affairs private and civil through planning while we possess full capacity and before any significant diminishment in mental cognitive function. People do not plan to have a contentious and public incapacity court proceeding. Still, the failure to plan almost always ensures that what was desired and unexpressed will not be realized. Of course, planning does not guarantee results, and business interests owned by a family raise the stakes and likelihood of a dispute. Looking at Sumner Redstone, despite having more wealth than 99% of all Americans and an elaborate estate plan for his property and business, even he still had to participate in public proceedings in California and Delaware about his mental capacity and control of a publicly owned business.[119] Ultimately, what is in our control is to plan for and decide about the inevitable death by understanding our mental health.

Key Takeaways

Individual family members who own a business venture, some with control and others without, some employed and involved in the business and others

---

119 Cullins, A. (2019b, January 23). Sumner Redstone had capacity to change estate plan, judge rules. *The Holly-wood Reporter*. https://www.hollywoodreporter.com/business/business-news/sumner-redstone-had-capaci-ty-change-estate-plan-judge-rules-1178467/; James, M. (2018, December 18). Sumner Redstone is declared incapacitated. Court doesn't rule on media mogul's competency – Los Angeles Times. *Los Angeles Times*. https://www.latimes.com/business/hollywood/la-fi-ct-sumner-redstone-incapacitated-20181217-story.html; B Stewart, J., & Abrams, R. (2023). *Unscripted: The Epic Battle for a Media Empire and the Redstone Family Legacy*. Penguin Press., see also Foy, C. (2023b, February 21). *Are mental disorders increasing over time? | FHE Health*. FHE Health. https://fherehab.com/mental-health-disorders-increasing.

who are not involved, can all benefit from having a will and living will/ power of attorney for health care, no matter how small their estate or simple their wishes.

When working with a family business, it is increasingly common that advisors and family members will have to deal with addiction or mental capacity issues. Understanding family systems, as described in Chapter 2: Thriving Together, will aid in advising the constituency to get plans in place.

- Understanding the underpinnings of the law, we realize that the mental capacity to act is fundamental, and there are straightforward steps that promote family harmony and business succession. Family members will decide their wishes in binding documents, and they will appoint agents (many of whom will be agents that are other family members) to fulfill their wishes.

- Understanding that emergent situations that accompany most lack of capacity instances, the law determines decision-making. If there is controversy such that judicial intervention is necessary, it will be public, potentially undignified, and protracted.

- Proactive planning is a recommended best practice by advisors. When dealing with any family business, more often than not, there will also be mental health issues to address by advisors and family members.

CHAPTER TWELVE

Raising Sensitive Subjects

by Diana Clark, JD, MA

As consultants specializing in behavioral, mental, and cognitive health, my team and I are often given a wide berth at conference social hours. No one wants to talk to the "alcohol police" over cocktails. We were, therefore, surprised that Bill, an executive from a thriving family enterprise, approached us after our "Raising Sensitive Subjects" session and jokingly said, "Can I take six hours of your time today to describe the situation I find myself in with my company?"

Bill started by discussing the family system and couldn't talk fast enough. The family, most of whom were employed by the family business, was rife with difficulties, including depression, substance use disorders, overspending, adults who failed to launch, and a matriarch who was showing signs of cognitive decline. However, the biggest concern at that moment was Chuck, a 38-year-old who recently appeared at the office dressed in fatigues with a hunting rifle and appeared agitated in his speech and demeanor. Bill wanted to address the whole family system's health and wellness, but his immediate concern was ensuring that Chuck wasn't a risk to himself or others.

Several red flags were apparent when we asked more questions about Chuck's history. Once employed by the enterprise, Chuck left months earlier in events shrouded in secrecy, and even Bill was not privy to the details despite his executive status. Chuck had long-standing addiction issues and a strong genetic predisposition towards substance use. He began using alcohol and marijuana at age 14, and the data shows that individuals who start using at that age have a 47 percent chance of developing an addictive disorder later in life. (Those who first use at the age of 21 have a 10 percent chance.)[120]

Chuck's dad, Bobby, was a successful serial entrepreneur who created enough wealth for the family to live for generations but died in his early 60s from medical complications due to chronic alcohol use. It wasn't a huge surprise to hear that Chuck's brother, John, also struggled with alcoholism.

We also learned from Bill that the family shunned clinical involvement: "He is from a very recognizable family name in a small town, and the whole family is concerned with preserving their image. They spend more of their efforts trying to look good instead of looking at the genuine problems with their family members. They are the largest donors to the local hospital system, where most services like therapists and psychiatrists are located." Indeed, Chuck was brought to the local hospital for evaluation after drunkenly hitting a tree with his automobile and was immediately seen and given a "pass" by the hospital doctors when Chuck said that his recent car crash was a "one-off mistake." The doctors, Chuck, and the family all colluded to downplay the acuity of Chuck's recent episode. Nothing changed with Chuck's behavior. Chuck's story is not uncommon. It is only one of many examples of conversations families avoid, particularly families tied together by both love and business.

Substance Use Disorders are not the only commonly occurring issues left undiscussed that get worse as a result. Others include eating disorders, hoarding, compulsive behaviors such as gambling, psychosis, destructive relationships, and spending. Stigma and the fear it generates are barriers for the people needing care to come forward, and their families, fearful as well, often walk on eggshells supporting the stance. Similarly, and importantly, given the ages of baby boomers, cognitive decline and dementia disorders are also left

---

120   Hingson, R. W., Heeren, T., & Winter, M. R. (2006). Age at drinking onset and alcohol dependence. *Archives of Pediatrics & Adolescent Medicine, 160*(7), 739. https://doi.org/10.1001/archpedi.160.7.739

undiscussed by family members and a large percentage of medical professionals. This silence exacerbates the sense of isolation and despair.

In family businesses where those suffering may have integral roles in the enterprise's success, silence is problematic from an operational and emotional standpoint. Conflict among family members tends to surface when concerns are avoided, and other enterprise employees begin to lose confidence. Beyond the pragmatic concerns of employee retention problems and stalled enterprise growth, the emotional costs are high. Simply stated, silence only promotes isolation for those struggling and creates fertile ground for the other family members' mental unwellness. It is estimated that for every person struggling with a mental health disorder, four others are struggling as well with higher rates of anxiety and mood disorders, often appearing more emotionally volatile than the individual with the actual disorder.

Notwithstanding these pitfalls of silence and the likelihood of the need to have difficult conversations, it is the rare person or family member who feels confident in the task. We, therefore, tend to avoid it. A classic example is a child's avoidance of meaningful conversations despite symptoms of a parent's decline. Instead of taking steps towards addressing the uncomfortable, they often focus on reasons to avoid:

- "Mom still plays tennis and volunteers; her drinking can't be that bad."

- "We talk to one another; my grandmother does not need to see a professional."

- "My brother feels bad for Dad and doesn't want to embarrass him by bringing this up."

- "I fear how my mother will react when raising this issue with her."

- "He still is a maven at sales—we would lose business without him."

- "He just works hard and plays hard."

Often, the people closest to the person in need of help are so steeped in the dailiness of the symptoms and avoiding crisis that they are the least equipped to see the large picture or are so terrified of rocking the boat that everyone stays silent. While those who specialize in the treatment of substance use disorders might use the word enabling to describe the silence, a kinder, perhaps more nuanced word is "protecting." In that case, the family member, advisor, medical professional, or employer seeks to protect the status quo or that person's reputation, ego, or self-image through silence or other compensating behaviors, which leaves the issue unaddressed. Simply put; by seeking to protect the individual from discomfort, we are protecting the dysfunction and the disorder.

Prepare for the Likely

In our consultant's vision of well-being, we should all have a plan for the inevitable. The "Not in my family" prerogative is disproved by statistics. We may not be struggling (now), but the likelihood that a family member will face mental health challenges in the future is alarmingly high. In an ideal world, therefore, families in general, particularly those whose financial and emotional well-being are integrally tied, would develop a plan that addresses concerns and challenges when they arise.

The elements of the plan should include:

- Selection of the professional(s) to coordinate the process and facilitate future discussions

- Development of a list of genetic predispositions and mental health challenges, both current and historical

- A professionally curated and frequently updated list of potential professional resources with expertise in those predispositions

- Organization of a team composed of a professional facilitator, no more than five interested family members, and a non-family member with the gravitas and insight into the family to offer more objective insight

- Schedule regular meetings with a cadence of four times per year in non-crisis periods and more frequently during active concern.

The team's role in the family system is to become facile with uncomfortable conversations when emotions are calm so that when emotions are heightened during a crisis, the process for a difficult discussion is already developed, and the potential options for care are readily accessible.

An agenda for such a council might sound like:

1. Current family/business news

2. Concerns for individual and family wellbeing

3. Possible strategies to address the concern

4. Resources needed and approach

Having the Conversation

While outside professional assistance often enhances the outcomes of difficult conversations, for those individuals seeking to have fewer formal forums for communication or for those who feel compelled to go it alone, we recommend the following steps:

Gather Data

Like attorneys going into court, emotionally charged conversations are best done when we are well-prepared with the facts. Here is a checklist that can help determine whether it is time to speak up:

- An individual's substance use has increased in severity as to kind and or frequency.

- Their social culture supports the frequent use of substances, including alcohol.

- They suffered legal consequences for their use of substances.

- They are dressing and talking in uncharacteristic ways.

- They display confusion or disorientation.

- There is a new overreaction to challenges and a need for coping skills.

- They are isolated from those closest to them.

- They exhibit signs of significant weight loss.

- They are spending in ways that are excessive or uncharacteristic.

- They are missing scheduled meetings or visits.

- They no longer respond punctually to phone outreaches.

- Their job performance has declined.

- They exhibit noticeable changes in mood or temperament.

- They reveal a sense of paranoia, increased suspiciousness, or uncharacteristic grandiosity.

- They show a new loss of usual tact or uncharacteristically uninhibited behavior.

- There is a new relationship that is uncharacteristically close.

Determine Who Will Participate

Approaching anyone with information suggesting an untreated substance use disorder or other mental or cognitive health condition is likely to be met with resistance and often anger. After all, when we are either frightened or seeking to protect the status quo, the best defense can be an offense. Therefore, the initiator (s) must be well-prepared for all possible responses.

In our practice, we often suggest that the "willing" person seek a second person to aid the conversation and support the intended goal. This third person in the conversation can mitigate the possibility that it gets misdirected from the purpose. As a consultant who regularly facilitated difficult conversations, I was often confronted with the ingenuity of resistance. Ancient wounds were revealed, blame sprayed, and tears shed, all to avoid the difficult change. Therefore, anyone making such an effort needs to be well-prepared and well-fortified. Moreover, the conversation initiators must be able to come from a place of goodwill, compassion, and, if possible, love.

Determining who is the most appropriate emissary is also not simple. For example, if a parent is struggling, their children, regardless of age, may not be the best person to approach. The parent/child relationship has a power differential that may result in failure to listen and hurt the child. Sometimes, a dear old friend is the best person; sometimes, it is a business partner. Boiled down when enlisting the emissary, the primary consideration should be selecting the people who will most be heard as loving or wise voices.

A voice outside the family is often best positioned to name the difficulties and suggest resources for help. For example, trustees regularly confide in my team and me that one of their most difficult tasks is not the protection or investment of the trust corpus. Instead, it is to protect the trust from the beneficiaries who would use it for purposes well outside the grantor's intended scope. They feel it is incumbent upon them to raise the problem or be accused of trust mismanagement later.

Ben was one such trustee. He was responsible for managing a multi-generational trust without precise parameters yet had a strong belief that he understood the grantor's intentions. When one of the trust beneficiaries, 26-year-old Emma, was showing concerning signs of a mental health crisis, he called for advice. He described a once lively young woman who did well in college, had ambitions to be a writer, and had a full social life deteriorate over the last several months. Lately, he heard rumblings from other family members that she had cut them off and refused to see them without any apparent reason for the break. In the preceding month, she emailed her family, stating that she was working on herself and that they shouldn't expect to hear from her for a while. Ben also relayed that her once reliable personality had done a 180-degree turn. She was now missing appointments with him, and when she did show up, he observed she had lost a great deal of weight and was very thin even by current standards. Ben became concerned and called us. He was in a quandary about what to do. We wrestled with the options:

- Call Emma's parents and seek to get more information about their observations of Emma and collaborate in a conversation or

- Have the conversation with her trust team and her.

In either event, Ben was committed to acting. He relayed that the family was angrier than they were concerned by the changes in Emma and didn't think they could table that resentment to have a productive conversation. Upon hearing about the fractures in those relationships and the absence of other obvious supportive ones, we suggested Ben prepare himself and his team for the uncomfortable discussion.

In family enterprises, the non-family executives or advisors often highlight the need for action and are willing to be part of a plan. For example, we received a call from Roger, the president of a successful boutique packaging enterprise started by Audrey. With Roger's help, Audrey began the business when her five children, now aged 25 to 32, were young. Fast forward 15 years: All were out of college, and four of the five were actively employed in the business. The fifth, Alex, was happily engaged elsewhere. The older two children, Anne and Thomas, flourished at work, and the relationship with Audrey and Roger was comfortable and collegial. The other two, Everett, age 29, and Kira, age 26, were doing less well. Everett hated his job and regularly arrived hours behind the remainder of the employees, disheveled and smelling of marijuana. Kira struggled with a depressive disorder and regularly missed long stretches of work, and her assignments often fell to other employees on the team. Audrey acknowledged to Roger that while she is a skilled and direct business negotiator with others, she tends to placate her children. After a rare but contentious conversation between Roger and Audrey, Audrey agreed to seek assistance.

We met with Audrey and Roger, listened to the situation, and asked: What conversations about work performance have been initiated with Everett and Kira? Audrey replied sheepishly that she often began conversations with Everett, but he responded angrily about the unfairness of life, and she dropped the issue and changed the subject. Her conversations with Kira were softer yet equally unproductive. Both needed therapeutic help, but it was never recommended nor sought. Roger, the invested observer, relayed that critical employees outside of the family constellation are resentful and complain openly to Roger and are exploring other employment opportunities. Audrey was similarly frustrated with her children's work performance. However, both Roger and Audrey seemed to be missing the critical issue. While the issues of Everett and Kira surfaced at work, each struggled with an untreated mental health issue, and without support or direct conversations, they were unlikely to improve. We strongly suggested that the focus be redirected to Everett's and Kira's mental health struggles. Roger volunteered to join Audrey in these conversations but asked for advice about approaching the subject.

The result: Conversations with Everett and Kira were productive, and each agreed to accept support. Everett made the decision to leave the company and seek employment elsewhere, and Kira was prescribed medication that reduced her symptoms of depression, and her work performance drastically improved.

Plan the Approach

Sensitive conversations require forethought. While criticized in recent years as potentially harmful when misused or ill-facilitated, the formal process of a surprise "Intervention" as a tool to address substance use disorders follows a fairly thorough planning rubric, much of which is transferable to other types of conversations, namely:

- Development of a formal team of individuals with the ability to present care and concern without anger or an alternate agenda to a struggling individual and follow the recommendations and direction of a facilitator

- Ascertainment of appropriate resources for the mental, behavioral, or cognitive health concern and verification of costs, admission practices, and availability

- Scheduled dates for the pre-intervention meeting (s) designed to provide psychoeducation about the disorder and allow the participants an opportunity to express concerns and doubts

- Clear advisement on how to approach and format for approach

- Scheduled date, time, and place of the meeting with the struggling individual

- Identification of logistical needs, including airline tickets, intake at selected program completed, and financial arrangements made

The format of the statements in a formal intervention often uses letters for communication. A letter is written by the concerned individuals and read to the struggling one during a formal intervention meeting. While the exact format differs depending on the interventionist/facilitator, common elements include:

- Statements of care and love

- A description of witnessed concerning events or behavior

- A request to accept the help offered

- A statement of healthy boundaries

In times of less urgency, or when a formal meeting using letters is clinically inappropriate due to trauma, psychosis, previous bad experience, or many other reasons, the following may be helpful when initiating a sticky conversation:

- **Ask permission to raise a sensitive subject.** In our experience, the person receiving the information is less likely to find it an intrusion if asked, as it allows them to ready themselves for something difficult. While some family members have argued that this only gives them time to build up a defense, our experience differs. It could sound like:

  "May I raise a sensitive subject?" Or "I think we're close enough for me to raise a sensitive subject. Is that true?" Or "Is there a good time for us to sit down and have a serious conversation?"

- **Verbalize concern and compassion.** Starting with a destigmatizing statement like the following is helpful: "Everybody is so stressed these days. How are you coping?" Or "I'm worried about your stress level (isolation or mood)." Or "Hey, I see that you are struggling, and I don't want you to struggle alone." Or "It's not in my definition of care to let you struggle without offering support or help."

- **Normalize the situation.** The expression "Every family/person has something" is true in our experience. With affluent and or high-achieving families, this is particularly true. While affluence can be a gift to afford the best care, the stigma attached might be greater or the resistance deeper for those with means or success. Here are some sample expressions to normalize the situation: "I know many families, and every family has its issues." Or "Everybody struggles at one time or another."

- **Offer help.** Expressions of care, love, and concern may prompt temporary vulnerability and willingness to accept support. Unfortunately, the window of openness is often short-lived, and the force of the status quo is mighty. Therefore, we highly recommend the conversation be accompanied by suggestions of resources or other offers of help to enhance the odds that the conversation will be productive. Here are a few ways to express this: "I'd like to help you with this, and I sourced some names of people and organizations that could be a resource for you." Or "I'm not surprised you are struggling with this issue given your genetics, and I have researched some options." Or "I'd like for us to go see a specialist. I've made an appointment. Will you join me?"

- **Anticipate resistance.** It is a rare person who can be presented with concern and not get defensive, at least momentarily. Our approach is that this is the moment when silence is our friend. Allow the resistance. Then you might say: "I might be angry too if I were in your position." Or "I know this makes you angry, and that's okay. I care about you enough to withstand that." Or "I hear that I should look in the mirror, and I will do that, but today we are here about you." Or "Your anger frightens me but doesn't change the truth that you need help." Or "What would need to happen for you to feel comfortable making a change?"

- **Request they accept the help offered.** Once emotions run high, the purpose of the meeting often gets lost. Having resources ready and possible support contacted before the meeting counter this. Ways to address this include: "Let's see if we can get this professional on the line while we're together," "Can I schedule an appointment?" and "Will you accept the help offered?"

- **Use the crisis as an opportunity.** One way to express this is: "This experience seemed to have scared you. Could we now explore treatment options?"

Consideration: Using a Professional Facilitator

Conversations without professional support are often less successful, and the family or enterprise remains stuck. Those families tend not just to have business repercussions but also family strife. For example, Andrew and his four brothers, Tim, Bob, and David, began a successful computer sales and repair company 20 years ago. Each brother brought a specific skill to the enterprise: Andrew managed contracts and finance, Tim managed the repair division, Bob managed installation, and David managed sales.

A gifted salesperson, David traveled extensively and was wining and dining potential clients multiple days per week. After ten years of success, the brothers noted a sales drop and diminished enthusiasm for the work. At first, they attributed the performance issues as a result of a contentious divorce, but when the issue continued well past that, they decided to explore other reasons. David's ex-wife had always claimed that alcohol use disorder was the issue between them. Still, the brothers ignored those claims despite his successful sales career and thought she was just a dramatic Harridan, as David asserted. Then David was stopped by police for erratic driving with his children in the car. This event triggered not only legal and parental ramifications but also highlighted for the brothers that alcohol was, in fact, an issue. Unaided by professional advice, they confronted him with anger, demanding he stop drinking or leave the company. He capitulated in the meeting but didn't change his behavior. He continued to drink but switched to a less noticeable beverage and tried to hide it.

Two years later, Andrew called back and asked if we could meet again. He explained that David continued to drink and was now showing up in the office intoxicated. Other employees were concerned and angry; his children no longer spoke to him. When asked whether he had received help for his alcohol use disorder, they said no and relayed that he refused, as demanded, to go to Alcoholics Anonymous. The brothers were now considering legal action to buy out David's share, and this once successful enterprise was in shambles.

We suggested one more try at a conversation with David before a legal division of the asset. We proposed a professionally facilitated conversation between David and the rest of the brothers to provide David with appropriate support, including residential treatment. We explained that simply demanding change without providing clinical support is only a partial measure. They agreed, and we facilitated the meeting. David accepted the help and later relayed that despite the discomfort at again being the identified focus in the room, this time felt different, and the experience was more one of care and concern than blame and shame.

Key Takeaways

- Silence does more than promote stigma and delay. With behavioral and cognitive health issues, the unaddressed can lead to exacerbation of problems, harm to family members, and foster frustration and conflict among all interested parties.

- Casual conversations without planning and forethought can lead to relationship ruptures instead of intended outcomes and make a thoughtful encounter more difficult in the future.

- Professional facilitators can add messaging direction, facilitation of challenging conversations and aid in the development of a thoughtful plan of care.

- Thoughtful planning, including the who, what to say, and how to help, can turn the tide and lead to more open, healthy discussions and lasting change.

CHAPTER THIRTEEN

Concluding Thoughts: Research on Mental Health in Family Businesses: What Do We Know, and Where Should We Go?

by Anneleen Michiels, PhD and Torsten M. Pieper, PhD

Mental health is important for every individual and organization, and family businesses are no exception. Indeed, *"mental health conditions have profound implications not only for the individual and their family, but also their business."*[121] The dual nature of family businesses, blending family and business systems, can exacerbate and mitigate mental health challenges, as noted in studies exploring the unique stressors and supports within family businesses.[122] The overlap introduces specific stressors, such as succession planning and role conflicts, which can heighten mental health risks.[123] On the flip side, the familial aspect of these enterprises can foster strong support networks, promoting resilience and mental well-being.[124]

Despite the growing recognition of this issue (73% of all studies identified by Arijs and Michiels were published after 2010), research remains

121 Tetzlaff, E., Jaskiewicz, P., & Wiklund, J. (2023). Implications of mental health for business families and family businesses: Toward a holistic research agenda. In (Vol. 36, pp. 284-295): SAGE Publications Sage CA: Los Angeles, CA.

122 Distelberg, B., & Blow, A. (2010). The role of values and unity in family businesses. *Journal of Family and Economic Issues, 31*, 427-441.

123 Kets de Vries, M. F., & Miller, D. (1984). Neurotic style and organizational pathology. *Strategic Management Journal, 5*(1), 35-55.

124 Danes, S. M., Stafford, K., Haynes, G., & Amarapurkar, S. S. (2009). Family capital of family firms: Bridging human, social, and financial capital. *Family Business Review, 22*(3), 199-215.

fragmented. Studies call for a more comprehensive understanding of mental health within family businesses, emphasizing the need for an interdisciplinary approach to unravel the complexities involved.[125] Recent review and conceptual articles on the topic by Miller, Wiklund, and Yu[126], Arijs and Michiels[127], and Tetzlaff et al.[128] all identify a significant gap in empirical research and theory development in this area.

In this chapter, we seek to consolidate current knowledge, identify research gaps, and propose directions for future studies, providing a foundational perspective on mental health in family business contexts. Addressing these mental health challenges is imperative for practitioners, researchers, and policymakers, given the unique position of family businesses straddling personal well-being and organizational health.

Where Are We Now? Understanding the Family Business Context

The context of a business family and a family business introduces unique dynamics that are likely to affect mental health significantly. Emotional bonds intertwine with business decisions in a family business where members often occupy overlapping roles as family and business stakeholders.[129] Additionally, addressing mental health concerns within the family business context is challenging, as it may provoke conflicts that affect not just the business but also personal and familial relationships and individual well-being. While families

---

125   Strike, V. M. (2012). Advising the family firm: Reviewing the past to build the future. *Family Business Review, 25*(2), 156-177.

126   Miller, D., Wiklund, J., & Yu, W. (2020). Mental health in the family business: A conceptual model and a research agenda. *Entrepreneurship Theory and Practice, 44*(1), 55-80.

127   Arijs, D., & Michiels, A. (2021). Mental health in family businesses and business families: A systematic review. *International Journal of Environmental Research and Public Health, 18*(5), 2589-2589.

128   Tetzlaff, E., Jaskiewicz, P., & Wiklund, J. (2023). Implications of mental health for business families and family businesses: Toward a holistic research agenda. In (Vol. 36, pp. 284-295): SAGE Publications Sage CA: Los Angeles, CA.

129   Jaskiewicz, P., & Rau, S. B. (2021). *Enabling next generation legacies: 35 questions that next generation members in enterprising families ask*: Family Enterprise Knowledge Hub Publishing.

can be supportive resources in mental health recovery, [130;131] the privacy valued by business families[132] often leads to underreporting of mental health issues. This secrecy can perpetuate stigma and hinder recovery, negatively impacting the individual, the family, and the family business.[133]

This unique context also means that we cannot just extrapolate findings on the prevalence and consequences on mental health conditions from either family psychology or management literature to the family business context. For instance, the overlapping roles of family members can lead to role ambiguity, increasing stress, and potentially leading to burnout or other mental health issues.[134] Also, succession issues might generate psychological stress and anxiety among siblings.[135] This complexity is compounded by the emotional attachment of family members to the business, often expressed through the socioemotional wealth perspective, which posits that family members value the emotional returns from their business involvement, sometimes even more than financial gains.[136]

Current State of Knowledge

In addressing the current state of knowledge on mental health in business families and family businesses, we observe a dispersed landscape, and little is known about the unique antecedents and consequences of mental health

130 Crowe, A., & Lyness, K. P. (2014). Family functioning, coping, and distress in families with serious mental illness. *The Family Journal, 22*(2), 186-197.

131 Lucksted, A., McFarlane, W., Downing, D., & Dixon, L. (2012). Recent developments in family psychoeducation as an evidence-based practice. *Journal of Marital and Family Therapy, 38*(1), 101-121.

132 Bork, D. (1986). *Family business, risky business*. AMACOM, American Management Association.

133 Tetzlaff, E., Jaskiewicz, P., & Wiklund, J. (2023). Implications of mental health for business families and family businesses: Toward a holistic research agenda. In (Vol. 36, pp. 284-295): SAGE Publications Sage CA: Los Angeles, CA.

134 Distelberg, B., & Blow, A. (2010). The role of values and unity in family businesses. *Journal of Family and Economic Issues, 31*, 427-441.

135 Zheng, V. (2002). Inheritance, Chinese family business and economic development in Hong Kong. *Journal of Enterprising Culture, 10*(04), 287-312.

136 Gomez-Mejia, L. R., Cruz, C., Berrone, P., & De Castro, J. (2011). The bind that ties: Socioemotional wealth preservation in family firms. *Academy of Management Annals, 5*(1), 653-707.

conditions in family businesses (see also recent review articles by Tetzlaff et al.[137] and Arijs and Michiels.[138] As mentioned above, although research from family psychology and family therapy on the relationship between family dynamics and mental health conditions and management and entrepreneurship research on mental health conditions in the workplace can be informative, we cannot expect the findings to be similar in a context where family and business systems overlap.

Some studies have pointed to the prevalence of mental health issues in family businesses, where the line between the personal and professional is inherently blurred. For instance, research indicates a heightened vulnerability to stress and anxiety due to the overlapping spheres of family and business.[139] These dynamics are compounded by the expectations of maintaining socio-emotional wealth the non-financial aspects of the firm that meet the family's affective needs, which can either buffer against or exacerbate mental health issues.[140] For example, the idea of carrying on a long-lasting family legacy may instill passion and pride among some successors. But the same idea may cause great levels of anxiety and stress among others.

The impact of mental health on business performance and family well-being cannot be overstated. The double ABCX model of family stress, originally developed by sociologist Reuben Hill[141] to understand how families cope with stress and adapt to it, has been adapted to the family business context to explain how business-related stressors can affect family well-being and vice versa

---

137   Tetzlaff, E., Jaskiewicz, P., & Wiklund, J. (2023). Implications of mental health for business families and family businesses: Toward a holistic research agenda. In (Vol. 36, pp. 284-295): SAGE Publications Sage CA: Los Angeles, CA.

138   Arijs, D., & Michiels, A. (2021). Mental health in family businesses and business families: A systematic review. *International Journal of Environmental Research and Public Health, 18*(5), 2589-2589.

139   Distelberg, B., & Blow, A. (2010). The role of values and unity in family businesses. *Journal of Family and Economic Issues, 31*, 427-441.

140   Berrone, P., Cruz, C., & Gomez-Mejia, L. R. (2012). Socioemotional wealth in family firms: Theoretical dimensions, assessment approaches, and agenda for future research. *Family Business Review, 25*(3), 258-279.

141   Hill, R. (1958). Generic features of families under stress. *Social Casework, 39*(2-3), 139-150.

(Miller et al., 2020).[142] The model has been instrumental in understanding this interplay, positing that the accumulation of stressors (A), combined with the family's resources (B) and perception of the stressors (C), lead to a range of adaptive outcomes (X).[143] This model helps us understand how families in business appraise and respond to mental health challenges, often navigating complex emotional landscapes to maintain business continuity and family harmony.

Emerging research has begun to map the types of mental health issues prevalent in family businesses, with studies pointing to a spectrum that ranges from mood and anxiety disorders to substance abuse and burnout. The research and theoretical models available, such as the socioemotional wealth and double ABCX model, provide a foundational understanding but also highlight the need for more in-depth studies that address the heterogeneity of family businesses and the various cultural contexts in which they operate. In synthesizing existing research, it becomes evident that families and family businesses possess unique characteristics that demand bespoke mental health strategies and interventions. The academic community has made some strides in documenting and theorizing these phenomena. Yet, there remains an imperative for ongoing empirical research to deepen our understanding and provide evidence-based guidance for practitioners.

Antecedents and Consequences

Understanding the antecedents and consequences of mental health issues within business families and family businesses is essential to developing effective interventions. These **antecedents** can often be traced to the unique pressures of overlapping family and business roles and systems. Everyday stressors

---

142 Miller, D., Wiklund, J., & Yu, W. (2020). Mental health in the family business: A conceptual model and a research agenda. *Entrepreneurship Theory and Practice, 44*(1), 55-80.

143 McCubbin, H. I., & Patterson, J. M. (2014). The family stress process: The double ABCX model of adjustment and adaptation. In *Social stress and the family* (pp. 7-37): Routledge.

include the high expectations for succession, the burden of legacy, the complexities of managing interpersonal family dynamics within a professional setting, or not achieving goals.[144;145;146] The intergenerational transfer of leadership and ownership, for instance, is a particularly poignant phase, replete with emotional and operational challenges that can precipitate stress and anxiety.[147;148] A recent study by Clark, Wittmer, and Jones[149] highlights the unique struggles of family business leaders who are owners and family members and the important role of workaholism in the work-family dynamics of these individuals. Employing family members who suffer from a medical disorder can be the motivation for some individuals to start family businesses, and some findings indicate that owners who employ other family members experience significantly higher levels of work-family conflict.[150] Finally, some studies have focused on adolescents working in the family business and found that this is associated with less drug and alcohol use[151] and a greater sense of psychological well-being.[152]

The **consequences** of such stressors are manifold, impacting not only the individuals but the business as a whole. On a personal level, these can manifest as mental health disorders such as depression or anxiety. In contrast, on a

---

144   Astrachan, J. H., & Jaskiewicz, P. (2008). Emotional returns and emotional costs in privately held family businesses: Advancing traditional business valuation. *Family Business Review, 21*(2), 139-149.

145   Davis, P. S., & Harveston, P. D. (2001). The phenomenon of substantive conflict in the family firm: A cross-generational study. *Journal of Small Business Management, 39*(1), 14-30.

146   Sharma, P., & Irving, P. G. (2005). Four bases of family business successor commitment: Antecedents and consequences. *Entrepreneurship Theory and Practice, 29*(1), 13-33.

147   Handler, W. C. (1994). Succession in family business: A review of the research. *Family Business Review, 7*(2), 133-157.

148   Zheng, V. (2002). Inheritance, Chinese family business and economic development in Hong Kong. *Journal of Enterprising Culture, 10*(04), 287-312.

149   Clark, M. A., Wittmer, J. L., & Jones, A. (2023). When business is personal: A mixed methods examination of workaholism in family business leaders. *Community, Work & Family*, 1-23.

150   Boles, J. S. (1996). Influences of work-family conflict on job satisfaction, life satisfaction and quitting intentions among business owners: The case of family-operated businesses. *Family Business Review, 9*(1), 61-74.

151   Hansen, D. M., & Jarvis, P. A. (2000). Adolescent employment and psychosocial outcomes - A comparison of two employment contexts. *Youth & Society, 31*(4), 417-436.

152   Houshmand, M., Seidel, M. D. L., & Ma, D. G. (2017). The impact of adolescent work in family business on child-parent relationships and psychological well-being. *Family Business Review, 30*(3), 242-261.

business level, they may result in diminished performance, lower employee morale, and, in severe cases, business failure.[153;154;155] The emotional toll on family relationships can be substantial, often leading to conflict, reduced cohesion, and, in some cases, complete familial estrangement.[156]

A range of factors can either mitigate or exacerbate the impact of these stressors on mental health in family businesses. Family dynamics, characterized by strong kinship ties and shared values, can play a protective role, fostering resilience and providing emotional support during challenging times.[157] Conversely, dysfunctional family relations can heighten stress and impede effective coping mechanisms.[158]

The culture within the family business also serves as a moderating factor. Businesses that promote open communication, emotional intelligence, and a supportive work environment can create a buffer against mental health issues.[159] Furthermore, adopting formal governance structures, such as family councils and boards, can help clarify expectations and roles, reducing ambiguity and conflict. [160;161;162]

---

153 Kets de Vries, M. F. (1991). *Organizations on the couch: Clinical perspectives on organizational behavior and change.* Jossey-Bass.

154 Kets de Vries, M. F., Carlock, R., & Florent-Treacy, E. (2007). Family business on the couch. *UK: Wiley Online Library.*

155 Kets de Vries, M. F., & Miller, D. (1984). Neurotic style and organizational pathology. *Strategic Management Journal, 5*(1), 35-55.

156 Davis, P. S., & Harveston, P. D. (2001). The phenomenon of substantive conflict in the family firm: A cross-generational study. *Journal of Small Business Management, 39*(1), 14-30.

157 Zellweger, T. M., Eddleston, K. A., & Kellermanns, F. W. (2010). Exploring the concept of familiness: Introducing family firm identity. *Journal of Family Business Strategy, 1*(1), 54-63.

158 Kidwell, R. E., Kellermanns, F. W., & Eddleston, K. A. (2012). Harmony, justice, confusion, and conflict in family firms: Implications for ethical climate and the "Fredo effect". *Journal of Business Ethics, 106,* 503-517.

159 Miller, D., Wiklund, J., & Yu, W. (2020). Mental health in the family business: A conceptual model and a research agenda. *Entrepreneurship Theory and Practice, 44*(1), 55-80.

160 Neubauer, F., & Lank, A. G. (2016). *The family business: Its governance for sustainability.* Springer.

161 Qiu, H., & Freel, M. (2020). Managing family-related conflicts in family businesses: A review and research agenda. *Family Business Review, 33*(1), 90-113.

162 Suess, J. (2014). Family governance–Literature review and the development of a conceptual model. *Journal of Family Business Strategy, 5*(2), 138-155.

Strategies employed by business families and family businesses to cope with mental health challenges are diverse. These include seeking external advice from psychologists and business advisors, implementing formal mental health policies, and investing in employee well-being programs. Recognizing and addressing mental health proactively benefits the individuals involved and can enhance business performance and sustainability.[163]

Where Should We Go from Here?

While Strides have been made, significant research gaps persist in understanding and treating mental health in family businesses. One such area is the long-term impact of mental health issues on the sustainability of family firms. The nuanced ways these issues influence succession planning and intergenerational leadership transfer still need to be explored. Additionally, the intersection of culture, gender, and mental health in family business settings is ripe for investigation, especially across diverse geographic and economic contexts. Future research should also examine the efficacy of specific mental health interventions within the family business context. Methodologically, longitudinal studies could yield insights into the chronicity and evolution of mental health challenges. Qualitative approaches could provide depth to the understanding of individual and collective experiences of mental health within family firms.

The call for interdisciplinary approaches is strong, urging the integration of psychological, sociological, and business management perspectives. Empirical studies employing mixed methods can offer a more holistic view, capturing the complexity of mental health in these unique business environments.

For practitioners, the implications are clear: There is a need for proactive mental health strategies tailored to the family business context. Owners,

---

163   Miller, D., Wiklund, J., & Yu, W. (2020). Mental health in the family business: A conceptual model and a research agenda. *Entrepreneurship Theory and Practice, 44*(1), 55-80.

managers, and advisors should consider implementing regular mental health assessments and creating an open dialogue about mental well-being. Such strategies include developing family business-specific mental health resources and training programs. Promoting mental health and well-being in family businesses requires a multifaceted approach. This may involve establishing clear boundaries between family and business roles, creating formal support structures for those facing mental health challenges, and fostering a culture prioritizing psychological safety and emotional intelligence. Incorporating these practices will address the immediate well-being of family members and employees but will also serve as a strategic investment in the long-term health and viability of the business family itself.

Conclusion

The family system that empowers these enterprises can be both an advantage and a source of distress, necessitating a balance that respects the individual's well-being and the collective business character. The journey towards understanding and addressing mental health in family businesses is incomplete. The path forward calls for rigorous and multidisciplinary research coupled with practical applications tailored to the distinctive needs of business families.

For practitioners, this chapter serves as a call to action. It is an invitation to incorporate mental health into the business strategy and build resilient frameworks supporting individual, family, and business health. As family businesses continue to be a cornerstone of the global economy, their success and longevity will increasingly hinge on their members' mental and emotional fortitude.

Author Biographies

Ellen Astrachan-Fletcher, PhD, FAED, CEDS-S

Ellen Astrachan-Fletcher, PhD, FAED, CEDS-S, is Regional Clinical Director at Eating Recovery Center and Pathlight Mood and Anxiety Center. She is a lecturer at the Feinberg School of Medicine, Northwestern University and Associate Professor of Psychiatry at UIC. She has 30 years of clinical and teaching experience in the field. She is a nationally recognized expert in the field of DBT and RO DBT and is a frequent presenter at national conferences. She co-authored *The Dialectical Behavior Therapy Skills Workbook for Bulimia: Using DBT to Break the Cycle and Regain Control of Your Life* (2009), which is used at eating disorders treatment facilities throughout the country. She also recently co-authored the *Radically Open DBT Workbook for Eating Disorders: From Overcontrol and Loneliness to Recovery and Connection* (2022).

Joseph H. Astrachan, PhD

Chairman of Generation6 Family Enterprise Advisors, Joe's family-owned businesses, including Meindersma, (Dutch pharma) and the Seatrain Lines. He is former Editor of *Family Business Review* and *Journal of Family Business Strategy*, has over 40 years of experience working with business families in over 60 countries, and has sat on the boards of 22 family businesses, currently serving on 11. Joe is Emeritus Professor of Management at Kennesaw State University, has academic affiliations at Cornell, JIBS, and Witten/Herdecke, and received many awards for research and service. Joe earned BA, MA, MPhil and PhD degrees from Yale.

Diana Clark, JD, MA

President of Intent Clinical. She is a renowned family recovery advocate in mental health and behavioral health treatment. She has developed and facilitated numerous workshops for family members and professionals and also authored a coordinating book *"Addiction Recovery: A Family's Journey"* specifically designed for family members of those struggling with substance use disorders and mental health concerns. As both a specialist in family systems and parenting she is a recognized force of clear speech, logic and loving acceptance, and has helped thousands of family members establish healthy boundaries, manage expectations appropriately, and develop plans for their families.

R. Trent Codd, III. EdS, LCMHC

VP of Clinical Services for the Carolinas, Refresh Mental Health. He is a Diplomate, Fellow, and Certified Trainer/Consultant for the Academy of Cognitive and Behavioral Therapies.

Trent has authored or co-authored several peer reviewed publications and books including *The Stoicism Workbook: How the wisdom of Socrates can help you build resilience and overcome anything life throws at you.*

Alyce Jurgensen, LCSW-C

Alyce is a licensed clinical social worker with two decades of experience helping individuals navigate life's challenges. Alyce's experience includes assisting those facing trauma, anxiety, and depression. Her current focus is supporting clients as they master the delicate balance of maintaining their individuality within relationships. In addition to her clinical work, Alyce is actively involved in her family business, serving on the board of directors since 2006 and playing a pivotal role in navigating its transition from the first to the second generation.

Andrew Keyt

Andrew is a Founder, CEO and Advisor of Generation6 Family Enterprise. He brings over 25 years of professional family business consulting experience working with the largest and most complex family businesses in the world. He is also the author of *Myths & Mortals: Family Business Leadership and Succession Planning.* Prior to founding Generation6, Andrew was the Executive Director and Clinical Professor in Family Business at the Loyola University Chicago Family Business Center and President of the Family Business Network USA. Andrew holds an Executive MBA for Families in Business, an MS in Marital and Family Therapy, and a BA in Psychology.

Fran Langdon, MD, ABAM

Fran Langdon is Diplomate of the American Board of Internal Medicine, and the American Board of Addiction Medicine is an internal medicine physician at Positive Sobriety Institute and medical director of Above and Beyond Family Recovery Center. Her focus is on diagnosing and treating chronic medical conditions and pain that may contribute to the development of an addiction disorder and impact a professional's workplace. For 15 years Dr. Langdon served as the medical director of the Northwestern University Eating Disorder Program and academic positions at Northwestern University School of Medicine.

Edward P. Monte, PhD

Edward Monte, PhD has specialized in family business consulting for the last 32 years. His primary concentration is on parents and adult children relationship issues that impact family business — particularly the dynamics between fathers and sons. He has taught for 30 years in the Family Business Center at Loyola's Quinlan School of Business. He retired from his clinical practice of couple and family therapy in 2020 leaving the multi-disciplinary clinical practice he founded in New Jersey and Pennsylvania in 2015. For almost 25 years, he taught graduate-level couple therapy at the University of Pennsylvania.

Anneleen Michiels, PhD

Anneleen Michiels is Associate Professor of Finance and Family Business at Hasselt University, Belgium, and a family business advisor at Generation6 | Family Enterprise Advisors. Her research, published in both academic and practitioner-oriented journals, investigates the complex role of finance in family enterprises and the families that run them. She founded and coordinates executive courses tailored for family wealth advisors at Hasselt University. Anneleen is an editorial board member of the Journal of Family Business Strategy, a board member at the International Family Enterprise Research Academy and a former family business chair of the European Academy of Management.

Torsten Pieper, PhD

Torsten Pieper is Associate Professor of Management at UNC Charlotte and Editor-in-Chief of the Journal of Family Business Strategy, the second-most-cited academic journal dedicated to the scientific study of family businesses. As an advisor with Generation6, Torsten assists families in business and family office leaders on the topics of family cohesion, longevity, strategy and governance.

Gail Silverstein, PhD

Gail Silverstein has a PhD in Clinical Psychology, a Post-Doctoral Certificate in Neuropsychology, and over four decades of experience in the field. Over the last fifteen years, she has developed a specialty in comprehensive neuropsychological testing for family business members. Testing provides insight into how people think and problem-solve which can be used to enhance performance. It also supplies useful input into business personnel decisions, such as which family member will have what role in the business now and in the future. Dr. Silverstein is licensed in Pennsylvania and has a PSYPACT APIT Certificate which allows her to work across state lines.

Anne Smart

Anne Smart is a senior advisor at Generation6 Family Business Advisors. Before joining Generation6, she spent 15 years working with family businesses at the Loyola University Family Business Center, retiring as the Director in 2022. She is a gifted group facilitator, speaker, coach, and advisor to multi-generational families in business. Professional and personal experiences with families experiencing substance use disorder motivate her to help families access reliable, credible resources for themselves, their families and their businesses.

Domingo P. Such III, JD

Domingo Such focuses his practice on excellence in the delivery of legal advice. He serves as the firm-wide chair of the Family Office Services practice, a multi-disciplinary practice representing family offices and quasi-family office arrangements comprised of operating companies, boards of directors, fiduciaries, and beneficiaries. Domingo also serves on the Perkins Coie LLP Firmwide Executive Committee which manages the strategic policymaking and governance of the firm. Using his MBA education and business acumen, he advises public and private businesses and single and multi-family offices (including trustees and trust companies), serving as outside general counsel in strategically significant and complex matters.

www.ingramcontent.com/pod-product-compliance
Lightning Source LLC
Chambersburg PA
CBHW070349200326
41518CB00012B/2178